Contents

GROWING UP
JEWISH

Other **GROWING UP** *Titles*
from Avon Books

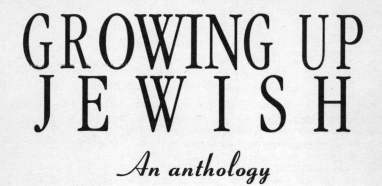

GROWING UP JEWISH

An anthology

Edited and with an Introduction by

JAY DAVID

AVON BOOKS  NEW YORK

AVON BOOKS
A division of
The Hearst Corporation
1350 Avenue of the Americas
New York, New York 10019

The William Morrow edition contains the following Library of Congress Cataloging in Publication Data:

Growing up Jewish : an anthology / edited and with an introduction
  by Jay David.—1st ed.
     p. cm.
   1. Jews—United States—Biography. 2. Jewish youth—United
States—Biography. I. Adler, Bill.
E184.J5G763   1996
973'.04924'00922—dc20
[B]
                                  95-26106
                                     CIP

First Avon Books Trade Printing: December 1997

AVON TRADEMARK REG. U.S. PAT. OFF. AND IN OTHER COUNTRIES, MARCA REGISTRADA, HECHO EN U.S.A.

Printed in the U.S.A.

OPM   10 9 8 7 6 5 4 3 2 1

Acknowledgments

Many thanks to Menachem Youlus of the Jewish Bookstore of Greater Washington, Rochelle Gottlieb, Bonni Goldberg, Lisa Swayne, and Arthur Magida for their guidance in choosing these selections.

Contents

CONTENTS

Introduction

Unlike other American minorities, Jews are well represented in our country's collection of writings. With their propensity for education and letters, America's Jews have given the world plenty of stories of their lives and dreams. Some are passed down from generation to generation and never leave the family. Others are collected as memoirs or published in widely read and loved books—these are the stories collected in this anthology. They can be read many ways, but they are offered to you here as examples of the various interpretations of what it is to be Jewish in America.

The last time Jews agreed on what being Jewish meant was when Moses came down from the mountain carrying the Ten Commandments. Since then, it's been widely disputed: a spiritual quest, a cultural heritage, a nation, a race, a people—and what makes an *American* Jew is no better defined. This differing of opinions, of voices, is reflected by the differences found within the stories themselves. Authors find varying interpretations and transliterations for the Yiddish and Hebrew words they use. Some authors feel the need to translate non-English vocabulary, while other authors are happy to let the words speak for themselves. These differences have been kept, to preserve the original intent of the authors.

Too often in world history, other people have had the power to decide what a Jew would be, and the power has had no good end: pogroms, Jewish ghettos, the Holocaust. It's different in America, because Jews here can set their own agendas. Jews in America could and did change Judaism to suit their new lives and freedom. Life in America offers so many choices. Little by little, they were able to do what other Jews around the world could not: assimilate, take a new name, and disappear. Or, Jews in America could become even more religious than those in the old country. Though many Jews got off to a rough start, things changed quickly.

When the first Jewish settlers arrived in the New World in 1654, they were nearly refused admittance. And when they were permitted to settle in New Amsterdam, they were barred from claiming rights granted to other citizens: the right to hold land, trade with Native Americans, hold public office, or practice their religion in a public place or synagogue. Jewish settlers fought for their rights to freedom of religion and won, as did many other settlers in America. Jewish immigration continued at a trickle after the first settlers arrived. By the time of the American Revolution, Jews numbered close to three thousand.

The first Jews settled throughout the colonies and prospered through hard work and sacrifice. As more and more Jewish families made America their home, a mass wave of immigrants arrived in the 1840s. These Jews were fleeing persecution in their homelands of Austria, Bavaria, Germany, Northern Italy, and other European countries. They sought a peaceful life here. For the most part, they found it. Many immigrants became peddlers and successful shopkeepers.

The new wave of Jewish immigrants moved south and west across the country. Galveston, Texas, had a Jewish mayor in the 1850s. Although some Jews met with discrimination, it occurred more on an individual than an institutional basis. Average Americans of the time didn't even know a Jew, and when they did, they regarded Jews generally as Germans. This generation of Jews had an easier time settling into American ways, and quickly exchanged old ways for new. The stories collected in *Growing Up Jewish* reaffirm the belief held by many immigrants that America was a land of opportunity. Nowhere is this more apparent than in the determination of the children in these stories to learn, to work, and to play in the streets of America.

In 1880, about a quarter of a million Jews lived in America. Then came the "huddled masses." Between 1880 and 1924, when immigration quotas were drastically tightened, millions of Jews fled eastern Europe and came to America. It's estimated that the vast majority of Jews in America today descend from these eastern European immigrants. They came individually and in families—entire villages immigrated. Unlike many earlier immigrants, these Jews weren't all well educated or well off. And there wasn't work for all of them in the crowded urban landscapes they inhabited. The Great Depression saw many Jewish families go through hard times where finding enough to eat could be a daily occupation. At the same time, many immigrants had to decide between religious and social customs from the Old World and those from the New.

While many Jewish immigrants went to Boston, Baltimore, St. Louis, the majority who arrived at New York's Ellis Island went from there to the Lower East Side of Manhattan. Some went on west, but most Jewish immigrants to New York stayed within a twelve-square-mile area, along with other immigrants of the time. In 1880, there were eighty thousand

Jews in New York City; by 1910, there were estimated to be a million and a quarter. The accounts from this time period reflect the hope these immigrants brought—and the patriotism instilled in them when they arrived.

Part I of *Growing Up Jewish* explores the experiences of some first-generation immigrants. Although their experiences could be as different as Edna Ferber's midwestern childhood, Maurice Hexter's recollection of Cincinnati, or Meyer Birnbaum's Brooklyn origins, still Judaism was a theme common to their lives. Whether it manifested itself through weekly rituals like the Sabbath, life-cycle rituals like bar mitzvah, or, sadly, through anti-Semitism, growing up Jewish in America had its own distinct influence.

Jewish immigration dropped sharply after the great influx at the turn of the century, but subsequent waves, though small, were powerful. Before World War II, a hundred and forty thousand refugees managed to escape the Nazis in Germany and Austria. After the war, survivors of the Holocaust came. They became a vocal minority, and their very presence inspired American Jews to become more politically active. Among these immigrants were some of the most Orthodox Jews, the Hasidim; twelve thousand of them settled in the Williamsburg section of Brooklyn. In Part Two of this anthology, Chaim Potok deftly examines the world of the Hasidic Jews in an excerpt from *The Chosen*. Other pieces explore growing up as an American-born Jew after the turn of the century.

The stories in Part II show how Jewish life gradually became Americanized. Sometimes, the conflicting feelings that assimilation brought on could be comical, as they are in Grace Paley's story "The Loudest Voice." In this piece, a young Jewish girl is given a starring role in her school's Christmas pageant, creating confusion at home. In the excerpt from *Deborah, Golda, and Me*, Letty Cottin Pogrebin examines how Judaism created an awkward yet vital bond between herself and her father. Whether they are excerpts about being at home in the suburbs, in elite boarding schools from Paul Cowan's *An Orphan in History*, or coming of age in Faye Moskowitz's story "And the Bridge Is Love," American culture and society are always present.

But Jewish tradition also endured in the hearts of Jewish writers. In *The Search for God at Harvard*, the weekly ritual of Sabbath dinner offered young Ari Goldman something solid, dependable, and beautiful in his otherwise tumultuous childhood. Kate Simon recalls looking forward to Passover in an excerpt from *Bronx Primitive* as a time of Jewish celebration and food. In many of these stories, children look to parents and grandparents for wisdom from the Old World.

Part III brings us experiences of Jews growing up in America today. While writers Adam Schwartz, Rebecca Goldstein, and Michael Chabon do not look at themselves as Jewish first, they still carry strong ties to the Jewish religion.

As much as immigrant Jews absorbed American culture, they changed it. Although they've never been a large percentage of the American population, they've been an influential minority. From the Supreme Court of the United States to the Congress, from entertainment to universities, the American Jew is represented. Many of the dreams and aspirations held by children have been realized with success in business, the arts, sciences, service to society, and fruitful family life. America has embraced what Jews have to offer.

The stories in *Growing Up Jewish* capture the feeling for the experience of Jewish children in America. Future generations of Jewish children will add to the story with their own accomplishments.

PART I

Making Their Way:

Jewish Immigrants

Come to America

"AMERICA AND I"

ANZIA YEZIERSKA

Symbolic of her own experience, this short story by Anzia Yezierska illustrates the hardships that a young Jewish girl faces building a new life in America. "I arrived in America," she says. "My young, strong body, my heart and soul pregnant with the unlived lives of generations clamoring for expression. . . . I was in America, among the Americans, but not of them."

Resentment at the treatment of Jews figures prominently in Yezierska's work, and her characters often don't find the American dream, only American social workers to frustrate their ambitions.

The author immigrated to the United States in 1901 from Plinsk, Russia. She and her family settled on New York's Lower East Side where Anzia worked as a sweatshop seamstress, a cook, a domestic for a wealthy family, and a factory worker before beginning her career as a writer. The publication of her first two books led to a brief screenwriting career in Hollywood. Her novels include The Bread Givers; Red Ribbon on a White Horse; Arrogant Beggar; *and* All I Could Ever Be.

As one of the dumb, voiceless ones I speak. One of the millions of immigrants beating, beating out their hearts at your gates for a breath of understanding.

Ach! America! From the other end of the earth from where I came, America was a land of living hope, woven of dreams, aflame with longing and desire.

Choked for ages in the airless oppression of Russia, the Promised Land rose up—wings for my stifled spirit—sunlight burning through my darkness—freedom singing to me in my prison—deathless songs tuning prison bars into strings of a beautiful violin.

I arrived in America. My young, strong body, my heart and soul pregnant with the unlived lives of generations clamoring for expression.

What my mother and father and their mother and father never had a chance to give out in Russia, I would give out in America. The hidden sap of centuries would find release: colors that never saw light—songs that died unvoiced—romance that never had a chance to blossom in the black life of the Old World.

In the golden land of flowing opportunity I was to find my work that was denied me in the sterile village of my forefathers. Here I was to be free from the dead drudgery for bread that held me down in Russia. For the first time in America, I'd cease to be a slave of the belly. I'd be a creator, a giver, a human being! My work would be the living joy of fullest self-expression.

But from my high visions, my golden hopes, I had to put my feet down on earth. I had to have food and shelter. I had to have the money to pay for it.

I was in America, among the Americans, but not of them. No speech, no common language, no way to win a smile of understanding from them, only my young, strong body and my untried faith. Only my eager, empty hands, and my full heart shining from my eyes!

God from the world! Here I was with so much richness in me, but my mind was not wanted without the language. And my body, unskilled, untrained, was not even wanted in the factory. Only one of two chances was left open to me: the kitchen, or minding babies.

My first job was as a servant in an Americanized family. Once, long ago, they came from the same village from where I came. But they were so well-dressed, so well-fed, so successful in America, that they were ashamed to remember their mother tongue.

"What were to be my wages?" I ventured timidly, as I looked up to the well-fed, well-dressed "American" man and woman.

They looked at me with a sudden coldness. What have I said to draw away from me their warmth? Was it so low from me to talk of wages? I shrank back into myself like a low-down bargainer. Maybe they're so high up in well-being they can't anymore understand my low thoughts for money.

From his rich height the man preached down to me that I must not be so grabbing for wages. Only just landed from the ship and already thinking about money when I should be thankful to associate with "Americans."

The woman, out of her smooth, smiling fatness, assured me that this was my chance for a summer vacation in the country with her two lovely children. My great chance to learn to be a civilized being, to become an American by living with them.

So, made to feel that I was in the hands of American friends, invited to share with them their home, their plenty, their happiness, I pushed out from my head the worry for wages. Here was my first chance to begin my life

4

in the sunshine, after my long darkness. My laugh was all over my face as I said to them, "I'll trust myself to you. What I'm worth you'll give me." And I entered their house like a child by the hand.

The best of me I gave them. Their house cares were my house cares. I got up early. I worked till late. All that my soul hungered to give I put into the passion with which I scrubbed floors, scoured pots, and washed clothes. I was so grateful to mingle with the American people, to hear the music of the American language, that I never knew tiredness.

There was such a freshness in my brains and such a willingness in my heart that I could go on and on—not only with the work of the house, but work with my head—learning new words from the children, the grocer, the butcher, the iceman. I was not even afraid to ask for words from the policeman on the street. And every new word made me see new American things with American eyes. I felt like a Columbus, finding new worlds through every new word.

But words alone were only for the inside of me. The outside of me still branded me for a steerage immigrant. I had to have clothes to forget myself that I'm a stranger yet. And so I had to have money to buy these clothes.

The month was up. I was so happy! Now I'd have money. *My own, earned* money. Money to buy a new shirt on my back—shoes on my feet. Maybe yet an American dress and hat!

Ach! How high rose my dreams! How plainly I saw all that I would do with my visionary wages shining like a light over my head!

In my imagination I already walked in my new American clothes. How beautiful I looked as I saw myself like a picture before my eyes! I saw how I would throw away my immigrant rags tied up in my immigrant shawl. With money to buy—free money in my hands—I'd show them that I could look like an American in a day.

Like a prisoner in his last night in prison, counting the seconds that will free him from his chains, I trembled breathlessly for the minute I'd get the wages in my hand.

Before dawn I rose.

I shined up the house like a jewel box.

I prepared breakfast and waited with my heart in my mouth for my lady and gentleman to rise. At last I heard them stirring. My eyes were jumping out of my head to them when I saw them coming in and seating themselves by the table.

Like a hungry cat rubbing up to its boss for meat, so I edged and simpered around them as I passed them the food. Without my will, like a beggar, my hand reached out to them.

The breakfast was over. And no word yet from my wages.

Gottuniu! I thought to myself. *Maybe they're so busy with their own things they forgot it's the day for my wages. Could they who have everything know what I was to do with my first American dollars? How could they, soaking in plenty, how could they feel the longing and the fierce hunger in me, pressing up through each visionary dollar? How could they know the gnawing ache of my avid fingers for the feel of my own, earned dollars? My dollars that I could spend like a free person. My dollars that would make me feel with everybody alike.*

Lunch came. Lunch past.

Oi-i weh! Not a word yet about my money.

It was near dinner. And not a word yet about my wages.

I began to set the table. But my head—it swam away from me. I broke a glass. The silver dropped from my nervous fingers. I couldn't stand it any longer. I dropped everything and rushed over to my American lady and gentleman.

"*Oi weh!* The money—my money—my wages!" I cried breathlessly.

Four cold eyes turned on me.

"Wages? Money?" The four eyes turned into hard stone as they looked me up and down. "Haven't you a comfortable bed to sleep, and three good meals a day? You're only a month here. Just came to America. And you already think about money. Wait till you're worth any money. What use are you without knowing English? You should be glad we keep you here. It's like a vacation for you. Other girls pay money yet to be in the country."

It went black for my eyes. I was so choked no words came to my lips. Even the tears went dry in my throat.

I left. Not a dollar for all my work.

For a long, long time my heart ached and ached like a sore wound. If murderers would have robbed me and killed me it wouldn't have hurt me so much. I couldn't think through my pain. The minute I'd see before me how they looked at me, the words they said to me—then everything began to bleed in me. And I was helpless.

For a long, long time the thought of ever working in an "American" family made me tremble with fear, like the fear of wild wolves. No—never again would I trust myself to an "American" family, no matter how fine their language and how sweet their smile.

It was blotted out in me all trust in friendship from "Americans." But the life in me still burned to live. The hope in me still craved to hope. In darkness, in dirt, in hunger and want, but only to live on!

There had been no end to my day—working for the "American" family. Now rejecting false friendships from higher-ups in America, I turned back to the ghetto. I worked on a hard bench with my own kind on either side of me. I knew before I began what my wages were to be. I knew what my hours were to be. And I knew the feeling of the end of the day.

From the outside my second job seemed worse than the first. It was in a sweatshop of a Delancey Street basement, kept up by an old, wrinkled woman that looked like a black witch of greed. My work was sewing on buttons. While the morning was still dark I walked into a dark basement. And darkness met me when I turned out of the basement.

Day after day, week after week, all the contact I got with America was handling dead buttons. The money I earned was hardly enough to pay for bread and rent. I didn't have a room to myself. I didn't even have a bed. I slept on a mattress on the floor in a rat-hole of a room occupied by a dozen other immigrants. I was always hungry—oh, so hungry! The scant meals I could afford only sharpened my appetite for real food. But I felt myself better off than working in the "American" family, where I had three good meals a day and a bed to myself. With all the hunger and darkness of the sweatshop, I had at least the evening to myself. And all night was mine. When all were asleep, I used to creep up on the roof of the tenement and talk out my heart in silence to the stars in the sky.

Who am I? What am I? What do I want with my life? Where is America? Is there an America? What is this wilderness in which I'm lost?

I'd hurl my questions and then think and think. And I could not tear it out of me, the feeling that America must be somewhere, somehow—only I couldn't find it—*my America*, where I would work for love and not for a living. I was like a thing following blindly after something far off in the dark!

"Oi weh!" I'd stretch out my hand up in the air. "My head is so lost in America! What's the use of all my working if I'm not in it? Dead buttons is not me."

Then the busy season started in the shop. The mounds of buttons grew and grew. The long day stretched out longer. I had to begin with the buttons earlier and stay with them till later in the night. The old witch turned into a huge greedy maw for wanting more and more buttons.

For a glass of tea, for a slice of herring over black bread, she would buy us up to stay another and another hour, till there seemed no end to her demands.

One day, the light of self-assertion broke into my cellar darkness.

"I don't want the tea. I don't want your herring," I said with terrible boldness. "I only want to go home. I only want the evening to myself!"

"You fresh mouth, you!" cried the old witch. "You learned already too much in America. I want no clockwatchers in my shop. Out you go!"

7

I was driven out to cold and hunger. I could no longer pay for my mattress on the floor. I no longer could buy the bite in my mouth. I walked the streets. I knew what it is to be alone in a strange city, among strangers.

But I laughed through my tears. So I learned too much already in America because I wanted the whole evening to myself? Well America has yet to teach me still more: how to get not only the whole evening to myself, but a whole day a week like the American workers.

That sweatshop was a bitter memory but a good school. It fitted me for a regular factory. I could walk in boldly and say I could work at something, even if it was only sewing on buttons.

Gradually, I became a trained worker. I worked in a light, airy factory, only eight hours a day. My boss was no longer a sweater and a bloodsqueezer. The first freshness of the morning was mine. And the whole evening was mine. All day Sunday was mine.

Now I had better food to eat. I slept on a better bed. Now, I even looked dressed up like the American-born. But inside of me I knew that I was not yet an American. I choked with longing when I met an American-born, and I could say nothing.

Something cried dumb in me. I couldn't help it. I didn't know what it was I wanted. I only knew I wanted. I wanted. Like the hunger in the heart that never gets food.

An English class for foreigners started in our factory. The teacher had such a good, friendly face, her eyes looked so understanding, as if she could see right into my heart. So I went to her one day for an advice:

"I don't know what is with me the matter," I began. "I have no rest in me. I never yet done what I want."

"What is it you want to do, child?" she asked me.

"I want to do something with my head, my feelings. All day long, only with my hands I work."

"First you must learn English." She patted me as if I was not yet grown up. "Put your mind on that, and then we'll see."

So for a time I learned the language. I could almost begin to think with English words in my head. But in my heart the emptiness still hurt. I burned to give, to give something, to do something, to be something. The dead work with my hands was killing me. My work left only hard stones on my heart.

Again I went to our factory teacher and cried out to her: "I know already to read and write the English language, but I can't put it into words what I want. What is it in me so different that can't come out?"

She smiled at me down from her calmness as if I were a little bit out of my head. "What *do you want* to do?"

8

"I feel. I see. I hear. And I want to think it out. But I'm like dumb in me. I only feel I'm different—different from everybody."

She looked at me close and said nothing for a minute. "You ought to join one of the social clubs of the Women's Association," she advised.

"What's the Women's Association?" I implored greedily.

"A group of American women who are trying to help the working girl find herself. They have a special department for immigrant girls like you."

I joined the Women's Association. On my first evening there they announced a lecture: "The Happy Worker and His Work," by the Welfare director of the United Mills Corporation.

Is there such a thing as a happy worker at his work? I wondered. *Happiness is only by working at what you love. And what poor girl can ever find it to work at what she loves?* My old dreams about my America rushed through my mind. Once I thought that in America everybody works for love. Nobody has to worry for a living. Maybe this welfare man came to show me the *real* America that till now I sought in vain.

With a lot of polite words the head lady of the Women's Association introduced a higher-up that looked like the king of kings of business. Never before in my life did I ever see a man with such a sureness in his step, such power in his face, such friendly positiveness in his eye as when he smiled upon us.

"Efficiency is the new religion of business," he began. "In big business houses, even in up-to-date factories, they no longer take the first comer and give him any job that happens to stand empty. Efficiency begins at the employment office. Experts are hired for the one purpose, to find out how best to fit the worker to his work. It's economy for the boss to make the worker happy." And then he talked a lot more on efficiency in educated language that was over my head.

I didn't know exactly what it meant—efficiency—but if it was to make the worker happy at his work, then that's what I had been looking for since I came to America. I only felt from watching him that he was happy by his job. And as I looked on this clean, well-dressed, successful one, who wasn't ashamed to say he rose from an office boy, it made me feel that I, too, could lift myself up for a person.

He finished his lecture, telling us about the Vocational-Guidance Center that the Women's Association started.

The very next evening I was at the Vocational-Guidance Center. There I found a young, college-looking woman. Smartness and health shining from her eyes! She, too, looked as if she knew her way in America. I could tell at the first glance: Here is a person that is happy by what she does.

"I feel you'll understand me," I said right away.

She leaned over with pleasure in her face: "I hope I can."

"I want to work by what's in me. Only, I don't know what's in me. I only feel I'm different."

She gave me a quick, puzzled look from the corner of her eyes. "What are you doing now?"

"I'm the quickest shirtwaist hand on the floor! But my heart wastes away by such work. I think and think, and my thoughts can't come out."

"Why don't you think out your thoughts in shirtwaists? You could learn to be a designer. Earn more money."

"I don't want to look on waists. If my hands are sick from waists, how could my head learn to put beauty into them?"

"But you must earn your living at what you know, and rise slowly from job to job."

I looked at her office sign: VOCATIONAL GUIDANCE. "What's your vocational guidance?" I asked. "How to rise from job to job—how to earn more money?"

The smile went out from her eyes. But she tried to be kind yet. "What *do* you want?" she asked, with a sigh of last patience.

"I want America to want me."

She fell back in her chair, thunderstruck with my boldness. But yet, in a low voice of educated self-control, she tried to reason with me.

"You have to *show* that you have something special for America before America has need of you."

"But I never had a chance to find out what's in me, because I always had to work for a living. Only, I feel it's efficiency for America to find out what's in me so different, so I could give it out by my work."

Her eyes half closed as they bored through me. Her mouth opened to speak, but no words came from her lips. So I flamed up with all that was choking in me like a house on fire.

"America gives free bread and rent to criminals in prison. They got grand houses with sunshine, fresh air, doctors and teachers, even for the crazy ones. Why don't they have free boarding schools for immigrants—strong people—willing people? Here you see us burning up with something different, and America turns her head away from us."

Her brows lifted and dropped down. She shrugged her shoulders away from me with the look of pity we give to cripples and hopeless lunatics.

"America is no Utopia. First you must become efficient in earning a living before you can indulge in your poetic dreams."

I went away from the vocational-guidance office with all the air out of my lungs. All the light out of my eyes. My feet dragged after me like dead wood.

Till now there had always lingered a rosy veil of hope over my emptiness, a hope that a miracle would happen. I would open up my eyes some
day and suddenly find the America of my dreams. As a young girl hungry
for love sees always before her eyes the picture of lover's arms around
her, so I saw always in my heart the vision of Utopian America.

But now I felt that the America of my dreams never was and never could
be. Reality had hit me on the head as with a club. I felt that the America
that I sought was nothing but a shadow—an echo—a chimera of lunatics
and crazy immigrants.

Stripped of all illusion, I looked about me. The long desert of wasting
days of drudgery stared me in the face. The drudgery that I had lived
through, and the endless drudgery still ahead of me rose over me like a
withering wilderness of sand. In vain were all my cryings, in vain were all
frantic efforts of my spirit to find the living waters of understanding for
my perishing lips. Sand, sand was everywhere. With every seeking, every
reaching out I only lost myself deeper and deeper in a vast sea of sand.

I knew now the American language. And I knew now, if I talked to the
Americans from morning till night, they could not understand what the
Russian soul of me wanted. They could not understand *me* any more than
if I talked to them in Chinese. Between my soul and the American soul
were worlds of difference that no words could bridge over. What was that
difference? What made the Americans so far apart from me?

I began to read the American history. I found from the first pages that
America started with a band of Courageous Pilgrims. They had left their
native country as I had left mine. They had crossed an unknown ocean
and landed in an unknown country, as I.

But the great difference between the first Pilgrims and me was that they
expected to make America, build America, create their own world of lib-
erty. I wanted to find it ready-made.

I read on. I delved deeper down into the American history. I saw how
the Pilgrim Fathers came to a rocky desert country, surrounded by Indian
savages on all sides. But undaunted, they pressed on—through danger—
through famine, pestilence, and want—they pressed on. They did not ask
the Indians for sympathy, for understanding. They made no demands on
anybody, but on their own indomitable spirit of persistence.

And I—I was forever begging a crumb of sympathy, a gleam of understanding from strangers who could not understand.

I, when I encountered a few savage Indian scalpers, like the old witch
of the sweatshop, like my "Americanized" countryman, who cheated me
of my wages—I, when I found myself on the lonely, untrodden path

through which all seekers of the new world must pass, I lost heart and said: "There is no America!"

Then came a light—a great revelation! I saw America—a big idea— a deathless hope—a world still in the making. I saw that it was the glory of America that it was not yet finished. And I, the last comer, had her share to give, small or great, to the making of America, like those Pilgrims who came in the *Mayflower*.

Fired up by this revealing light, I began to build a bridge of understanding between the American-born and myself. Since their life was shut out from such as me, I began to open up my life and the lives of my people to them. And life draws life. In only writing about the ghetto I found America.

Great chances have come to me. But in my heart is always a deep sadness. I feel like a man who is sitting down to a secret table of plenty, while his near ones and dear ones are perishing before his eyes. My very joy in doing the work I love hurts me like secret guilt, because all about me I see so many with my longings, my burning eagerness, to do and to be, wasting their days in drudgery they hate, merely to buy bread and pay rent. And America is losing all that richness of the soul.

The Americans of tomorrow, the America that is every day nearer coming to be, will be too wise, too openhearted, too friendly-handed, to let the least last-comer at their gates knock in vain with his gifts unwanted.

from

A PECULIAR TREASURE

EDNA FERBER

A Peculiar Treasure, *originally published in 1938, is the first of two autobiographies and the only one in which Edna Ferber describes growing up in Ottumwa, Iowa. Ottumwa was a small midwestern town with only five or six Jewish families and no synagogue, and Ferber was faced with "the brutality and ignorance" of the people who lived there. Anti-Semitism—young boys yelling "Hello, sheeny!" on the way to school or adults refusing to shop in her parents' store—was a way of life.*

Despite its depiction of the difficulties of living in Iowa, this excerpt from A Peculiar Treasure *is filled with the strength of Edna Ferber's family and its ability to come together. She writes, "I can't account for the fact that I didn't resent being a Jew. Perhaps it was because I liked the way my own family lived, talked, conducted its household and its business. I admired immensely my grandparents, my parents, my uncles and aunt."*

Edna Ferber won the Pulitzer Prize in 1924 for her best-selling novel So Big. Show Boat, *published in 1926, was adapted for the stage and has been in production almost continually since 1927. She coauthored five plays with George S. Kaufman, including* Dinner at Eight *and* Stage Door *and wrote eleven additional novels.*

My father had decided that Chicago was not, after all, the ideal spot on which to lay the foundations of our future fortunes. A year had gone by during which we had stayed on in the house on Calumet Avenue. During that year my father was off for days at a time looking for a business location. He realized that he might much better have stayed on in Kalamazoo, but it was too late to think of that now. Perhaps he had discovered that the steps toward becoming a second Marshall Field or Carson Pirie Scott & Company were not so simple. He had, after all, been a small-town man always. Some miracle of mischance led him to a small Iowa coal-

13

mining town distinguished by the Indian name of Ottumwa. The word is said to mean Place of Perseverance. Whatever Ottumwa means in the Indian language, it meant only bad luck for the Ferbers. My father had been told that there was absolutely no general store in the town. Ottumwa clamored, apparently, for Ferber's Bazaar. He inspected the place (he must have been blindfolded) and returned with glowing stories of this Iowa town in a farming and coal-mining district. The fact that it boasted more than sixteen thousand population without a decent shop for china, toys, notions, and all sorts of household goods should have been significant enough to serve as a warning.

My mother was anguished. She had left Kalamazoo happy at the thought of again becoming a Chicagoan. Now she was to live in an Iowa coal-mining town apparently for the rest of her days. Heavy-hearted with misgivings she gathered up her household goods and her two children, left Chicago and her people behind her, and came to Ottumwa. As soon as she had a good look at the sordid, clay-and-gully Iowa town, she knew. There it lay flanked by the muddy Des Moines River; unpaved, bigoted, anti-Semitic, undernourished. Julia Ferber's days of youth and peace and happiness were over.

Those next seven years—from 1890 to 1897—must be held accountable for anything in me that is hostile toward the world in which I live. Child though I was, the brutality and ignorance of that little town penetrated to my consciousness, perhaps through casual talk as I heard it between my young parents; certainly as it was visited upon me.

I have since visited the town once, some ten years ago, and I found it a tree-shaded, sightly, modern American town of its size; clean, progressive. I had planned to stay overnight in the new and comfortable hotel. Memory was too strong. At eight that evening I drove through the starlit night back to Des Moines, past the rich black-loam farmlands of Iowa, past the substantial square-built fine farm homes, certainly the most modern and even luxurious farmhouses in the world. It was a purple velvet spring night; the air was rich with the smells of freshly turned earth and the first flowers; the highway ran its flawless length, mile on mile; the sky was lavish with brilliants.

For the first time in my life, out of the deep well of repression where they had so long festered, I dragged those seven years of my bitter little girlhood and looked at them. And the cool clean Iowa air cleansed them, and I saw them then, not as bitter corroding years, but as astringent strengthening years; years whose adversity had given me and mine a solid foundation of stamina, determination, and a profound love of justice.

My mother kept a sort of skeleton diary through the years, and the scant line-a-day covering the Ottumwa years forms a human document, bare as it is, containing all the elements of courage, vitality, humor, sordid tragedy, high tragedy. Through it all, I may add, the Ferber family went to the theater. Bitter Iowa winters, burning Iowa summers; death, business crises, illness—the Ferber family went to the theater when any form of theater was to be had in the boundaries of that then-benighted little town.

We moved into a new eight-room house on Wapello Street at the foot of a steep hill. The town ran from almost perpendicular hill streets to the flats near the Des Moines River. In the wintertime it was thrilling to be able to coast, gaining rocketlike velocity, down the length of Wapello or Marian Street hill. It was before the day of automobiles, there was little danger of being run down as you whizzed past street intersections. An occasional team, plop-plopping along in the snow, pulled up at the hill-street crossings. In the summer Wapello hill was almost as exciting because you could count on the runaways. There were runaway horses every few days and, as we lived at the foot of the hill, they usually wound up with a grand flourish and splintering of wood and screaming of occupants practically in our laps. Faulty brakes, steep hill and frightened horse combined to bring about this state of affairs. The best runaway I remember was a heavily laden hay wagon whose driver, helpless, sat perched atop his precarious load. I still can see the unwieldy mass careening wildly down the hill like a vast drunken fat woman. The usually phlegmatic farm horses, teased by the overladen wagon nipping at their heels, had taken fright, had galloped frantically down the steep slope, the mass had overturned, and the farmer lay unconscious, his head bleeding, his arm dislocated at the shoulder and broken. It was midmorning. There were no men about. I remember the doctor, hastily summoned, looking about him in his shirt-sleeves for likely help in this emergency.

"Which one of you ladies will pull this man's arm with all your strength while I set it?"

Julia Ferber came forward. "I will." And she pulled with all her strength while the sweat poured down the doctor's face and that of the groaning farmer.

My sister Fannie and I were left increasingly alone as my mother realized that there was more to my father's business than opening a store, stocking it, and waiting for customers. With instinctive common sense, though she knew nothing of business, she felt that something was amiss, and she set about finding out what this might be. She was still too young, too newly married, and too life-loving to admit the whole structure was wrong. She got into the way of going to the store early after midday and staying there through the afternoon. There was the hired girl to look after my sister and myself, and we lived the normal outdoor life of small-town children.

The American maid-of-all-work, known then as the hired girl, was an institution in the middle-class life of that day and until the emigration restrictions largely stopped her. She should have a rich, colorful, and important book all to herself. The American hired girl was, in that day, a farm girl, daughter of foreign-born parents; or she was an immigrant newly landed; perhaps at most of five years' standing in this country. She was any one of a half-dozen nationalities: Irish, German, Swedish, Bohemian, Hungarian, Polish. Poverty, famine, persecution, ambition, a spirit of adventure—any one of these may have been the force which catapulted her across the ocean and into the melting pot. She brought into the Eastern and Midwestern middle-class American household a wealth of European ways, manners, customs in speech, cooking, religion, festivals, morals, clothing. If Hungarian, she brought the household such dishes as goulash and strudel; if Irish, stew and shortbread; if Bohemian, noodlekraut; if Swedish, meat balls and flaky pastry; if Austrian, wienerschnitzel and the best of coffee. She brought her native peasant costume overseas in her funny corded trunk and could be coaxed to don it for the entertainment of the children of the household. To them, too, she brought old-world folk tales, dances, myths, songs. She was warmhearted, simple, honest, and had to be taught to brush her teeth. Her hair, tightly braided, was wound around her head or skewered into an eye-straining knot. She rose at five-thirty to start the kitchen fire; she rose at four on Mondays to do the family wash. Numbers of her you will see queening it now in American so-called society. She loved to dance, she loved to sing, she loved to work. She might be uncouth or graceful, sullen or sunny, neat or slovenly, but she was the American hired girl of the '50s, '60s, '70s, '80s, and '90s, and as such she influenced the manners, morals, and lives of millions of American-born children. I always have thought that English children brought up by English maids, French children cared for by French maids, and so on through the countries of Europe, have missed a lot of variety and fun.

Of the Ottumwa hired girls the first I remember is Sophy. Sophy was swarthy, rather heavily mustached, a superb cook and definitely "touched." Her mental maladjustment was, however, confined to one narrow theme. She thought all men were in love with her. I don't know whether she was Polish or Hungarian. She was somewhere in her forties, very plain. She spoke with an accent, and she was always rushing in, after her days off, with an account of the passionate advances of some strange male encountered in her girlish perambulations. These stories were considered very amusing as told among the married couples of my parents' acquaintance. My sister and I listened, awestruck, while she regaled us with accounts of her amorous adventures.

"I vass walking on the street and pretty soon I know somebody vass following after me, so I hurry but he catch up wiss me, he is tall and handsome wiss black mustache and black eyes and curly hair. And he says, 'So! You are de vooman I am seeking.' " This last word became *sikking* in her accent. " 'You must come wit me, my beauty, or I will keel you.' " In those simple and rather cruel days this story was repeated with the accent complete, and greeted by shrieks of mirth. No one seemed to realize that here was a middle-aged virgin in the throes of a mild sex mania. She was devoted to us children and we loved her, but it was not our childish love she wanted.

After Sophy there was Sarah, a dear Welsh girl. Sometimes I used to go to early Mass with her. During my childhood I often went to early Mass when the household maid happened to be Catholic. I liked the drama of it; the color, the rich robes, the procession, the choir boys' fresh young voices; the sweetish prick of incense. Once or twice I went with Sarah to the little cottage where her parents lived, near the mines, and my first trip down into the deep black shaft of a coal mine was made with Sarah and her father. We stumbled through the eery galleries where the men were at work, their tiny cap lamps casting weird shadows. I remember being shocked to learn that people worked in the earth like grubs. I felt sorry for them, and when we came up into the open air again I was relieved. I somehow had felt doomed never to see daylight again.

More and more of my mother's time was spent at the store, though she did little but watch and learn. It was as though scales and scales were falling from her eyes and she were seeing the hard world as it was for the first time. On Saturdays she was there until nine or ten o'clock waiting for her husband, for Saturdays and Saturday nights were the busy times. The farmers and their wives would come in to sell their produce and put in supplies; and the miners would spend their pay. The coal mines lay very near the town. The miners were, for the most part, Welshmen, brought over from the black pits of Cardiff. I would see them coming home from work in the evening, their eyes grotesquely rimmed with black, their trade caps, with the little miner's lamp, on their heads, their tin lunch pails in their tired hands. A lean gaunt lot with few enough quarters and half-dollars to exchange for goods at Ferber's Bazaar.

The town swirled down Main Street on Saturday night. On Saturday afternoon my sister and I went to a matinee if there happened to be a stock company in temporary residence. On Saturday night I was allowed to sit in a tiny chair in a corner and survey the crowds shuffling by. This I insisted on doing. I don't know why a child of five or thereabouts should have enjoyed this diversion, but I did, and I do to this day. My notion of bliss would be to sit in an armchair at the corner of Broadway and Forty-second, or State and Madison, or any other busy intersection in America, and watch the town go by. The passerby does not notice you or care about you; they, the people, are intent on getting somewhere, their faces are open to the reader; they betray themselves by their walk, their voices, their hands, clenched or inert; their feet, their clothes, their eyes.

Well, there I sat at my ease, an intent and obnoxious little student of the human race, fascinated, God knows why, as I saw this cross section of America go shuffling by in a little Iowa town. At about nine o'clock my sister and I would be sent home, either with the hired girl who had come for us, or hand in hand alone through the dark streets and into the empty house. Perhaps that's why I don't understand what women mean when they say that they are timid about being alone on the street at night. All my life I've walked at night. It is my favorite tramping time.

If it was not too late we were allowed to read at night. Our reading was undirected, haphazard. By the dining-room kerosene lamp we read and read and read. We read the Horatio Alger books in which the newsboy helped the white-headed gentleman with the gold-headed cane across perilous Lexington Avenue, and was promptly adopted by the old gentleman (who later turned out to have been his long-lost grandfather all the time). By the time I was nine I had read all of Dickens, but I also adored the Five Little Pepper books, the *St. Nicholas* magazine, all of Louisa Alcott, and the bound copies of *Harper's Bazaar; Hans Brinker and the Silver Skates*; the novels of The Duchess (the Kathleen Norris of her day); *Thelma; Between Two Worlds; The First Violin*. Good and bad, adult or infantile, I read all the books in the house, all the books in the store stock, all the books in the very inadequate little public library, for this was before the day of Andrew Carnegie's omnipresent Greek temple. I remember that when Fannie [Edna Ferber's sister] and I were simultaneously stricken with measles, and lay in separate rooms, she in the spare bedroom, I in our everyday bed, my mother sat in the hall between the two rooms so that we both might hear plainly as she read aloud from *A Texas Steer*, a gusty tale which we relished enormously. Of the standbys in the household bookcase there was one book of which I never tired. It was known familiarly as the Green Book, because of the color of its worn binding. Its official name was *The World of Wit and Humour*. I read it to tatters. I still have it, its worn pages held together now by skillful binding, its leaves yellow and dog-eared, but its cover still the old original bilious cloth of the Green Book. Between those boards I was introduced to Bret Harte and George Eliot, Samuel

Lover and William Allen Butler, author of the immortal *Flora M'Flimsey of Madison Square*. There I read of Samuel Warren's *Tittlebat Titmouse*; Oliver Wendell Holmes's *Ballad of the Oysterman*; there were Artemus Ward, Charles Lever, Mark Twain. Jokes, poems, Mrs. Caudle's Curtain Lectures—the Green Book was a mine of riches, and is to this day. Curiously enough, a friend of my mother subscribed to *Puck* and the English humorous magazine *Punch*. These she saved for me, and I spent an occasional Saturday afternoon curled up, ecstatically happy, with a pile of these papers. In *Puck* there was one series I particularly loved. It depicted its characters as very plump, round-cheeked pop-eyed creatures, in type a good deal like the Betty Boop cartoons, but infinitely more human and varied.

If all this sounds stuffy I hasten to say that it wasn't. Ottumwa of that day was a tough town. There were seven murders in it one year, and no convictions. This annoyed certain of the citizenry. They decided to take steps. Consequently, one day as I was rounding the corner of Main Street I saw people running and I was aware of a strange and blood-curdling sound, not human. It was like the sound made by animals as I remembered them in Chicago's Lincoln Park Zoo at their mealtime. I quickened my steps and cleared the corner just in time to see an odd bundle jerking its way in midair up the electric light pole. It had legs and arms that waved like those of an insect, then they ceased to wave, the thing straightened itself and became decorous and limp, its head drooping as though in contrition. The animal sounds from the crowd below swelled, then ceased. Suddenly they melted away, seeming to flow up and down the streets in all directions. I heard the clang of the police patrol wagon.

Whatever there was to see I saw. Yearly there were held Methodist camp meetings in a great tent. People "got religion," they came down the aisle clapping their hands and shouting, rolling their eyes, shrieking and sobbing in an hysteria of induced emotion. They would drop to the floor at the foot of the platform. I was astonished to learn that these frenzies were occasioned by religious fervor. I had thought of religion as something dignified, solemn and a little sad.

Somehow or other I attended Chautauquas, revival meetings, political rallies, political parades, ten-twenty-and-thirties, the circus. We always went to the circus at night because my parents could not very well get away in the daytime. I pitied my small friends who were obliged to be content with the afternoon performance. I thought it must be very dull to see this strange world by daylight exposed beneath a blazing sun. Under the gas flares it was mysterious, romantic. Spangles glittered, color blazed, there was more menace in the snarls and growls of the wild animals. Then, too, there was the added thrill of being up so late. When we stumbled out after the performance, drunk with sound and color and dazzling sights, the smaller tents already had been whisked away like an Arabian Nights dream; hoarse men were shouting to one another and charging about with poles and weird canvas bundles. One heard the thick rich sound of heavy circus wheels on the roadway, like no other sound in the world. It stirred something in me, vague and terrible—something that went back, back, perhaps to Egyptian days and the heavy wheels of chariots.

The political parades were fine things. The marchers carried torch flares and wore colored hatbands and ribbons fastened crosswise from shoulder to waist, and there were huge signs and painted banners on poles held high in the air. I was in the dense crowd that heard Bryan's Cross of Gold speech. He spoke at the Opera House; the throng waiting for the door to be opened was unmanageable. It was then I came by my lifelong horror of close-packed crowds. The doors were opened, the eager hundreds surged forward, I lost my father's hand, I felt myself suffocating, being trampled, I screamed at the top of a none-too-dulcet voice, a man picked me up out of the welter of trampling feet and crushing knees and swung me up to his shoulder, where I sat perched above the heads of the mob and from which vantage point I calmly listened to the impassioned Mr. Bryan in his historic speech, not a word of which I can recall, for some hidden reason.

I saw Coxey's Army, a pitiful tatterdemalion crew, floating down the muddy Des Moines River on flat boats and rafts, hungry, penniless, desperate, on their way to demand food and work of a government which, at that time, had not even dreamed of Relief, of Social Security, of Old Age Pensions, of PWA Projects. The Panic of 1893 had struck America a violent blow, and the whole country was writhing in terror and misery.

It is not for me to say whether all this was good or bad for me. Probably bad and good. Certainly it made for an interesting childhood. Perhaps it is just as well that I never have had a child. I am afraid I should have wanted to bring him or her up in this way—fending for itself, moving from place to place, seeing all that there is to see. I hear mothers and fathers debating whether or not to allow their offspring to see *Snow White and the Seven Dwarfs*. They discuss its possible psychological and physical effects on little Junior or Sister. I know they're modern and right and wise and oh, how glad I am that I was not thus sheltered in my childhood. Always to be cared for and serene seems to me to be much like living in a climate where it is always summer. Never to know the bitter nip of winter's cold, and to brace oneself against it and fight it; never to long for the coming of spring and then to witness, in ecstasy, the marvel of the first pale lemon-green haze; not to know the voluptuous luxury of rare hot summer sun on basking flesh. No. Summer's only fun if winter is remembered.

Going to school, playing with Ora Burney and Maude Hayward and the Trost boys, I had plenty of normal childish pleasure. But there in Ottumwa it was smirched with constant and cruel persecution. Through the seven years during which we lived in Ottumwa I know that I never went out on the street without being subjected to some form of devilment. It was a fine school for a certain sort of fortitude, but it gave me a strong dash of bitterness at an early age, together with a bewildered puzzlement at what was known as the Christian world. Certainly I wasn't wise enough or old enough at five, six, seven, eight, nine, ten, to philosophize about this. But these people seemed to me to be barbarians.

On Saturdays, and on unusually busy days when my father could not take the time to come home to the noon dinner, it became my duty to take his midday meal down to him, very carefully packed in a large basket; soup, meat, vegetables, dessert. This must be carried with the utmost care so as not to spill or slop. No one thought of having a sandwich and a cup of coffee in the middle of the day, with a hot dinner to be eaten at leisure in the peace of the evening.

This little trip from the house on Wapello Street to the store on Main Street amounted to running the gantlet. I didn't so much mind the Morey girl. She sat in front of her house perched on the white gatepost, waiting, a child about my age, with long red curls, a freckled face, very light green eyes. She swung her long legs, idly. At sight of me her listlessness fled.

"Hello, sheeny!" Then variations on this. This, one learned to receive equably. Besides, the natural retort to her baiting was to shout, airily, "Red Head! Wets the bed!"

But as I approached the Main Street corner there sat a row of vultures perched on the iron railing at the side of Sargent's drugstore. These were not children, they were men. Perhaps to me, a small child, they seemed older than they were, but their ages must have ranged from eighteen to thirty. There they sat, perched on the black iron rail, their heels hooked behind the lower rung. They talked almost not at all. The semicircle of spit rings grew richer and richer on the sidewalk in front of them. Vacant-eyed, they stared and spat and sat humped and round-shouldered, doing nothing, thinking nothing, being nothing. Suddenly their lackluster eyes brightened, they shifted, they licked their lips a little and spat with more relish. From afar they had glimpsed their victim, a plump little girl in a clean starched gingham frock, her black curls confined by a ribbon bow.

Every fiber of me shrieked to run the other way. My eyes felt hot and

21

wide. My face became scarlet. I must walk carefully so as not to spill the good hot dinner. Now then. Now.

"Sheeny! Has du gesak de Isaac! De Moses! De Levi! Heh, sheeny, what you got!" Good Old Testament names. They doubtless heard them in their Sunday worship, but did not make the connection, quite. They then brought their hands, palms up, above the level of their shoulders and wagged them back and forth, "Oy-yoy, sheeny! Run! Go on, run!"

I didn't run. I glared. I walked by with as much elegance and aloofness as was compatible with a necessity to balance a basket of noodle soup, pot roast, potatoes, vegetable and pudding.

Of course it was nothing more than a couple of thousand years of bigotry raising its hideous head again to spit on a defenseless and shrinking morsel of humanity. Yet it all must have left a deep scar on a sensitive child. It was unreasoning and widespread in the town. My parents were subject to it. The four or five respectable Jewish families of the town knew it well. They were intelligent men and women, American born and bred, for the most part. It probably gave me a ghastly inferiority, and out of that inferiority doubtless was born inside me a fierce resolution, absurd and childish, such as, "You wait! I'll show you! I'll be rich and famous and you'll wish you could speak to me."

Well, I did become rich and famous, and have lived to see entire nations behaving precisely like the idle frustrated bums perched on the drugstore railing. Of course Ottumwa wasn't a benighted town because it was cruel to its Jewish citizens. It was cruel to its Jewish citizens because it was a benighted town. Business was bad, the town was poor, its people were frightened, resentful, and stupid. There was, for a place of its size and locality, an unusually large rough element. As naturally as could be these searched for a minority on whom to vent their dissatisfaction with the world. And there we were, and there I was, the scapegoat of the ages. Yet, though I had a tough time of it in Ottumwa and a fine time of it in New York, I am certain that those Ottumwa years were more enriching, more valuable than all the fun and luxury of the New York years.

There was no Jewish place of worship in Ottumwa. The five or six Jewish families certainly could not afford the upkeep of a temple. I knew practically nothing of the Jewish people, their history, religion. On the two important holy days of the year—Rosh Hashana, the Jewish New Year; and Yom Kippur, the Day of Atonement—they hired a public hall for services. Sometimes they were able to bring to town a student rabbi who had, as yet, no regular congregation. Usually one of the substantial older men who knew something of the Hebrew language of the Bible, having been taught it in his youth, conducted the service. On Yom Kippur, a long day of fasting and prayer, it was an exhausting thing to stand from morning to sunset in the improvised pulpit. The amateur rabbi would be relieved for an hour by another member of the little improvised congregation. Mr. Emmanuel Adler, a familiar figure to me as he sat in his comfortable home talking with my parents, a quaint long-stemmed pipe between his lips, a little black skullcap atop his baldish head as protection against drafts, now would don the rabbinical skullcap, a good deal like that of a Catholic priest. He would open on the high reading stand the Bible and the Book of Prayers containing the service for the Day of Yom Kippur, and suddenly he was transformed from a plump middle-aged German-born Jew with sad kindly eyes and a snuffy gray-brown mustache to a holy man from whose lips came words of wisdom and of comfort and of hope.

The store always was closed on Rosh Hashana and Yom Kippur. Mother put on her best dress. If there were any Jewish visitors in the town at that time they were invited to the services and to dinner at some hospitable house afterward. In our household the guests were likely to be a couple of traveling salesmen caught in the town on that holy day. Jewish families came from smaller nearby towns—Marshalltown, Albia, Keokuk.

I can't account for the fact that I didn't resent being a Jew. Perhaps it was because I liked the way my own family lived, talked, conducted its household and its business better than I did the lives of my friends. I admired immensely my grandparents, my parents, my uncles and aunt. Perhaps it was a vogue, something handed down to me from no one knows where. Perhaps it was something not very admirable—the actress in me. I think, truthfully, that I rather liked dramatizing myself, feeling myself different and set apart. I probably liked to think of myself as persecuted by enemies who were (in my opinion) my inferiors. This is a protective philosophy often employed. Mine never had been a religious family. The Chicago Neumann family sometimes went to the temple at Thirty-third and Indiana, but I don't remember that my parents ever went there while in Chicago. In our own household there was no celebration of the informal home ceremonies so often observed in Jewish families. The Passover, with its Seder service, was marked in our house only by the appearance of the matzos or unleavened bread, symbolic of the hardships of the Jews in the wilderness. I devoured pounds of the crisp crumbling matzos with hunks of fresh butter and streams of honey, leaving a trail of crumbs all over the house, and thought very little, I am afraid, of the tragic significance of the food I was eating or of that weary heartsick band led by Moses out of Egypt to escape the Hitler of that day, one Pharaoh; or of how they baked and ate their unsalted unleavened bread because it was all they had, there in the wilderness. I still have matzoth (*matzos*, we always called them) in my house during the Passover, and just as thoughtlessly. Now they come as delicate crisp circlets, but they seem to me much less delicious than the harder, tougher squares of my childhood munching. Ours were not Jewish ways. My father and mother and sister Fan and I exchanged many friendly little calls with the pleasant Jewish families of the town—the Almeyers, the Adlers, Feists, Silvers, Lyons, living in comfortable well-furnished houses, conducting their affairs with intelligence and decorum, educating their children. They saw a little too much of one another. There was a good deal of visiting back and forth, evenings. At nine there would be served wine or lemonade and cake, a moment which I eagerly awaited. The Ferber specialty was a hickory-nut cake, very rich, baked in a loaf, for which I was permitted to crack the nuts and extract the meats. This was accomplished with a flat-iron between my knees and a hammer in my hand. The nuts went into the cake and into me fifty-fifty. Once baked, it was prudently kept under lock and key in the cupboard of the sitting-room desk, rather than in the free territory of the pantry.

My mother, more modern than most in thought and conduct, had numbers of staunch friends among the non-Jewish townspeople, and these enormously enjoyed her high spirits, her vitality, her shrewd and often caustic comment. She, too, was an omnivorous reader, so that when life proved too much for her she was able to escape into the reader's Nirvana. Certainly she was the real head of the family, its born leader; unconsciously she was undergoing a preliminary training which was to stand her in good stead when she needed it.

It is interesting (to me) to note that all this time I never wrote a line outside my schoolwork and never felt the slightest urge toward original composition. But the piece-speaking went on like a house afire. I recited whenever I could. In school we had recitations every Friday afternoon, and a grand burst of entertainment at the end of each term and on that world-rocking occasion, the Last Day of School, in June. I was by this time a confirmed show-off and a chronic reciter. At the slightest chance I galloped to the front of the room and began my recitation, with gestures. My bliss was complete on those days when we went from room to room giving our programs as visiting artists before an entire class of helpless listeners. To a frustrated actress like myself it is significant now to read a phrase that recurs again and again in that hastily scribbled line-a-day kept by Julia Ferber. "Edna recited," it says. No comment, no criticism. Edna recited.

During the Ottumwa period my sister and I used to be taken to Chicago once a year, in the summer, to visit Grandma and Grandpa Neumann. By this time money was scarce, and we—my mother and the two of us—sat up all night in the coach. Children of six were allowed to ride free. I was bundled up in a shawl for a supposed nap, and told to make myself very small. There I lay, trembling and sweating, until the conductor had passed on his ticket-collecting trip. He always looked exactly the same, though perhaps he wasn't. Perhaps he only followed the pattern of the Midwest American train conductor—grizzled, spectacled, brownish spots on the backs of his hands; an Elks and a Masonic emblem; service stripes on his sleeve, a worn, patient, and rather benevolent face, strangely unembittered by the pettiness, bad manners, and vagaries of the American traveling public.

He would cast a doubting eye on the plump mound under the shawl. "Looks like a big girl to me, ma'am."

"She's big for her age."

Which I undeniably was.

Always I watched and waited with enormous anticipation for the first glimpse of the Mississippi River. I can't explain why it held such fascination for me. Perhaps I had been impressed by what I had learned of it in school—three thousand miles long, tributaries, floods, currents, Mark Twain. For an hour before it was time to cross the great bridge that spanned the stream my face was pressed against the car window. With my own eyes I had seen its ruthless power reflected in the wild antics of our Des Moines River, its tributary. Every year, in the spring, we heard stories of the Mississippi's wild career, how it went berserk and destroyed farms and lives with a single lash of its yellow tail, or gobbled up whole towns in one dreadful yawning of its gigantic jaws. It was always a living thing to me. A monster. When we actually sighted it I eagerly knelt up at the window and watched it out of sight—its broad turbulent bosom, its swift current, its eddies, its vast width, like a mighty lake rather than a river.

The lowlands of Ottumwa, and especially the low-lying Main Street which embraced the chief business section of the town, frequently were flooded. I am here rather embarrassed to admit that I was quite old enough to have known better—such was the terror of the rivers in that part of the country—before I realized that the long laden trains of boxcars and flatcars that crept and puffed so slowly and cautiously along the tracks by the side of the Des Moines River were not 'fraid trains, but freight trains.

It was because of these floods that I knew how rivers behaved. I saw bridges as they swayed, cracked, then, with screams of despair, were swept downstream in the flood. I saw houses tossing like toys in midstream, while sheep, cows, pianos, rocking chairs, bedsteads floated and bobbed by. People sat marooned on rooftops as their houses took to the nautical life.

In the beginning chapters of the novel *Show Boat* there is a description of the Mississippi at floodtime. I found I did not need to consult books or ask old-timers to relate their river experiences. I just took my childhood memories of the Mississippi and the Des Moines at floodtime out of the back of my head where they had been neatly stored for so many years and pinned them down on paper.

It is a method every writer can use and one which all experienced writers do use. Sometimes (this may be scientifically disputed, but I believe it nevertheless) the memory goes back, back, beyond one's actual lifetime experience, into the unknown past. Most writers must have had the odd sensation of writing a line, a paragraph, a page about something of which they have had no actual knowledge or experience. Somehow, inexplicably, they know. It writes itself. Of course the everyday storehouse method is merely a matter of having a good memory and a camera eye, with the mental films all neatly filed away for future development when needed. That is why, no matter what happens, good or bad, to a professional writer, he may count it as just so much velvet. Into the attic it goes. This can better be illustrated, perhaps, by describing a shabby old yellow trunk kept in the storeroom of the Ferber household in my childhood. When you lifted the rickety lid there was wafted to you the mingled odor of mothballs, lavender, faint perfumery, dyes, and the ghostly emanation peculiar to cast-off garments. Inside, the trunk foamed with every shade and variety of material. There were odds and ends and scraps and bolts and yards of silk, satin, passementerie, beads, ruchings, insertion, velvet, lace, ribbon, feathers, flower trimmings, bits of felt, muslin. When my mother needed trimming for a dress or a hat for herself or for my sister Fannie and myself she merely dived into the old trunk, fished around in the whirlpool of stuffs, and came up with just the oddment or elegancy she needed.

from

LIFE SIZE

M A U R I C E   H E X T E R

Maurice Hexter was born in Cincinnati. Although his father was an Orthodox Jew, young Hexter managed to worm out of his religious duties as a young boy, due in part to the lack of a Jewish community in Ohio that otherwise might have steered him to religious classes.

Because his life turned out so well, Hexter could look back on his childhood with cheer and humor, but it had been a difficult existence. Like many Jewish children, he had had to find work to help his family, and the work took him away from them. Although secular life in America distanced him from his German-Jewish roots, he still maintained a strong bond to the Jewish people. That bond can be seen in this selection from his autobiography, Life Size.

Hexter became quite successful working for various Jewish charities, most of them formed by established German-American Jews to assist the new Eastern European Jewish immigrants. These charities were essential in helping assimilate new immigrants.

Later in life, Hexter earned a Ph.D. at Harvard. He served as superintendent of United Jewish Charities and as executive director of the Federation of Jewish Charities. Before Israel's creation as an independent state, Hexter went to Palestine to direct emergency relief and later to oversee the changeover from British to Israeli rule. He also helped found several social-work schools in the United States—among them, those at Hunter College, Brandeis University, and Yeshiva University.

According to the ancient rhyme, I was born "full of grace," as a Tuesday child. I was also a middle child, four years behind my brother, Leo, and three years ahead of Betty. Modern researchers conclude that a middle child manifests "greater dependency behavior"; seeks more adult help and approval than the first or later born; spends more time in individual activity; is generally more talkative. Middle children also tend to be more creative

27

than firstborns. Of course no one knew this back then, which was probably just as well for me.

All this commenced on June 30, 1891, in a lower-middle-class section of Cincinnati. It was not a particularly vintage year for emerging, but Averill Harriman also arrived that year, in far grander circumstances. Eighteen ninety-one was also the year Carnegie Hall opened and Herman Melville closed. And the first of the Sherlock Holmes stories started appearing in London.

My father, Max Hexter, was born in Hoechst, Germany, the site of a large chemical company. "Hexter" is surely derived from that name. My mother, Sarah Beck, came from a town near Dresden and was related to the famous Rabbi Baeck. My father had come to America when he was in his mid-twenties and had a little capital. I never found out how he came to invest most of it in an oil well in Ohio. The drilling ran out and the oil didn't. (Years later a Rockefeller company got the lease on the well and brought in a minor gusher by going down another two hundred feet.)

My parents met here through cousins, the Blocks. After marriage, my father opened a little candy store near the old Cincinnati & Ohio railway station. But he clearly wasn't intended for retailing. For one thing, he was hard of hearing, with a middle-ear condition. Still, Cincinnati wasn't a bad place for promising beginnings. The Kroger chain started there; so did the Snyder Ketchup Company, which later became Campbell's Soup.

We had a small apartment behind the store. We spoke German at home, as half of the city's families probably did. (As a result of my early German fluency, which I still have, I sometimes will favor a sentence structure with the verb at the end.)

At five I was enrolled in the nearby 5th District School, which was next to Hughes High School. My first day at school was a shameful catastrophe and I had to be sent home: The newly imposed disciplines, the hostile environment, made me pee in my pants. Worse was to follow. It now appeared that I had inherited my father's hard-of-hearing condition. *Genetics* was barely a word then, let alone a science, but the connection was made. It became more certain when it turned out that my sister, Betty, was also afflicted. I wasn't a particularly dutiful student—I'm sure that my inability to hear well was a factor—and I encountered the disciplinary process often. Usually I would be banished to the clothing closet for a spell. Or merely receive a sharp rap on the knuckles with a long ruler.

Money was tight. At eight, I started selling newspapers—almost at the same time I started reading Horatio Alger stories of *Dan the Newsboy, Pluck and Luck*, and *Paddle Your Own Canoe*. I had two newsboy careers, morning and afternoon. It was quickly apparent that I was a morning person, and getting up at 4:45 wasn't a great hardship. I'd take the streetcar to a downtown printing plant that turned out a very special daily called the Court Index, a mini-version of dailies like the *New York Law Journal*. It provided the only information for lawyers on which courtrooms were to be used for what cases at what time. I had a key to the plant and I would find the corner where the big sheets of the index were placed. First I had to fold them down into smaller sheets. That was easy. The hard part was delivery of 135 copies to lawyers' offices, nearly all of them in fairly high office buildings: eighteen stories at the First National Bank Building, fourteen at the Atlas National Bank, a mere ten at the Union Trust. As a rule elevators weren't running that early in the morning. If I got lucky I'd find an elevator that was taking up the cleaning women, but mostly it was a lot of hiking up and down.

I was finished by 8:00 A.M. and walked to school by way of a Greek candy store, Marooden's, where I had breakfast of a kind—a chocolate sundae, for three cents. (I always asked them to put on lots of chocolate.) After a while I'd be greeted when I came in with a "Good morning, Lots." I'd get a flat $1.50 a week for delivery of the Court Index, minus fifteen cents carfare, or a net of $1.35—it sounds impossibly minuscule today but you have to keep in mind that in those days a pound of round steak cost thirteen cents and a dozen eggs twenty-one cents. You could rent a fairly decent apartment for eighteen dollars a month.

After school let out, at 3:00 P.M., I'd go to the newspaper plants of the *Cincinnati Post* and the *Times-Star*. I'd pay half a cent per paper and sell them for two cents. But before I picked up the papers I'd stop at a little restaurant called Riggs Manhattan, started by a couple from New York. I'd have an order of hotcakes with maple syrup—and you could have all of the syrup you wanted. (Chocolate *and* maple syrup every weekday! No, I never had acne.)

Sundays meant getting to the *Cincinnati Inquirer* plant about 4:00 A.M. to get a bundle of the much thicker Sunday papers. These cost two cents and were supposed to sell for a nickel. Mostly I did residential deliveries right to the door, and every now and then I'd get a windfall: a quarter or even a fifty-cent piece from a big spender. I made at least two dollars on Sundays.

My father was an orthodox Jew who attended a conservative congregation. He walked to it on Saturdays, even though it was a very long walk. He recited his morning prayers, went to *schul* regularly, and I'm sure obeyed the 613 commandments. Naturally, we had a kosher home. (To this day I can't eat pork.) My father saw to it that I was enrolled in the Saturday- and Sunday-school classes. On Saturdays I managed to get evicted in about twenty minutes by talking and I'd run to the public library to read far more interesting volumes, such as Mark Twain's. I probably was a premature agnostic.

When I was ten I made an interesting discovery. Ordinary people paid regular prices for daily newspapers, but there was a sizable element in the city that was far more generous to a newsboy who would come to them. At the turn of the century Cincinnati had a red-light district with hundreds of bordellos. St. Louis and Cincinnati were the only two American cities that ever attempted to control prostitution by registering and inspecting the whores.

By selling papers in the district, usually for five or ten cents, I did much better. I also got to know the various houses and their pricing policies, an odd specialty that later led to a nice windfall.

Propinquity breeds attempt—or contempt, some cynic once said. I was physically eligible but much too frightened of the women I sold to. This was an age long, long before sex had become a commonplace for young-sters. (As for contempt: They were staunch loyal customers who always overpaid. Bless them.)

I was a young man with ferocious energy. What else did I do to earn money? The corn-silk connection. Farmers would come into town with fresh vegetables. During the corn season I'd go under their wagons and pick up the corn silk in the husks that had been pulled from the ears to show the customer what he was getting. There was a market for corn silk: The W. S. Merril Chemical Company paid five cents a pound. It was used somehow in their patented cough syrup.

I discovered basic business principles early. I could add to my earnings by buying the corn silk from other young gatherers for three cents a pound because they wanted to avoid the long trip to the chemical company. I usually made one dollar a day net—and I never tried to smoke corn silk. Much too valuable.

I was introspective and shy. Partial deafness didn't help, but I must have been persuasive. Every morning on the way to pick up papers I'd pass the Berry Bros. Varnish Company. In the window was a red express wagon available as a premium for buying varnish. By my fifth or sixth try I persuaded the owner to give me the little wagon, which became an enor-mous help in carrying my newspapers and the corn silk.

Things also improved at home. The candy store had long vanished and now my father managed to get a loan to buy an oil-delivery route and a horse-drawn tank wagon that carried oil and naphtha to residential customers, who used them for cooking and lighting. I often joined him. We'd go through the streets ringing our bell to announce our presence. We went into apartment houses, took the empty cans, filled them at the faucets of the truck, and then collected the money. It was a big day when my father collected six dollars, because that threw off a net of two dollars. We usually took sandwiches from home and stopped at a saloon to have a beer with the sandwich. Our favorite was a German "Zum Huenerhloch" (chicken's behind). Things got better and my parents were able to buy a house at 912 Richmond Street, a big step up. It cost three thousand dollars, a lot of money then. We lived on the first floor and had a tenant upstairs. We even had a phone installed when it was still a comparative rarity.

I had two good friends: Sidney, the boy who lived upstairs, and Rachel Manischewitz, who lived nearby. Ray's family baked matzos and were on their way to become a Jewish tradition. (As I write this the old firm was worth forty-five million dollars.) Sidney's family moved to Hamilton, Ohio, twenty miles from us and easily traveled on the interurban trolley. There was a large reservoir and Sidney and I chipped in to buy a used canoe. Once we canoed from Hamilton down the Miami River, a three-day trip, and then back. I picked up a tent and sometimes I would take the canoe up the Ohio River and set up my tent for the weekend. There was a Coney Island-like resort on the river to which steamboats would carry people to and from the city. To get to my primitive little camp I'd sometimes get on the stern of the boat at the wharf and ride up to where my tent was located, jump in the river, and swim for shore. It wasn't the only idiotic daring I displayed in those years.

I had an insatiable curiosity about places and people—particularly raffish ones—and one of the particular attractions was the Latonia racetrack, over the river in Kentucky. It was a sleazy, second-rate dirt track. Generally the Latonia Jockey Club was given a thirty-day running season in June.

I got a job as a hot walker, a stablehand who walks horses after an exercise run. When I was twelve I got promoted to jockey and rode in ten or twelve races, which paid me fifty dollars per. (The owner provided the silks and boots.) I was about five feet four inches and weighed 110 pounds, not ideal jockey statistics, but permissible. I think if I had ever won there would have been great embarrassment all around. Of course, I didn't know then that jockeys couldn't get life insurance. Racing was considered even riskier than steeple-jacking. I'm sure it wouldn't have mattered if I *had* known. Kids have no intimations of mortality.

Inevitably came time for my bar mitzvah. It called for intense make-up study, because I had not been a good student at the Saturday- and Sunday-Hebrew school sessions. With the concentrated study came an awareness of the religious community around me. I was fascinated by a neighboring family, the Isaacs, who were *really* orthodox. On Friday night they'd disconnect their telephone so it wouldn't ring on the Sabbath. One of the men in the family, a heavy cigar smoker, would smoke a lot on Friday and blow the smoke into test tubes, which he would cork. On Saturdays when he couldn't smoke he'd open the test tubes, one at a time, and inhale deeply.

Religion began playing an increasingly divisive role in our own family. My father decided that his first-born, Leo, should become a rabbi, and should go to Hebrew Union College. Leo didn't last long there and dropped out. It led to a bitter time between my father and my brother and contributed, I'm sure, to Leo's lack of focus in his life. A terrible waste: I considered myself pretty bright, but Leo was far smarter. But he was in the wrong family at the wrong time. For many years he retreated into gambling and heavy drinking.

It was a particularly difficult time for him and my father because by then my parents had bought a larger house on Avondale. We occupied the whole house and in order to make the mortgage payments my mother took in boarders, mostly students at Hebrew Union College, which then had no dormitories. One of the students my mother took care of was Julius Mark, who later became Rabbi Mark of Temple Emanu-El in New York. The contrast between good-student Julius Mark and my brother was too marked. For a time, Leo ran away.

I sold papers through most of my intermediate and some high-school years. I was a good student, somehow, and skipped at least two grades, in spite of playing hooky from time to time. Corporal punishment was still approved—when I got whacked by the principal, it was the last time I skipped school.

In Hughes High School I was introduced to anti-Semitism. The common cry was, "Hughes, Hughes, niggers and Jews." Cincinnati was just north of the Mason-Dixon Line and had been once a key stop on the underground railway for escaped slaves. But Blacks and Jews were a distinct minority in the school. I had become a prodigious reader and didn't mind in the least that there were no Jewish fraternities in high school.

Out of the blue came my great gift from Uncle Sam himself. Well, one of his minions: the Bureau of Immigration. The bureau was conducting a nationwide study on the importation of prostitutes into America—even though experts had told them there was more than enough local talent— and now the investigators had come to Cincinnati. The white slave trade was a very hot subject then. One of the investigators talked to a local newspaper editor, who thought a moment and recommended a young twelve-year-old hustling newsboy who knew the red-light district better than anyone. A kid who sold more *Times-Star* papers to whores and their customers than anyone else. Me.

I managed to keep my mouth closed when they mentioned the "expert" fee they could pay me: ten dollars a day. (Twenty dollars a week was a good salary then.) For that I was to guide them through the district and give them the pricing level of each house: which were the $2, $3, the $5, and even the plush $10, the top of the line. There were hundreds of houses, so it could not be done in a day. The task took ten days, which gave me one hundred dollars and a minor mention somewhere in the voluminous report the immigration people finally did on the subject.

In my senior year we had talks about college. I hoped to get away from home to a private college in the Northeast, but my father said there just wasn't enough money. So college would have to be the University of Cincinnati, which was then the second city-run liberal arts college in the nation. (CCNY, now City College of the City University of New York, was the first.) Tuition at Cincinnati was two hundred dollars a year and I'd have to earn it.

There were jobs at school for willing students. My first was typing—although I never learned the touch system—for a geology professor. I transcribed his handwritten notes. The pay was better than selling newspapers and it didn't involve long trips and a lot of carrying.

Other opportunities emerged. I began teaching English three evenings a week to some of the new immigrants at the Jewish Settlement House. This was 1910, when I was a junior, and the great influx of East European Jews was reaching a peak. Another job, much less proper: One of our rich local ladies, Helen Trounstein, was making a study of the dance halls. She was certain that they were being used to induce girls to enter prostitution. There was a law that no one under eighteen could enter those halls, but she was certain it wasn't being enforced. Thus my job: to find out how old the girls were. To get to the dance halls I needed a car and she lent me her Model-T Ford, which I learned to operate in an afternoon. At the halls I had to dance with the girls and find out who was under eighteen and where they lived. I then discovered two things about myself: I don't like dancing and I don't like being a snitch. More than half the girls were under eighteen and Helen Trounstein, a minor local power, managed to get a lot of the dance halls closed.

In college I also began working for Professor Robert C. Brooks, a political scientist, who gave me research tasks. It was congenial work and by my junior year I wondered out loud to Professor Brooks if, after all, I might not think of a career of college teaching. He shook his head, sadly, and pointed out that as far as he knew there wasn't a single Jew teaching political science then at the college or university level anywhere in the country. The odds were bad, he said. (The prevailing academic anti-Semitism had a remarkably long run: it didn't die until after World War II.)

There was a certain consistency of the policy. A couple of gentile friends who were presidents of their fraternities apologized for not being able to propose me for membership.

As a sweetener for this disappointment Brooks came up with a possible consolation prize. The National Municipal League was meeting in Cincinnati—then one of the most corrupt cities in the country—and from the balance of the convention funds they announced a prize essay contest with a two-hundred-dollar first prize. Professor Brooks urged me to try for it. I took three days off from school and banged out a longish piece on how American cities could obtain the reform so badly needed. A few months later my mother told me she had forgotten to give me a letter. I opened it and there was a congratulatory letter and a check for two hundred dollars. A marvelous sum for those days—a full year's tuition.

If I wasn't to go into college teaching there was only one other path: law school. Under local rules that prevailed at a lot of colleges until World War II you could spend your senior year as a first-year student in law school, if your grades were good enough. I elected that path and long before the year was out realized this was not for me. I had some adolescent moral qualms: If I won a case it meant someone had to lose, and so on. But in truth I simply felt uncomfortable in law study.

I graduated from college in 1912—my one year in law school counted as my senior year—but I was not at the ceremony, because I had agreed to help my mentor, now my friend, Professor Robert Brooks, in two matters: He had taken a job with Swarthmore College and he was doing a study for the National Education Association on teachers' salaries. I was working on that.

In the fall I was the beneficiary of a nationwide reform movement that led to the creation of the Municipal Research Bureau. I did several jobs for them: on police personnel policies; on local traffic rerouting, which led to my being called "Expert Hexter" in the *Cincinnati Times*. But expert or no, I still didn't have a real *job*. Just then fate intervened forcefully and I was firmly set on a path that was to endure for many decades, with interesting detours here and there. The instrument of fate was Dr. Boris Bogen, a Russian immigrant who had managed to get a doctorate in education at the University of Moscow—which had far worse restrictions on Jewish students than we had here—and had come to America. Here he took up social service, which was just a notion then. So in January 1913, at the age of twenty-two, I entered the office of the United Jewish Charities of Cincinnati, which had been formed in 1896. (Boston had been the first, in 1895, to unite its Jewish charities.)

He had asked me to work for him, he later told me, because he liked the way I handled the evening English classes at the Settlement House when I was in college. "I liked the way you stayed put when the bell rang," he said. "You didn't rush out but remained to answer questions for ten or fifteen minutes." That, he added, made him think that I could be trained for social work.

In a way, he constituted the first major Jewish social-work school. The pay was not great—fifty dollars for the first three months and then fifty dollars a month—but considering the tuition was free, it was riches. And, of course, I was living at home.

Dr. Bogen had a large family, with four boys and three girls and an interesting, well-educated wife. In time I became one of the family.

from

LIEUTENANT BIRNBAUM:
A SOLDIER'S STORY

MEYER BIRNBAUM

Meyer Birnbaum grew up in an Orthodox family in Brooklyn during the Depression. His mother and father were Polish immigrants who observed Orthodox Judaism's rules, and the children were raised in a religious household despite the many diversions America offered the family.

Birnbaum became quite active in Young Israel, a youth organization, and, interestingly, became part of a backlash against older Jews, whom youths deemed not religious enough. Notable in this excerpt is Birnbaum's recollection of his bar mitzvah, a dramatic contrast to many of today's boisterous and lavish affairs.

Because of his activities with Young Israel, Birnbaum had an opportunity to meet respected Jewish scholars. He served in the United States Army during World War II and participated in the Normandy invasion. Later in the war, Birnbaum was at the liberation of Buchenwald and Ohrduff. Taking the love of Israel instilled in him as a child and the skills he gained in the U.S. Army, he trained Israeli youngsters in the tactics they'd need for the War of Independence. Later in life, he moved to Israel.

I was born in 1918, and three other siblings followed in the next six years—two sisters and a brother.

Any way you look at it, we were poor. During the Great Depression, of course, we were far from the only ones struggling for every penny, and that made being poor somewhat easier to take. Still, you have to put food on the table and clothes on your back.

My father worked for the Works Progress Administration and brought home eighteen dollars a week. My mother did not work, and when I was about eight years old, she lost her sight in one eye. That only made our situation worse since even the housework became much more difficult for her. From the time I was ten or eleven, I used to skip Friday afternoon classes in the winter months so that I could help my mother clean the house and prepare for *Shabbos*. Even though I was only an average student, my principal was sympathetic and gave me permission to leave at lunchtime. This continued through my first two years in high school.

We were so poor that we couldn't afford to pay the electric bills and we lit the house with gas lanterns. Even toilet paper was beyond our means. I used to go to fruit stores and take the tissue paper in which the fruits were packed. All our clothing was handed down from our cousins. One of my uncles bought me my bar mitzvah suit. It was the first new clothing I had ever worn. A new pair of shoes was a major financial crisis. My mother would buy shoes that were several sizes too large for us and stuff them with newspaper. As our feet grew, we would remove the newspaper from the toes. Every two or three months, I would go to Woolworth's and buy new rubber soles for my shoes and for those of my younger siblings. Then I would scrape the soles, put on a special glue, and replace the worn-out ones.

My first two years in high school were spent in an annex of Thomas Jefferson High School, which was several miles from my home. It was a long walk, especially in the winter, when the snowdrifts piled up and the wind was blowing. The better-off kids took the subway, but I couldn't afford the fare.

My aunt and uncle, who lived downstairs from us, owned a wholesale fruit business. Once a week, there would be a package of fruits and vegetables left at the bottom of the steps. Potatoes were the staple of our diet. My mother could make anything with potatoes.

My friends and I hit upon a stratagem for supplementing our supply of potatoes. There was a railroad siding that divided Brownsville from East New York. Railroad cars carrying produce for the Brooklyn Terminal Market were brought there. The cars were guarded to make sure that no one tried to steal the produce. We would go down to the rail yard and throw pebbles against the cars. When the guards heard the ping of stones hitting the cars, they would start throwing potatoes and onions, or sometimes coal, back at us. They couldn't chase us because they were afraid to leave the cars unguarded. When we had enticed them into throwing enough to fill the scrub pails we brought with us, we would gather up whatever was lying around and scurry home. While today I'm not proud of this story, it gives you an idea of the poverty of the times.

My bar mitzvah celebration was fully commensurate with our economic status. I had an *aliyah* on Monday morning at the Malta Street *shul* down the block from us. After *davening*, a *minyan* of men from the *shul* came back to our house, where my mother served them egg *kichlech*, herring, and coffee. Not a single friend of mine was present. Such quiet, unostentatious bar mitzvahs were not at all uncommon in those days. Most of my friends celebrated their bar mitzvahs in exactly the same way.

On one thing, however, there was no scrimping: my *tefillin*. I can still remember my mother taking me to a *sofer* on Riverdale Avenue in East New York to purchase them. They cost between twenty and twenty-five dollars which, my mother told me later, almost bankrupted us, but they were truly kosher. My mother asked the *sofer*, a chassidic man with a long beard, to give me a *berachah*, something she did whenever we met an older religious Jew.

Like most kids, I wanted a little spending money, which I obviously wasn't going to get from my parents. I got my first job when I was eight years old. My mother told me that she couldn't give me a penny for some candy, and I decided to go out and earn the money myself. Across the street from us there was a soda manufacturer by the name of Chester Club. When I walked in and asked for a job, the owner took one look at me and started laughing. But in the end he gave me a job as a bottle washer. In three or four hours after school, I could make fifty to seventy-five cents plus a soft drink, which I would save for *Shabbos*.

My other job at that age was the traditional one of shining shoes. As people came off the IRT on Pennsylvania Avenue, I'd shout, "Shoe shine, shoe shine, five cents, five-cent shoe shine." It took fifteen minutes for that nickel shine, and if we were lucky, the customer would add a nickel tip.

I hated shining shoes. I found kneeling down on my hands and knees in front of someone degrading. Even with a kneepad, my knees used to bleed after a while. I vowed that when I grew up, I would never let anyone shine my shoes for me.

One of those whose shoes I shined was the infamous Louis Lepke, the head of Murder, Incorporated. He was raised in Brownsville and used to return to the area to visit his family. He came from a traditional Orthodox family; his brother, a sweet man, was a pharmacist in the neighborhood. The paradox of a gangster growing up in a traditional home and still maintaining ties to the old neighborhood was typical of those days—strange as it may seem today. Lepke was nice to us kids. He never tipped me less than a dime, and near the holidays he sometimes threw me a dollar. When I got that type of tip, you can be sure that my workday was done.

During the long summer vacation, I used to sell Big Bear ice creams at Coney Island. We would pick up wooden boxes filled with dry ice from the Big Bear plant on Blake Avenue in Brownsville and from there take a forty-five-minute ride out to Coney Island, where we walked along the beach selling our ice cream pops to the bathers. We'd pay three cents apiece for the pops and sell them for five cents. Sometimes at the end of the day, I would give my mother as much as two or three dollars—which was not bad for a ten-year-old—and she would praise me, "*A gutter. Er is azoi gut*—A good person. He's so good."

One of the occupational hazards of this job was that it was illegal. There were concession stands along the boardwalk, and moving vendors were prohibited. When the owners of the concession stands caught sight of us, they would call the police. The bathers, of course, sided with the cute little kids against the cops, and they would warn us of the cops' approach and sometimes even run interference for us. When we saw the policemen coming, we would run out into the water. The cops would not wade out after us, but would stand on the beach threatening us. After a while they usually wandered away and the people on the beach who had been jeering at them would call out, "It's okay, kid; the coast is clear."

I was once collared from behind by a policeman in the midst of a big sale and hauled off in a paddy wagon to the police station on West 8th Street in Coney Island. The ice cream boys whom the police had caught that day were all placed together in the police station garage, which is also where they took the bodies of drowning victims. We sat there trembling at the thought of the bodies covered with newspaper. We made a deal that whichever boy's parents arrived first would take out the other kids as well.

Another of my summer jobs made me the envy of all my friends. An older cousin managed a roller coaster called the Cyclone. Each seat held two people. Whenever there was a lone rider, especially if it was a young child, I would ride next to him to make sure he did not lean forward and hit his head on the bar in front of him. Actually, the ride quickly became boring, despite the delirious screaming of the riders, but the five dollars my brother and I picked up in a day seemed like a fortune to us.

Some of the jobs really built me up physically. One of these was as a "puller" in a commercial laundry. I had to lean over a large bin of wet laundry and separate the large from the small pieces as I pulled them out. Sopping wet laundry can get pretty heavy, and this job strained me to the utmost until my body adjusted.

But the hardest job of all was cleaning windows. By my last two years of high school, I had become a pretty serious student. In order to have time to study at night, I took a job cleaning windows early in the morning. Getting up long before sunrise was just one of the job's hardships. In the wintertime, I had to work very quickly—first getting the water off the sponge so that it did not freeze and render the sponge useless, and then removing the water from the windows before it froze. We used to put alcohol in the water to prevent it from freezing. By the time I finished my hands were ice, and the rest of me was not much warmer.

Despite my mother's determination to raise us as *frum* Jews, I had little formal Jewish education as a child and teenager. Perhaps because my mother was raised in an environment so permeated with *Yiddishkeit* and her own faith was so firm, she did not realize how important yeshiva training was for an American boy. In addition, the East New York section of Brooklyn in which we lived had no yeshivos in those days. To get to the Lower East Side, where most of the yeshivos were, would have involved taking two trolley cars and several trains, something beyond the capacity of most young kids.

In any event, I was a regular public school kid all the way. All my friends were nonreligious. In the afternoons, I would play ball with them wearing my homemade *yarmulke*. They would laugh at me when the *yarmulke* fell off as I was running the bases, but I got used to it. I learned early in life not to be fazed by being laughed at, and that ability served me well during my years in the army.

What little formal Jewish education I had consisted of an hour a day after school with a private *rebbe*. Six or seven other boys and I would recite *aleph-beis* (or in later years, *Chumash*), while the *rebbe* sat there paying more attention to the onions or potatoes he was peeling to help his overburdened wife than to us. It was very discouraging. By my bar mitzvah, I told my mother that she was wasting her money and that I should go to yeshiva instead.

My only real teacher as a young boy was my mother. Every day she would come down to where I was playing ball and escort me to *shul* for *Minchah-Maariv* services. I was always the only young kid there and someone would invariably ask, "Do you have to say *Kaddish*?" In the worst winter weather, my mother would open up the window and call out for me to go to *shul*. She would watch me from the window the entire way to make sure I went. Whenever I looked back, I would see my mother in the window—watching.

What is interesting is that I do not remember ever resenting my mother's close supervision. Her authority was unchallenged. I never told her, "Oh Ma, leave me alone." I didn't try to fool my mother or forget *cheder* or *davening* whenever the ballgame got too exciting, as other boys did.

Not one of my mother's ten older brothers and sisters remained religious. I don't have even one religious cousin. One of my uncles used to take off my *yarmulke* and tell me that I would go bald from wearing such an old-fashioned thing on my head. My mother would grab it back, put it on my head, and lead me to a corner where she would console me. Eventually, we stopped visiting that uncle.

When I was sixteen or seventeen, a rich uncle offered me twenty-five dollars to work six nights a week, including *Shabbos*, at his stand in the Washington Square Market in Manhattan, which was then the largest wholesale fruit and vegetable market in the United States. Twenty-five dollars a week was a fortune to us—my father was then bringing home only eighteen dollars a week for full-time work. My mother's response was blunt: "There is not enough money in the world to buy *Shabbos*. We'll starve to death before Meyer works on *Shabbos*."

In those days, there were many who came from religious homes who were eager not only to give up religious observance themselves but also to lure others away. They must have felt guilty about having been unable to withstand the temptations of America, and the sight of others who had been able to resist was a constant reproach to them.

As a youngster, I was always asked at family celebrations to make *hamotzi* over the *challah*. No one else in the family could even make a blessing. When I got older, I refused. I sensed that my relatives were treating the blessing as some sort of joke. At family gatherings, my mother would stress to my siblings and me that we could not eat anything without her explicit permission.

Most important of all, my mother instilled in me a love of doing *chesed* (good deeds). If she looked out the window and saw someone carrying a number of packages or bags of groceries, she would send me outside to help. When I returned from these little missions, she would praise me so warmly that I could hardly wait for the next opportunity to help someone. She herself was a model of *chesed*. When people came door-to-door for donations, she always gave them a nickel and invited them in for coffee and cake or some pickled herring. Never did she just give someone money.

When I was younger, my mother was also a member of the *Chevrah Kadishah*, which prepares bodies for burial. Those who worked with her in this *chesed shel emes* (true *chesed*—i.e., one undertaken without any possibility of being reciprocated) told me years later how she was always the first one there for every *taharah* (purification of the body prior to burial). Though my mother was a small, slight woman, and the process of doing the *taharah* can be physically strenuous, she nevertheless had the strength for this great *mitzvah*.

My mother was a bastion of strength for every Jew in the neighborhood who needed encouragement to remain firm in his or her religious observance. It was not easy to be *frum* in those days. Besides the economic pressure to work on *Shabbos*, religious Jews were subjected to continual ridicule for holding on to their old-country ways. Whenever my mother felt people were in danger of succumbing to either the economic or social pressures, she would visit them and encourage them. Jews who felt their religious resolve weakening often came to see her. Her own faith was so rock hard that it inevitably strengthened those who were wavering.

From the time I was a little boy, I was always attracted to *Yiddishkeit*. By ten, I was a regular *kiruv* professional. On *Shabbos* afternoon, I would stand outside the movie theater. As boys came out I would speak to them and try to convince them to come to the Young Israel and experience some taste of *Yiddishkeit*. I was pretty good at this, and was even given a prize for bringing the most kids to the Young Israel. Some of my best friends to this day are those whom I picked up outside the Biltmore theater.

from

PREPOSTEROUS PAPA

LEWIS MEYER

Lewis Meyer, a Tulsa lawyer, television and radio personality, and bookstore owner, grew up in a small Oklahoma town. He had to travel to Tulsa for the High Holy Days, since Sapulpa had no synagogue. (As a matter of fact, between 1906 and 1916, Joseph Blatt of Temple B'nai Israel was the only rabbi in the state of Oklahoma.)

Lewis's father, Max, remedied this situation by building a temple in Sapulpa where Reform, Conservative, and Orthodox Jews could worship together. The following piece written by Lewis describes rather humorously what Jewish worship was like in a southwestern town in the first quarter of the twentieth century. Surely it was a far cry from the crowded neighborhoods of the large eastern cities.

Papa spoke Yiddish with an Arkansas accent. One of papa's distant relatives, who dropped in for a week on his way from New York to California, said to me, "I wish your father would stick to English. When he talks Yiddish he sounds like a Frenchman speaking Italian that he learned from a Swede."

His Yiddish was to Yiddish what Yiddish is to German. He had little opportunity to hear Yiddish spoken, but when he did hear it, he plunged into the conversation like a long-lost brother. The people he interrupted were considerably startled at this sudden torrent of pidgin Yiddish from what was surely a full-blooded Osage Indian. More than once, Papa's size was the only thing that saved him.

Papa never remembered anyone's having taught him to speak Yiddish, nor to read Hebrew. "I just absorbed 'em," he said. "Picked 'em up along the line."

Hebrew scholars who suddenly heard Papa's voice reading Hebrew prayers looked shocked and disbelieving. On the other hand, we who knew no Hebrew at all marveled at Papa's seeming ability to hold his own with the others.

Our prayer books had English on one page and Hebrew on the opposite page. Since those who prayed in Hebrew went faster than those who read the English, we children were always falling behind. During services, we'd constantly call Papa to us and demand to know the correct place at that moment. He'd look at us solemnly, moisten his index finger, and start flipping the pages of the prayer book we handed him.

He'd turn ten pages ahead, then back up fifteen. Hopelessly lost, he'd peer over the shoulders of an old-timer who knew where he was, glance at the page number, turn our book to the proper page, and hand it back to us with the pious admonition, "For Pete's sake, try to pray faster!"

My father believed in God, in prayer, and in doing right. Although he knew little if anything about the service itself, he preferred the Orthodox manner of worship to the Reform service in English. He was a good observer. He stood when others stood. He sat when they sat. He wore his tallith on his shoulders and his *yarmulka* on the back of his head.

During the responsive readings he chanted aloud in that quaint, queer Hebrew vernacular which was all his own. He was proud to be accepted as a fellow member by this group of deeply religious men.

"Do you understand what they're saying?" I asked him once.

"Do I have to understand to be blessed?" he hedged.

"What I mean is—wouldn't you get more out of it if you read the service in English the way the Reform Jews do?"

"Certainly not!" Papa stated emphatically. "The Orthodox Jews are the only real Jews. They pray the way the prayers were written to be prayed. They are religious because there are three hundred and sixty-five things they can't do. They can't eat pork. Can't mix milk with meat. Can't eat shrimp. Can't eat catfish. Can't ride on Saturday. Can't do lots of things. And by golly, they are happier not doin' all those things than the Reform Jews are who do anything and everything they please! Show me a man whose religion keeps him toein' the mark and I'll show you a good, moral, Godfearin' person. It's when the church gets so liberal that a member can do anything short of killin' with a clear conscience that the folks in it get into trouble."

Papa compromised, however, on the house of worship he built in Sapulpa. He made it possible for both Orthodox and Reform Jews to hold services in the same place. On the High Holy Days, the Orthodox group began at seven in the morning and took an intermission from ten until noon.

During this period the Reform worshippers trooped in and held their services in English. Then the Orthodox resumed their prayers until an afternoon break, when the Reform element took over again. Papa, who felt a Reform service was better than no service at all, stayed through it all.

When Papa first came to Oklahoma, he and Mama made what was then the long trip to Tulsa for the Jewish holidays. They had to choose a hotel close enough to the shul for them to walk to the services because Papa held to the Orthodox belief that it was a sin to ride in a car on holy days.

This meant that they had to arrive at the temple early in the morning, kill time between services, and stay until the closing prayers at sundown. Then they walked back to the hotel and began the drive back home. Four children complicated this system to the point where religion was almost a chore.

After taking a one-man poll of all elements in the county—strict Orthodox, Conservative, semi-Reform, strict Reform—Papa was convinced that there'd be a willing Jewish congregation right there in Sapulpa if they had a place to pray.

He had his eye on a large corner lot (which was two blocks from his house on Oak Street—a short walk to food after a fast day!), and without consulting anyone but himself, he bought it.

He then designed one of the strangest temples imaginable. From the street it looked like a neat, comfortable home. Indeed, the front door opened into what was a living room during the nonreligious days and a reception room for the congregation on the three or four holy days of the year. The five-room house took up one side of the structure.

The other side, which also opened onto the living-reception area, was a temple, large enough to accommodate a hundred worshippers. The walls were always neatly papered, the woodwork freshly painted. There was a rostrum at one end containing a large, raised prayer table. The east wall contained an enclosure which held the Holy Torah. The pews were highly varnished pine benches.

Papa was the autocrat of this little temple. His was the responsibility for keeping it clean. He made decisions about repairs. He decided when new prayer books should be purchased. He listened to members' complaints on every subject from too-soft soap to too-hard seats.

It was Herschel Cohen who brought up the subject of the seats.

"Max," Herschel said, "it's not fault that I'm finding. Believe me, we're all loving the shul you built. It's very nice."

"But—" Papa anticipated.

"But maybe the seats are too hard. We all know what Mrs. Shapiro thinks of them. She tells everybody about her piles. But Irving and Rose Brodsky have rear-end trouble, too. Irving tells me that Rose had to leave in the middle of the Rosh Hashana service because she couldn't sit on that wood a minute longer.''

"I *like* the benches,'' Papa said. "A temple doesn't have to sit like a movie.''

Herschel pressed his point. "*Your tokis* is well padded, Max. You've got a natural cushion. You must look at the situation from all viewpoints.''

Papa couldn't help smiling. "All viewpoints! Front, rear, top, and bottom! Okay, Herschel. You win. I'll have some cushion pads made. We don't want any backsliders just because the seats are too hard on their backsides!''

The cushions not only helped increase the attendance. They made for a happier flock.

When strangers entered this bright and cozy place of worship, with its chintz curtains and its austerely clean look, they got a homey feeling. This was exactly the impression Papa wanted them to get.

"A temple should be like a home,'' he said, "because the Lord lives there.'' Papa's temple was compared at various times to everything from a small Congregational meetinghouse in New England to a prayer room in Israel. Among churches it was unique.

Papa footed the bill for the works—the lot, the house-temple, the modest furnishings, the prayer books, and the Holy Torah itself.

"It'll always be easy to find a nice couple to live in the house part,'' he said, "a man and his wife who won't mind our usin' their livin' room three or four times a year. We'll make the rent so low they'll stay a long time and keep the place nice. Won't be any taxes to pay because it's a church. The rent money will take care of the upkeep.''

"Dues and fees'' was a subject Papa expounded on with great feeling. "I've noticed that they do one tenth prayin' and nine tenths beggin' in a lot of churches,'' he said. "People don't need to be browbeaten into givin' to the Lord. They hate like hell to put it on a pay-as-you-pray basis. It burns a man up when someone tells him how much he oughta give to his church. The kibitzers who do it confuse themselves with Solomon! Once our little temple gets to goin' it won't cost anybody anything to come and worship God. It'll be plain-lookin' enough so's people won't have to feel that they have to dress up in fancy clothes just to enter it.''

Through the years it worked the way Papa planned it. The structure is still there, surrounded by giant trees, landscaped with shrubs (from the Max Meyer Nursery). What a rare temple it was! Free of debt from the beginning. Free of controversy, too. Nobody got mad, nobody resigned, nobody got upset—not even when Papa went for red-white-and-green candy-striped wallpaper (which was a trifle unsettling as you prayed on an empty stomach on Yom Kippur). It was, and still is, a very pleasant place to come to and be with God.

News of Papa's temple spread to all the small towns in the area. People who felt they could not afford the city temples where there were fixed prices for seats, and where most of the worshippers were expensively dressed, came to Sapulpa to worship in the little house-temple, temple-house. There was no choir, there were few trimmings, but everyone who came to pray went away with a good feeling.

Complications occasionally presented themselves, but people rose above them. On Yom Kippur, while the men fasted and prayed, small children ran up and down the narrow middle aisle between the benches eating bananas, apples, and bread-butter-and-jelly sandwiches.

Sometimes stone-deaf Teresa Braunstein, who went to the Christian Science Church fifty weeks a year and to the Sapulpa Jewish Temple the other two, carried on a toneless conversation with her cousin Sadie which drowned out completely the voice of the person leading the Reform service.

Sometimes old Mr. Finkelstein decided to stay in his seat through the Reform service after leading the Orthodox prayers. He read aloud from his own prayer book (in Hebrew) while the Reform leader valiantly read against him (in English). But, all in all, it was, and still is, more of a house of worship than many religious edifices infinitely more beautiful, more comfortable, and more financially embarrassed.

The entire congregation was unnerved the Yom Kippur Bea chose to elope with Harold Miller. Three times Harold had come to Sapulpa from St. Louis to ask for Bea's hand in marriage. Three times Papa had put him off. When Bea went back to enroll for her senior year at the university, she enrolled at the Marriage License Bureau instead and telephoned the tidings to Papa the night before Yom Kippur Eve.

Yom Kippur is a fast day but Papa was so upset at what his daughter had done that he began what amounted to a hunger strike. He ate no supper the night Bea called. Nor did he eat breakfast, dinner, or supper the next day.

All during the services he stayed apart, glowering and grieving over the elopement. No one in the congregation dared congratulate him. Mama, who was happy for Bea and knew that the marriage was good, told everyone, "Leave him alone. He'll get over it."

At the end of the Yom Kippur fast Papa had gone without food for two and a half days instead of the conventional twenty-four hours. Mama finally took one of her rare, but effective, stands.

"Max," she said, "if you go around looking like that one more day people will think our daughter has really done something wrong."

"How do I know she hasn't?" Papa muttered. "Elopin' like that without tellin' anybody!"

"They both tried to tell you for three years that they wanted to get married. You wouldn't listen. They are two normal young people in love. Now get to that telephone and call them up at the hotel in Chicago and tell them you forgive them."

"I'm not goin' to do it."

Mama didn't answer him. She went to her closet and started taking out her dresses. She called the children and told us we were going on a trip.

"What's the matter with *you*?" Papa asked uneasily.

"Nothing's the matter with me," Mama said quietly. "I'm not living another day with a man who goes to the temple and prays all day on Yom Kippur and then hasn't an ounce of forgiveness in his heart for his own daughter. I'm going to Texas and I'm taking the children with me." She paused. "I don't think I'll ever come back."

Papa called Bea and Harold that evening. He ate a big bowl of chicken soup first.

"LET GOD WORRY A LITTLE BIT"

GERTRUDE BERG

*Perhaps it goes unnoticed in the annals of American-Jewish history,
but in 1877, the German-Jewish banker Joseph Seligman and his
family were refused accommodations at a hotel in Saratoga Springs.
Not surprisingly, the Jewish community turned to its own resources,
building resorts where they could congregate with other Jews and
avoid anti-Semitism.*

*Because of its proximity to New York City, the Catskills became a
well-known resort for Jews and remained popular until shortly after
World War II when social views on Jews became more liberal. The
spirit of those mountain resorts in their heyday is artfully captured
by Gertrude Berg in this story about a summer in the Catskills.*

*Berg (the Jewish matriarch "Mollie Goldberg" to her millions of
radio and television fans) was born in Upper Manhattan. Her Yiddish
accent was assumed. "My sense of Jewishness," she once said,
"comes not from my father and mother so much as from my grandparents. We scarcely spoke Yiddish at home."*

*Her Jewish background, however, permeated her life, and although
she was acclaimed from 1929 on for her performance as the Jewish
mother whose gentle domination calmed strife, united enemies, and
ran the family, few knew that she also wrote the scripts for the
semifictitious Goldberg family. She drew her characters from life, and
in 1949, when the Goldbergs moved from radio to television, the
program included installments about vacations at Pincus Pines, based
on the Berg family's real life Catskills summer resort.*

"Money," my father used to say, "is of no consequence unless you owe
it."

It was a point of honor with him to pay all debts when due. But, beyond
that, Jake Edelstein was most casual about money. If an investment collapsed, as it frequently did, he'd say to Mother, "Dinah, it was money we
never had." When a real pinch came, and our household fund had to be
commandeered for a creditor, Father would feel slightly sheepish. "Let

God worry about us a little bit," he would say. Then he'd be off on his next business venture.

Over the years God must have worried a good deal. And the year I was fifteen I shared His concern.

For several summers, Father had run Fleischmann's Hotel in the Catskill Mountains, near the village of Griffins Corners. It was a shoestring operation. Each season he opened by the grace of the local butcher, baker, and hardware merchant; each Labor Day he paid off his debts. Then, consigning our worries to God, he would take us back to our New York flat and would work through the winter, managing a restaurant and saving toward another summer.

We loved the hotel; when, that spring, Father revealed that he just didn't have enough money to open it, I was crushed. But, being fifteen and sure of myself, I decided to take matters into my own hands. I went secretly to my grandfather.

Mordecai Edelstein had come to America as an immigrant tinsmith with a talent for hard work. After a lifetime of labor, he had retired from his sheet-metal business in New Jersey, a well-to-do and respected citizen. But the pride and independence that had made him what he was were matched in his son Jake, and as a result the two of them didn't get on well. The last man in the world Jake would have approached for a loan was his father.

"Grandfather," I said, "I've worked hard at the hotel every summer, and I think I should be a partner. Would you lend me the money to buy a partnership from Papa?"

Mordecai pulled at his white handlebar mustache. He understood the maneuver at once, and he knew that his son was ignorant of it. "So how much do you need?" he asked.

"Five thousand dollars."

"All right, but"—and he shook a bony finger under my nose—"remember *you're* the partner, not me."

When I presented the proposition to Father, he realized that my five-thousand dollars could have come only from Grandfather. But, so long as I didn't tell him, he could accept it, and that summer I endured for the first time the burden of debt. Every time a guest checked in, my heart was full of hope; every time one checked out, I was in despair. All I could think of was the money I owed.

We had learned from experience that August 21 was the day when the hotel would begin to go into the black—if it was to go at all. The number of guests we retained from then until Labor Day made the summer worthwhile or a failure, and from this day forward rain and boredom were our mortal enemies. They could empty the hotel like a plague.

On August 21 I awoke at dawn to hear horrible splashing on the roof. I ran to Father's room and cried out in a choking whisper, "It's raining!" Father nodded grimly and headed toward the kitchen.

"Everybody look pleasant!" he commanded the assembled waiters and busboys. A glazed smile was set on each countenance as it went out to face the breakfast guests. But the guests failed to respond. It was raining, and they took it as a personal affront from the management.

After breakfast they all filed out to the veranda to sit in the rocking chairs and look at the sky. It remained gray and wet. Luncheon was more dolorous than breakfast. After lunch they returned to the rockers and the rain. The last train for New York left at four o'clock, and I knew that the moment the first woman announced her departure the exodus would begin.

I also knew who would be first to make the move—a Mrs. Goldenson, whose boredom threshold was low. I kept my eyes on her. What I would do I wasn't sure. I couldn't tie her to the rocker, but something heroic would be demanded.

At 3:15, exactly time to pack and get to the station, Mrs. Goldenson sighed and stood up.

"Mrs. Goldenson!" I almost screamed from the far end of the porch. "How would you like your palm read, your fortune told?"

I was aghast to hear those words coming out of my mouth. I didn't know the first thing about palmistry.

Mrs. Goldenson hesitated. "Fortunes you teli?"

I whipped out a large handkerchief and tied it around my head. I bent over like an old woman and put a crack in my voice. "We gypsies know the future," I cackled.

Mrs. Goldenson smiled and winked at the others, but she sat down and extended her hand. The others crowded around. For a moment I studied her palm, and suddenly I *did* see her future.

All that summer, from my favorite reading spot—a big lobby chair by a window that opened on the porch—I had overheard the gossip and confidences exchanged by the ladies while they rocked. I had stored up everything I heard, and now it was my salvation.

Bending over Mrs. Goldenson's hand, I murmured, "You are a fortunate woman. You have the love of two men."

"Ah?" breathed the circle of kibitzers, pressing closer.

"One is rather short, middle-aged. I think he is bald. . . ."

"Herman," she said with pleased possessiveness.

"The other is young and tall and handsome."

"Stanley, my son," she announced to the ladies.

"I see the two of them close together . . . I think in an office . . ."

"Supreme Fashions," she said.

"I see a cloud coming between you and your son Stanley."

"Never! What kind of a cloud?"

"It's not clear. Perhaps . . . another woman. Yes, a woman. She's in the same office with your husband and son."

"Eunice Meyers!" cried Mrs. Goldenson, striking her forehead with the palm of the hand I was trying to read. "I told Herman not to hire that girl!"

"I see a wedding," I said.

"I'll die!" she wailed. Then she stood up and said, "I have to telephone New York."

A few minutes later she returned to the porch. "Miss Edelstein, please make another room available. My husband and my son Stanley will be coming up this weekend."

Grandfather's money was safe for another twenty-four hours! The following morning the blessed sun shone.

Day by day I watched the ledger figures creep toward the black until our sole debt was the one that weighed most heavily upon me: Grandfather's loan. What if it rained again? I couldn't count on fortune-telling a second time. Then came another inspiration.

At dinner one evening I announced the production of a children's play, with auditions the next morning. I sat up that night to write the play—a mixture of *Cinderella, Robin Hood,* and *Little Women.* My problem was one not of art but of numbers. Our guests were 50-percent women, 40-percent children, and 10-percent weekend commuting husbands. I hoped to tie down as many children as possible.

The auditions were successful beyond my wildest hopes. Every child in the hotel appeared, some voluntarily, some prodded—and suddenly I had a cast of thirty-five. Rehearsals were started, and after a week, the parents began to demand a performance. I explained that more rehearsals would be necessary. A Mrs. Lowen wasn't satisfied. "Why can't we have the play tomorrow?" she asked.

"The actors aren't ready," I explained. "We need at least another week."

"I'm not expecting to stay so long. Maybe I'll have to take Patty out of the play."

"Patty will be disappointed."

Mrs. Lowen made a wry face. Patty was a spoiled brat, and we both knew that she'd scream bloody murder if Mrs. Lowen attempted such a thing.

At last I set the date for the performance: Labor Day, the last day of the hotel season. And I suggested that it would be nice for the cast to invite their uncles and aunts and cousins to come for the weekend.

I think the play went off reasonably well. After the performance, however, I came face-to-face with Mrs. Lowen. ''Ten days I stayed over so Patty could be an actress,'' she said. ''And what does Patty have to say? One speech, six words—I counted them. That's less than a word a day!''

''Patty had to serve an apprenticeship,'' I said. ''Next year she'll have one of the leads.''

''Yoweeee!'' Patty exulted.

The morning after Labor Day, Father and I sat together in the tiny office while I ran up the figures on the adding machine. My hand trembled slightly as the total mounted. The final figure was $5,367.92.

''We made it!'' I cried.

I felt wonderfully free, and when Father pointed out that we would be practically broke after I had added interest to the loan, I said happily, ''Let God worry about us a little bit.''

Father laughed and threw his arms around me.

PART II

Discovering "Americanness"

"THE LOUDEST VOICE"

from

THE LITTLE DISTURBANCES OF MAN

GRACE PALEY

Fitting in is always difficult. With the annual school Christmas play as the backdrop, "The Loudest Voice" follows Shirley Abramowitz as she learns to balance her Jewish heritage while still participating in a Christian holiday. In the end, Shirley uses her voice to celebrate and rejoice for other people who are not loud enough to be heard themselves.

Grace Paley's short stories have appeared in The New Yorker, Esquire, *and* Atlantic Monthly. *Her collections include* The Little Disturbances of Man; Enormous Changes at the Last Minute; *and* Later the Same Day. *She was elected to the American Academy and Institute of Arts and Letters in 1980.*

There is a certain place where dumb-waiters boom, doors slam, dishes crash; every window is a mother's mouth bidding the street shut up, go skate somewhere else, come home. My voice is the loudest.

There, my own mother is still as full of breathing as me and the grocer stands up to speak to her. "Mrs. Abramowitz," he says, "people should not be afraid of their children."

"Ah, Mr. Bialik," my mother replies, "if you say to her or her father 'Ssh,' they say, 'In the grave it will be quiet.' "

"From Coney Island to the cemetery," says my papa. "It's the same subway; it's the same fare."

I am right next to the pickle barrel. My pinky is making tiny whirlpools in the brine. I stop a moment to announce: "Campbell's Tomato Soup. Campbell's Vegetable Beef Soup. Campbell's S-c-otch Broth . . ."

"Be quiet," the grocer says, "the labels are coming off."

"Please, Shirley, be a little quiet," my mother begs me.

In that place the whole street groans: Be quiet! Be quiet! but steals from the happy chorus of my inside self not a tittle or a jot.

There, too, but just around the corner, is a red-brick building that has been old for many years. Every morning the children stand before it in double lines which must be straight. They are not insulted. They are waiting anyway.

I am usually among them. I am, in fact, the first, since I begin with *A*.

One cold morning the monitor tapped me on the shoulder. "Go to Room 409, Shirley Abramowitz," he said. I did as I was told. I went in a hurry up a down staircase to Room 409, which contained sixth-graders. I had to wait at the desk without wiggling until Mr. Hilton, their teacher, had time to speak.

After five minutes he said, "Shirley?"

"What?" I whispered.

He said, "My! My! Shirley Abramowitz! They told me you had a particularly loud, clear voice and read with lots of expression. Could that be true?"

"Oh yes," I whispered.

"In that case, don't be silly; I might very well be your teacher someday. Speak up, speak up."

"Yes," I shouted.

"More like it," he said. "Now, Shirley, can you put a ribbon in your hair or a bobby pin? It's too messy."

"Yes!" I bawled.

"Now, now, calm down." He turned to the class. "Children, not a sound. Open at page thirty-nine. Read till fifty-two. When you finish, start again." He looked me over once more. "Now, Shirley, you know, I suppose, that Christmas is coming. We are preparing a beautiful play. Most of the parts have been given out. But I still need a child with a strong voice, lots of stamina. Do you know what stamina is? You do? Smart kid. You know, I heard you read 'The Lord is my shepherd' in Assembly yesterday. I was very impressed. Wonderful delivery. Mrs. Jordan, your teacher, speaks highly of you. Now listen to me, Shirley Abramowitz, if you want to take the part and be in the play, repeat after me, 'I swear to work harder than I ever did before.' "

I looked to heaven and said at once, "Oh, I swear." I kissed my pinky and looked at God.

"That is an actor's life, my dear," he explained. "Like a soldier's, never tardy or disobedient to his general, the director. Everything," he said, "absolutely everything will depend on you."

That afternoon, all over the building, children scraped and scrubbed the turkeys and the sheaves of corn off the schoolroom windows. Good-bye, Thanksgiving. The next morning a monitor brought red paper and green paper from the office. We made new shapes and hung them on the walls and glued them to the doors.

The teachers became happier and happier. Their heads were ringing like the bells of childhood. My best friend Evie was prone to evil, but she did not get a single demerit for whispering. We learned "Holy Night" without an error. "How wonderful!" said Miss Glacé, the student teacher. "To think that some of you don't even speak the language!" We learned "Deck the Halls" and "Hark! The Herald Angels." They weren't ashamed and we weren't embarrassed.

Oh, but when my mother heard about it all, she said to my father: "Misha, you don't know what's going on there. Cramer is the head of the Tickets Committee."

"Who?" asked my father. "Cramer? Oh yes, an active woman."

"Active? Active has to have a reason. Listen," she said sadly, "I'm surprised to see my neighbors making tra-la-la for Christmas."

My father couldn't think of what to say to that. Then he decided: "You're in America! Clara, you wanted to come here. In Palestine the Arabs would be eating you alive. Europe you had pogroms. Argentina is full of Indians. Here you got Christmas. . . . Some joke, ha?"

"Very funny, Misha. What is becoming of you? If we came to a new country a long time ago to run away from tyrants, and instead we fall into a creeping pogrom, that our children learn a lot of lies, so what's the joke? Ach, Misha, your idealism is going away."

"So is your sense of humor."

"That I never had, but idealism you had a lot of."

"I'm the same Misha Abramovitch, I didn't change an iota. Ask anyone."

"Only ask me," says my mama, may she rest in peace. "I got the answer."

Meanwhile, the neighbors had to think of what to say, too.

Marty's father said: "You know, he has a very important part, my boy."

"Mine also," said Mr. Sauerfeld.

"Not my boy!" said Mrs. Klieg. "I said to him no. The answer is no. When I say no! I mean no!"

The rabbi's wife said, "It's disgusting!" But no one listened to her. Under the narrow sky of God's great wisdom she wore a strawberry-blond wig.

Every day was noisy and full of experience. I was Right-hand Man. Mr. Hilton said: "How could I get along without you, Shirley?"

He said: "Your mother and father ought to get down on their knees every night and thank God for giving them a child like you."

He also said: "You're absolutely a pleasure to work with, my dear, dear child."

Sometimes he said: "For God's sakes, what did I do with the script? Shirley! Shirley! Find it."

Then I answered quietly: "Here it is, Mr. Hilton."

Once in a while, when he was very tired, he would cry out: "Shirley, I'm just tired of screaming at those kids. Will you tell Ira Pushkov not to come in till Lester points to that star the second time?"

Then I roared: "Ira Pushkov, what's the matter with you? Dope! Mr. Hilton told you five times already, don't come in till Lester points to that star the second time."

"Ach, Clara," my father asked, "what does she do there till six o'clock she can't even put the plates on the table?"

"Christmas," said my mother coldly.

"Ho! Ho!" my father said. "Christmas. What's the harm? After all, history teaches everyone. We learn from reading this is a holiday from pagan times also, candles, lights, even Chanukah. So we learn it's not altogether Christian. So if they think it's a private holiday, they're only ignorant, not patriotic. What belongs to history, belongs to all men. You want to go back to the Middle Ages? Is it better to shave your head with a secondhand razor? Does it hurt Shirley to learn to speak up? It does not. So maybe someday she won't live between the kitchen and the shop. She's not a fool."

I thank you, Papa, for your kindness. It is true about me to this day. I am foolish but I am not a fool.

That night my father kissed me and said with great interest in my career, "Shirley, tomorrow's your big day. Congrats."

"Save it," my mother said. Then she shut all the windows in order to prevent tonsillitis.

In the morning it snowed. On the street corner a tree had been decorated for us by a kind city administration. In order to miss its chilly shadow our neighbors walked three blocks east to buy a loaf of bread. The butcher pulled down black window shades to keep the colored lights from shining on his chickens. Oh, not me. On the way to school, with both my hands I tossed it a kiss of tolerance. Poor thing, it was a stranger in Egypt.

I walked straight into the auditorium past the staring children. "Go ahead, Shirley!" said the monitors. Four boys, big for their age, had already started work as propmen and stagehands.

Mr. Hilton was very nervous. He was not even happy. Whatever he started to say ended in a sideward look of sadness. He sat slumped in the middle of the first row and asked me to help Miss Glacé. I did this, although she thought my voice too resonant and said, "Show-off!"

Parents began to arrive long before we were ready. They wanted to make a good impression. From among the yards of drapes I peeked out at the audience. I saw my embarrassed mother.

Ira, Lester, and Meyer were pasted to their beards by Miss Glacé. She almost forgot to thread the star on its wire, but I reminded her. I coughed a few times to clear my throat. Miss Glacé looked around and saw that everyone was in costume and on line waiting to play his part. She whispered, "All right . . ." Then:

Jackie Sauerfeld, the prettiest boy in first grade, parted the curtains with his skinny elbow and in a high voice sang out:

> *Parents dear*
> *We are here*
> *To make a Christmas play in time.*
> *It we give*
> *In narrative*
> *And illustrate with pantomime.*

He disappeared.

My voice burst immediately from the wings to the great shock of Ira, Lester, and Meyer, who were waiting for it but were surprised all the same.

"I remember, I remember, the house where I was born . . ."

Miss Glacé yanked the curtain open and there it was, the house—an old haylott, where Celia Kornbluh lay in the straw with Cindy Lou, her favorite doll. Ira, Lester, and Meyer moved slowly from the wings toward her, sometimes pointing to a moving star and sometimes ahead to Cindy Lou.

It was a long story and it was a sad story. I carefully pronounced all the words about my lonesome childhood, while little Eddie Braunstein wandered upstage and down with his shepherd's stick, looking for sheep. I brought up lonesomeness again, and not being understood at all except by some women everybody hated. Eddie was too small for that and Marty Groff took his place, wearing his father's prayer shawl. I announced twelve friends, and half the boys in the fourth grade gathered round Marty, who stood on an orange crate while my voice harangued. Sorrowful and loud, I declaimed about love and God and Man, but because of the terrible deceit of Abie Stock, we came suddenly to a famous moment. Marty, whose remembering tongue I was, waited at the foot of the cross. He stared desperately at the audience. I groaned, "My God, my God, why hast thou forsaken me?'' The soldiers who were sheiks grabbed poor Marty to pin him up to die, but he wrenched free, turned again to the audience, and spread his arms aloft to show despair and the end. I murmured at the top of my voice, ''The rest is silence, but as everyone in this room, in this city—in this world—now knows, I shall have life eternal.''

That night Mrs. Kornbluh visited our kitchen for a glass of tea.

''How's the virgin?'' asked my father with a look of concern.

''For a man with a daughter, you got a fresh mouth, Abramovitch.''

''Here,'' said my father kindly, ''have some lemon, it'll sweeten your disposition.''

They debated a little in Yiddish, then fell in a puddle of Russian and Polish. What I understood next was my father, who said, ''Still and all, it was certainly a beautiful affair, you have to admit, introducing us to the beliefs of a different culture.''

''Well, yes,'' said Mrs. Kornbluh. ''The only thing . . . you know Charlie Turner—that cute boy in Celia's class—a couple others? They got very small parts or no part at all. In very bad taste, it seemed to me. After all, it's their religion.''

''Ach,'' explained my mother, ''what could Mr. Hilton do? They got very small voices; after all, why should they holler? The English language they know from the beginning by heart. They're blond like angels. You think it's so important they should get in the play? Christmas . . . the whole piece of goods . . . they own it.''

I listened and listened until I couldn't listen anymore. Too sleepy, I climbed out of bed and kneeled. I made a little church of my hands and said, ''Hear, O Israel . . .'' Then I called out in Yiddish, ''Please, good night, good night. Ssh.'' My father said, ''*Ssh* yourself,'' and slammed the kitchen door.

I was happy. I fell asleep at once. I had prayed for everybody: my talking family, cousins far away, passersby, and all the lonesome Christians. I expected to be heard. My voice was certainly the loudest.

from

A GIFT OF LAUGHTER

ALLAN SHERMAN

Allan Sherman joked about his typical Jewish background—his father, Percy Copelon, who came from Birmingham, Alabama, and his shy, retiring mother, who was "a swinger" and who won Charleston contests.

He came from a broken home—a somewhat atypical Jewish situation. He went from the twenty-one different grammar and high schools in New York, Illinois, California, and Florida, to army life, marriage, and a flight to the suburbs when his album "My Son the Folk Singer" became an overnight sensation. Sherman was a joke writer and comedy writer for television, but is perhaps most lastingly remembered for his song parodies, which include "The Twelve Gifts of Christmas" and "Hello Muddah, Hello Fadduh."

Throughout his life, the only real stability he remembers is connected to his grandparents' home in Chicago. It is a sadly sweet episode from one of those visits that he recalls here.

"Daddydaddydaddy!" that's how it came out—one long, excited word. He started yelling it at the top of the stairs, and by the time he bounded into the living room he really had it going good. I'd been talking to his mother about a money problem, and it stopped me mid-sentence.

"Robbie, *please*!" I said. Then I appealed to my wife. "Can't we have just five minutes around here without kids screaming?"

Robbie had been holding something behind his back. Now he swung it around for me to see. "Daddy, *look*!"

It was a picture, drawn in the messy crayon of a seven-year-old. It showed a weird-looking creature with one ear three times as big as the other, one green eye, and one red; the head was pear-shaped, and the face needed a shave.

I turned on my son. "Is *that* what you interrupted me for? Couldn't you wait? I'm talking to your mother about something *important*!"

His face clouded up. His eyes filled with bewilderment, rage, then tears. "Awright!" he screamed, and threw the picture to the floor. "But it's *your* birthday Saturday!" Then he ran upstairs.

I looked at the picture on the floor. At the bottom, in Robbie's careful printing, were some words I hadn't noticed: MY DAD by Robert Sherman.

Just then Robbie slammed the door of his room. But I heard a different door, a door I once slammed—twenty-five years ago—in my grandmother's house in Chicago.

It was the day I heard my grandmother say she needed a *football*. I heard her tell my mother there was going to be a party tonight for the whole family, and she had to have a football, for after supper.

I couldn't imagine *why* Grandmother needed a football. I was sure she wasn't going to play the game with my aunts and uncles.

She had been in America only a few years, and still spoke with a deep Yiddish accent. But Grandma wanted a football, and a football was something in *my* department. If I could get one, I'd be important, a contributor to the party. I slipped out the door.

There were only three footballs in the neighborhood, and they belonged to older kids. Homer Spicer wasn't home. Eddie Polonsky wouldn't sell or rent, at any price.

The last possibility was a tough kid we called Gudgie. It was just as I'd feared. Gudgie punched me in the nose. Then he said he would trade me his old football for my new sled, plus all the marbles I owned.

I filled Gudgie's football with air at the gas station. Then I sneaked it into the house and shined it with shoe polish. When I finished, it was a football worthy of Grandmother's party. All the aunts and uncles would be proud. When nobody was looking I put it on the dining-room table. Then I waited in my room for Grandma to notice it.

But it was Mother who noticed it. "Allan!" she shouted.

I ran to the dining room.

"You know your grandmother's giving a party tonight. Why can't you put your things where they belong?"

"It's not mine," I protested.

"Then give it back to whoever it belongs to. Get it out of here!"

"But it's for Grandma! She said she needed a football for the party." I was holding back the tears.

Mother burst into laughter. "A *football* for the party! Don't you understand your own grandma?" Then, between peals of laughter, Mother explained: "Not football. Fruit bowl! Grandma needs a fruit bowl for the party."

I was starting to cry, so I ran to my room and slammed the door. The worst part of crying was trying to stop. I can still feel it—the shuddering, my breath coming in little, staccato jerks. And each sputtery breath brought back the pain, the frustration, the unwanted feeling that had made me cry in the first place. I was still trying to stop crying when the aunts and uncles arrived. I heard their voices (sounding very far away), and the clink-clink of Grandma's good china, and now and then an explosion of laughter.

After dinner, Mother came in. ''Allan,'' she said, ''come with me. I want you to see something.'' I followed her into the living room.

Grandma was walking around the room like a queen, holding out to each of the aunts and uncles the biggest, most magnificent cut-glass bowl I'd ever seen. There were grapes and bananas in it, red apples, figs, and tangerines. And in the center of the bowl, all shiny and brown was Gudgie's football.

Just then my Uncle Sol offered Grandma a compliment. ''Esther,'' he said, ''that's a beautiful *football*. Real *cott gless*.''

Grandma looked at Uncle Sol with great superiority. ''Sol,'' she said, ''listen close, you'll learn something. This *cott gless* is called a *frutt boll*, not a *football*. This in the middle, *this* is a *football*.''

Uncle Sol was impressed. ''Very smot,'' he said. ''Very nice. But, Esther, now tell me something. How come you got a *football* in your *frutt boll*?'' He pronounced them both very carefully.

''Because,'' Grandma said, ''today mine Allan brought me a nice present, this football. It's beautiful, no?''

Before Uncle Sol could answer, Grandma continued, ''It's beautiful, yess—because from a child is beautiful, anything.''

. . . *From a child is beautiful, anything.*

I picked up Robbie's picture from the floor. It wasn't bad, at that. One of my ears *is* a little bigger than the other. And usually, when Robbie sees me at the end of the day, I *do* need a shave.

I went up to his room. ''Hi, Rob,'' I said.

His breath was shuddering, and his nose was running. He was packing a cardboard box, as he always does when he Leaves Home. I held up the picture. ''Say, I've been looking this over. It's very good.''

''I don't care,'' he said. He threw a comic book into the box and some Erector-set pieces. ''Tear it up if you want to. I can't draw, anyhow.''

He put on his cap and jacket, picked up the box, and walked right past me. I followed him with the picture in my hand.

When he got to the front door, he just stood there, his hand on the knob, the way he always does. I suppose he thinks of the same things I used to, whenever I Left Home. You stand there by the door, and pray *they* won't let you go, because you have no place to go, and if *they* don't want you, who does?

I got my coat and joined him. "Come on," I said. "I'm going with you." And I took him by the hand.

He looked up at me, very scared. "Where we going?"

"The shopping center is open tonight," I said. "We're going to buy a frame for this picture. It's a beautiful picture. We'll hang it in the living room. After we get the frame we're going to have an ice-cream soda and I'll tell you about something."

"About what?"

"Well, you remember that old football your great-grandma keeps in the cut glass bowl on her dining-room table?"

"Yes."

"Well, I'm going to tell you how she got it."

"Spells, Wishes, Goldfish, Old School Hurts"

CYNTHIA OZICK

In this autobiographical essay, which originally appeared in The New York Times, *Cynthia Ozick remembers growing up during the Depression in Pelham Bay, New York: sitting at the glass-top table at her parents' drugstore, Park View Pharmacy, choosing books from the boxes in front of the Traveling Library, and escaping into the stories of Louisa May Alcott, Charles Dickens, and Mark Twain. It is these pieces of her childhood that helped to form her life as a writer. She says, "Someday, when I am free of P.S. 71, I will write stories. Meanwhile, in the winter dusk, in the Park View, in the secret bliss of the* Violet Fairy Book, *I both see and do not see how these grains of life will stay forever."*

Cynthia Ozick is the author of three novels, three collections of short fiction, and dozens of essays. She is the recipient of the National Book Award and three O. Henry Prize Awards, including one for "The Shawl" and its sequel, "Rosa."

This is about reading; a drugstore in winter; the gold leaf on the dome of the Boston State House; also loss, panic, and dread. First, the gold leaf. (This part is a little like a turn-of-the-century pulp tale, though only a little. The ending is a surprise, but there is no plot.) Thirty years ago I burrowed in the Boston Public Library one whole afternoon, to find out—not out of curiosity—how the State House got its gold roof. The answer, like the answer to most Bostonian questions, was Paul Revere. So I put Paul Revere's gold dome into an "article," and took it (though I was just as scared by recklessness then as I am now) to *The Boston Globe*, on Washington Street. The Features Editor had a bare severe head, a closed parenthesis mouth, and silver Dickensian spectacles. He made me wait, standing, at the side of his desk while he read; there was no bone in me that did not rattle. Then he opened a drawer and handed me fifteen dollars. Ah, joy of Homer, joy of Milton! Grub Street bliss!

The very next Sunday, Paul Revere's gold dome saw print. Appetite for more led me to a top-floor chamber in Filene's department store: Window Dressing. But no one was in the least bit dressed—it was a dumbstruck nudist colony up there, a mob of naked frozen enigmatic manikins—tall, enameled, skinny ladies with bald breasts and skulls, and legs and wrists and necks that horribly unscrewed. Paul Revere's dome paled beside this gold mine. A sight—mute numb Walpurgisnacht—easily worth another fifteen dollars. I had a master's degree (thesis topic: "Parable in the Later Novels of Henry James") and a job as an advertising copywriter (9:00 A.M. to 6:00 P.M., six days a week, forty dollars per week; if you were male and had no degree at all, sixty dollars). Filene's Sale Days—Crib Bolsters! Lulla-Buys! Jonnie Mops! Maternity Skirts with Expanding Invisible Trick Waist! And a company show; gold watches to mark the retirement of elderly Irish salesladies; for me the chance to write song lyrics (to the tune of "On Top of Old Smoky") honoring our store. But "Mute Numb Walpurgisnacht in Secret Downtown Chamber" never reached *The Globe*. Melancholy and meaning business, the advertising director forbade it. Grub Street was bad form, and I had to promise never again to sink to another article. Thus ended my life in journalism.

Next: reading, and certain drugstore winter dusks. These come together. It is an eon before Filene's, years and years before the Later Novels of Henry James. I am scrunched on my knees at a round glass table near a plate-glass door on which is inscribed, in gold leaf Paul Revere never put there, letters that must be read backward: PARK VIEW PHARMACY. There is an evening smell of late coffee from the fountain, and all the librarians are lined up in a row on the tall stools, sipping and chattering. They have just stepped in from the cold of the Traveling Library, and so have I. The Traveling Library is a big green truck that stops, once every two weeks, on the corner of Continental Avenue, just a little way in from Westchester Avenue, not far from a house that keeps a pig. Other houses fly pigeons from their roofs, other yards have chickens, and down on Mayflower there is even a goat. This is Pelham Bay, the Bronx, in the middle of the Depression, all cattails and weeds, such a lovely place and tender hour. Even though my mother takes me on the subway far, far downtown to buy my winter coat in the frenzy of Klein's on Fourteenth Street, and even though I can recognize the heavy power of a quarter, I don't know it's the Depression. On the trolley on the way to Westchester Square I see the children who live in the boxcar strangely set down in an empty lot some distance from Spy Oak (where a Revolutionary traitor was hanged—served him right for siding with redcoats); the lucky boxcar children dangle their stick-legs from their train-house maw and wave; how I envy them! I envy the orphans of the Gould Foundation, who have their own private swings and seesaws. Sometimes I imagine I am an orphan, and my father is an impostor pretending to be my father. My father writes in his prescription book: 59330 Dr. O'Flaherty Pow .60/59331 Dr. Mulligan Gtt .65/59332 Dr. Thron Tab .90. Ninety cents! A terrifically expensive medicine; someone is really sick. When I deliver a prescription around the corner or down the block, I am offered a nickel tip. I always refuse, out of conscience; I am, after all, the Park View Pharmacy's own daughter, and it wouldn't be seemly. My father grinds and mixes powders, weighs them out in tiny snowy heaps on an apothecary scale, folds them into delicate translucent papers, or meticulously drops them into gelatin capsules.

In the big front window of the Park View Pharmacy there is a startling display: goldfish bowls, balanced one on the other in amazing pyramids. A German lady enters, one of my father's cronies—his cronies are both women and men. My quiet father's eyes are watercolor blue; he wears his small, skeptical, quiet smile and receives the neighborhood's life secrets. My father is discreet and inscrutable. The German lady pokes a punchboard with a pin, pushes up a bit of rolled paper, and cries out—she has just won a goldfish bowl, with two swimming goldfish in it. Mr. Jaffe, the salesman from McKesson & Robbins, arrives, trailing two mists: winter steaminess and the animal fog of his cigar, which melts into the coffee smell, the tarpaper smell, the eerie honeyed tangled drugstore smell. Mr. Jaffe and my mother and father are intimates by now, but because it is the 1930s, so long ago, and the old manners still survive, they address one another gravely as Mr. Jaffe, Mrs. Ozick, Mr. Ozick. My mother calls my father *Mr. O*, even at home, as in a Victorian novel. In the street my father tips his hat to ladies. In the winter his hat is a regular fedora; in the summer it is a straw boater with a black ribbon and a jot of blue feather.

What am I doing at this round glass table, both listening and not listening to my mother and father tell Mr. Jaffe about their struggle with "Tessie," the lion-eyed landlady who has just raised, threefold, in the middle of that Depression I have never heard of, the Park View Pharmacy's devouring rent? My mother, not yet forty, wears bandages on her ankles, covering oozing varicose veins; back and forth she strides, dashes, runs, climbing cellar stairs or ladders; she unpacks cartons, she toils behind drug counters and fountain counters. Like my father, she is on her feet until one in the morning, the Park View's closing hour. My mother and father are in trouble, and I don't know it. I am too happy. I feel the secret center of eternity, nothing will ever alter, no one will ever die. Through the window, past the lit goldfish, the gray oval sky deepens over our neighborhood wood, where all the dirt paths lead down to seagull-specked water. I am familiar with every frog-haunted monument: Pelham Bay Park is thronged with WPA art—statuary, fountains, immense rococo staircases cascading down a hillside, Bacchus-faced steles—stone Roman glories afterward mysteriously razed by an avenging Robert Moses. One year—how distant it seems now, as if even the climate is past returning—the bay froze so hard that whole families, mine among them, crossed back and forth to City Island, strangers saluting and calling out in the ecstasy of the bright trudge over such a sudden wilderness of ice.

In the Park View Pharmacy, in the winter dusk, the heart in my body is revolving like the goldfish fleet-finned in their clear bowls. The librarians are still warming up over their coffee. They do not recognize me, though only half an hour ago I was scrabbling in the mud around the two heavy boxes from the Traveling Library—oafish crates tossed with a thump to the ground. One box contains magazines: *Boy's Life, The American Girl, Popular Mechanics*. But the other, the other! The other transforms me. It is tumbled with storybooks, with clandestine intimations and transfigurations. In school I am a luckless goosegirl, friendless and forlorn. In P.S. 71, I carry, weighty as a cloak, the ineradicable knowledge of my scandal—I am cross-eyed, dumb, an imbecile at arithmetic; in P.S. 71, I am publicly shamed in Assembly because I am caught not singing Christmas carols; in P.S. 71, I am repeatedly accused of deicide. But in the Park View Pharmacy, in the winter dusk, branches blackening in the park across the road, I am driving in rapture through the *Violet Fairy Book* and the *Yellow Fairy Book*, insubstantial chariots snatched from the box in the mud. I have never been inside the Traveling Library; only grown-ups are allowed. The boxes are for the children. No more than two books may be borrowed, so I have picked the fattest ones, to last. All the same, the *Violet* and the *Yellow* are melting away. Their glass table, dreaming, dreaming. Mr. Jaffe is murmuring advice. He tells a joke about Wrong-Way Corrigan. The librarians are buttoning up their coats. A princess, captive of an ogre, receives a letter from her swain and hides it in her bosom. I can visualize her bosom exactly—she clutches it against her chest. It is a tall and shapely vase, with a hand-painted flower on it, like the vase on the second-hand piano at home.

I am incognito. No one knows who I truly am. The teachers in P.S. 71 don't know. Rabbi Meskin, my *cheder* teacher, doesn't know. Tessie the lion-eyed landlady doesn't know. Even Hymie the fountain clerk can't know—though he understands other things better than anyone: how to tighten roller skates with a skate key, for instance, and how to ride a horse. On Friday afternoons, when the new issue is out, Hymie and my brother fight hard over who gets to see *Life* magazine first. My brother is older than I am, and doesn't like me; he builds radios in his bedroom, he is already W2LOM, and operates his transmitter (*da-di-da-dit-da-da-di-da*) so penetratingly on Sunday mornings that Mrs. Eva Brady, across the way, complains. Mrs. Eva Brady has a subscription to *The Writer*; I fill a closet with her old copies. How to Find a Plot. Narrative and Character, the Writer's Tools. Because my brother has his ham license, I say, "I have a license, too." "What kind of license?" my brother asks, falling into the trap. "Poetic license," I reply; my brother can't abide me, but anyhow his birthday presents are transporting: one year *Alice in Wonderland, Pinocchio* the next, then *Tom Sawyer*. I go after Mark Twain, and find *Joan of Arc* and my first satire, *Christian Science*. My mother surprises me with *Pollyanna*, the admiration of her Lower East Side childhood, along with *The Lady of the Lake*. Mrs. Eva Brady's daughter Jeanie has outgrown her Nancy Drews and Judy Boltons, so on rainy afternoons I cross the street and borrow them, trying not to march away with too many—the child of immigrants, I worry that the Bradys, true and virtuous Americans, will judge me greedy or careless. I wrap the Nancy Drews in paper covers to protect them. Old Mrs. Brady, Jeanie's grandmother, invites me back for more. I am so timid I can hardly speak a word, but I love her dark parlor; I love its black bookcases. Old Mrs. Brady sees me off, embracing books under an umbrella; perhaps she divines who I truly am. My brother doesn't care. My father doesn't notice. I think my mother knows. My mother reads *The Saturday Evening Post* and the *Woman's Home Companion*; sometimes the *Ladies' Home Journal*, but never *Good Housekeeping*. I read all my mother's magazines. My father reads *Drug Topics* and *Der Tog*, the Yiddish daily. In Louie Davidowitz's house (waiting our turn for the rabbi's lesson, he teaches me chess in *cheder*) there is a piece of furniture I am in awe of: a shining circular table that is also a revolving bookshelf holding a complete set of Charles Dickens. I borrow *Oliver Twist*. My cousins turn up with *Gulliver's Travels, Just So Stories, Don Quixote*, Oscar Wilde's *Fairy Tales*, uncannily different from the usual kind. Blindfolded, I reach into a Thanksgiving grab bag and pull out *Mrs. Leicester's School*, Mary Lamb's desolate stories of rejected children. Books spill out of rumor, exchange, miracle. In the Park View Pharmacy's lending library I discover, among the nurse romances, a browning, brittle miracle: *Jane Eyre*. Uncle Morris comes to visit (his drugstore is on the other side of the Bronx) and leaves behind, just like that, a three-volume Shakespeare. Peggy and Betty Provan, Scottish sisters around the corner, lend me their *Swiss Family Robinson*. Norma Foti, a whole year older, transmits a rumor about Louisa May Alcott; afterward I read *Little Women* a thousand times. Ten thousand. I am no longer incognito, not even to myself. I am Jo in her "vortex"; not Jo exactly, but some Jo-of-the-future. I am under an enchantment: Who I truly am must be deferred, waited for and waited for. My father, silently filling capsules, is grieving over his mother in Moscow. I write letters in Yiddish to my Moscow grandmother, whom I will never know. I will never know my Russian aunts, uncles, cousins. In Moscow there is suffering, deprivation, poverty. My mother, threadbare, goes without a new winter coat so that packages can be sent to Moscow. Her fiery justice-eyes are semaphores I cannot decipher.

Someday, when I am free of P.S. 71, I will write stories; meanwhile, in winter dusk, in the Park View, in the secret bliss of the *Violet Fairy Book*, I both see and do not see how these grains of life will stay forever, papa and mama will live forever, Hymie will always turn my skate key.

Hymie, after Italy, after the Battle of the Bulge, comes back from the war with a present: *From Here to Eternity*. Then he dies, young. Mama reads *Pride and Prejudice* and every single word of Willa Cather. Papa reads, in Yiddish, all of Sholem Aleichem and Peretz. He reads Malamud's *The Assistant* when I ask him to.

Papa and mama, in Staten Island, are under the ground. Some other family sits transfixed in the sunparlor where I once read *Jane Eyre* and *Little Women* and, long afterward, *Middlemarch*. The Park View Pharmacy is dismantled, turned into a Hallmark card shop. It doesn't matter. I close my eyes, or else only stare, and everything is in its place again, and everyone.

A writer is dreamed and transfigured into being by spells, wishes, goldfish, silhouettes of trees, boxes of fairy tales dropped in the mud, uncles' and cousins' books, tablets and capsules and powders, papa's Moscow ache, his drugstore jacket with his special fountain pen in the pocket, his beautiful Hebrew paragraphs, his Talmudist's rationalism, his Russian-Gymnasium Latin and German, mama's furnaceheart, her masses of memoirs, her paintings of autumn walks down to the sunny water, her braveries, her old, old school hurts.

A writer is buffeted into being by school hurts—Orwell, Forster, Mann—but after a while other ambushes begin: sorrows, deaths, disappointments, subtle diseases, delays, guilts, the spite of the private haters of the poetry side of life, the snubs of the glamorous, the bitterness of those for whom resentment is a daily gruel, and so on and so on; and then one day you find yourself leaning here, writing at that selfsame round glass table salvaged from the Park View Pharmacy—writing this, an impossibility, a summary of how you came to be where you are now, and where, God knows, is that? Your hair is whitening, you are a well of tears, what you meant to do (beauty and justice) you have not done, Papa and Mama are under the earth, you live in panic and dread, the future shrinks and darkens, stories are only vapor, your inmost craving is for nothing but an old scarred pen, and what, God knows, is that?

"CHILDREN OF JOY"

from

RITES OF PASSAGE

J O A N N E   G R E E N B E R G

*Remembering the traditional ways of the old country and adjusting
to American mores are the bases for this short story by Joanne Greenberg. The narrator, a young girl dissatisfied with "false values and
materialism" of her generation, is surprised to hear her three great-
aunts lament what the girl sees as the simple truths of her Jewish
heritage. Interestingly, the young girl is baffled by what her aunts see
as progress: having enough food, being guaranteed basic freedoms.
Disenchanted by being "American," the young girl doesn't understand that she is disgusted by the very things that drove her family
to immigrate.*

Joanne Greenberg is the author of more than ten novels, including
Age of Consent *and* Of Such Small Differences, *and three collections
of short stories. Born in Brooklyn, New York, and a graduate of
American University, she lives in Colorado.*

They hadn't changed since I had grown up. The only difference was the
one that had always been there: the difference between what they were and
the way they appeared in the family stories. My names for them had
skipped the generation between. They were my great-aunts, really; Imah
was called *Imah* by my mother and so by me, though she was my grandmother. Once, impossibly, the aunt across the table had been a flirtatious
Hester, dance-mad and party-loving, who had spent a week's wages on
ribbons and been beaten for it. She was a large, soft woman now, her hair
white and scant.

Next to me, Aunt Ida was sniffing as she tossed a bad nut among the
shells on the table. Whenever I saw her, she would enter something new
into the catalogue of her illnesses: "conditions." I couldn't see or imagine
the girl who had been arrested and jailed for inciting a mob to riot, and
that at a time when women, especially immigrant women, did not command
attention.

Imah herself must have been other things before she was my grand-mother, but in 1890, people must have been different, born old, with only their bodies to age after that.

"I can feel the cold through the walls," Aunt Ida said.

Imah sighed. "I'll go turn up the thermostat."

"Thermostats don't make real heat." But Imah got up and went out of the kitchen and the aunts adjusted dutiful expressions on their faces.

"Enjoying your vacation?" Aunt Hester asked me.

"Yes. Before you came, Imah was telling me about the days in the old country, in Zoromin."

"A waste of time," Aunt Ida said. "Hitler chewed it up, but on its best day, in a good year, it wasn't anything to begin with."

I was shocked. "How can you say that when family life was so much closer, when the air was clean and the rivers and streams were unpolluted, when people ate natural foods and were so much richer spiritually than we are today?"

They looked at each other in what I could have sworn was confusion.

"I don't think they heard about all that in Zoromin," Aunt Hester said. "About the water—well, the women washed clothes in it, the horses drank, the tanner dumped into it. About clean water they didn't hear in Zoromin."

"At least things were what they seemed to be," I said. "You didn't look at everything through a plastic package. People, too. People were what they seemed to be, not packages with an 'image.' You didn't grow food for looks but for nourishment. People remember the old-fashioned cooking, and that's why."

"Oh, *that* cooking," Imah said, having come back and seated herself. She grinned and her hand went up to her mouth. Aunt Ida caught her eye and turned away, biting her lip. "Old-fashioned . . ." And then the three of them began to laugh.

I had gotten up to make more tea. I turned from the stove to look at them, chuckling comfortably above their bosoms.

"What's funny? What's the joke?"

They looked at me and laughed again, Aunt Ida checking the slipping wig she hadn't worn for years.

"You poor girl," Imah said. "You grew up in such a good home, you didn't have time to learn the simplest truths."

"It isn't her fault," and Aunt Ida wiped a crumb from her cheek. I came back to the table and began to clear a place among the nuts and shells.

"Listen," Ida went on, and impaled my arm with a forefinger. "First is a family so poor that there is no piece of cloth without a hole. Our father traveled, following the breezes of other men's moving. He sent money in years that ended with two and seven. We saw him coming and going when the road bent that way or when business was bad. Of course, we had our own work, painting the lead soldiers. All of us. I thought you knew about that.''

"Yes, but what does it have to do with cooking?''

She shook her head and clucked, then looked at me and shook her head again. ''God help us! What has happened to the Jewish mind? There *was* no cooking, only hunger. We ate potatoes and weak soup, and if you're hungry enough, it's a banquet.''

"But Uncle Reuben says—''

"Now there,'' Aunt Hester said, ''walks a sage. To this day, if a thing doesn't give him heartburn, he thinks it wasn't worth eating.''

Imah shook her head. ''What cook can match herself against hunger and memory?''

Aunt Hester said, ''We all carry a dream about Mama's chicken. If they set to music what we feel and remember of that chicken, Beethoven would be a forgotten article altogether.''

Ida mused, ''I think I know what chicken it was. It was the big one the Nachmansons gave us when they left to come to America.''

"Tell me something,'' Imah asked. ''What did it taste like, that chicken?''

"How should I know?'' Hester shrugged. ''We had to save it for Papa and the boys. By the time they finished, there wasn't anything left.''

"I don't think I had any either,'' Ida said. ''You see''—and she turned to me—''the chicken we didn't eat is the one we remember. That chicken is always tender.''

"You're both ashamed to tell me,'' Imah insisted. ''People took pieces of that chicken when it was still cooking.''

"I didn't touch it.'' Hester said. ''Not a shred.''

Imah smiled. ''Was I the only one? I thought maybe someone else did too. . . .''

"You little no-good, you! And Mama blamed Izzy!''

"Well, if you ate it, why did you ask what it tasted like?''

"Because I was so frightened, I just pushed it into my mouth and swallowed it and never tasted anything.''

Ida asked, ''If it was such a big chicken, how come there wasn't enough for us?''

"Wasn't there someone else?'' Imah murmured. ''I seem to remember—''

"My God, you're right!'' Hester cried. ''The Saint's children came!'' Her eyes sparkled and she sat smiling over this lost moment found among all the million since.

"It was an honor, the Saint's children. We must have invited them to come and eat with us—it wasn't often we could invite someone for *Shabbos* dinner. That was why there wasn't enough. . . ."

Her eyes were full of warmth. She turned to me. "Our Saint was a wonderful man. We looked up to him, you have no idea; more than a scholar. People used to quote him like Torah. . . ." Then she waved at herself deprecatingly. "Such a man, and look how I forgot him. I wonder where his children are now."

"His name was Simcha," Imah explained to me. "It means joy. People used to call his sons 'The Children of Joy.' "

"What a crew!" Ida said. "They were boils on the backside of Zoromin. I wonder on what backside they are boils now?"

"Ida, how can you say such a thing!" Heads came up, Imah and Hester's mouths widening in unison.

"What did I spit on something holy, that you should look so stunned? Your Saint was a madman who starved his wife and beggared his children. If it's all the same to you, I won't waste clearing my throat to bless him."

"It isn't right to talk that way," Imah said, motioning toward me. "Your talk is only confusing. It's enough the gentiles have stopped trying to tear down Judaism and left the job to Jews, who do it better."

Ida had her fire up. "Who said anything about Judaism? If that lunatic is Judaism, you can write me off the list—I'll dip myself tomorrow." She sat back, cracking righteously. Shells and nutmeats showered from her hands.

"Aunt Ida thinks he was crazy," I said to Hester, who was sulking. "What makes you think he was a Saint?"

"I'll tell you," Aunt Hester said, "and afterwards, Ida can have her say. I'll tell you the facts and you can judge for yourself. Zoromin has nothing to be ashamed of, and neither do the Jewish people. There was, in our town, in Zoromin, a very pious and saintly man—"

"That's facts?" Ida crowed.

"I *said*, a very pious and saintly man. Originally, the family was well off—or as well off as anyone gets in a town like that. Anyway, Simcha was raised with a warm coat in winter and a full belly and good, dry shoes. . . ."

"What a pity his children weren't as well off as he. . . ."

"Ida . . ."

"All right, go on."

"I don't know how it happened, but it was soon after he was married (a beautiful girl from a fine family. How she loved him and looked up to him!). Anyway, out of a clear sky, he came home one day, God-struck, changed. That day he gave away all his fine things, opened his house to the poor, and declared himself a refuge for anyone who was needy. During the day he walked miles, visiting the sick and hungry. Any penny extra went to the poor. He became even more pious than he had been before, and shamed many people who were more comfortable into being better Jews by his example.

"Well, his wife gave birth, and on each occasion he gave a party—not for the relatives, but for the poor, whose tongues didn't touch a piece of butter-cake from one year to the next. His Sabbaths were like the Sabbaths angels must have; his door was never closed.

"I remember most of all, his gentleness. The men in Zoromin worked like animals, sixteen, seventeen hours a day, in little shops, or walking to sell town to town, at the mercy of any robber or policeman on the way. Their lives and spirits became twisted because of it." She made a twisting motion with her old fingers.

"These men weren't gentle with their wives and they had no time to be loving to their children, or to say a pleasant word. What if they whipped a child by mistake and found it out later? They never apologized to that child or admitted the wrong, and if the child . . ."

Suddenly, she was that child who had always been waiting for the incident to be found again, the anger and despair fresh although the cause had passed seventy years, and the father and the mistake and the town itself were no more. Weren't the old supposed to have forgiven everything long ago?

It frightened me a little. Maybe it frightened her too, because she turned from it quickly and hunted her thought again.

"It was no easy place, Zoromin, but there was one man there who would pick up a child who fell in the mud, and brush its clothes off and comfort it. There was one man who would notice if a woman's basket was too heavy and would help her.

"There were women, certain women, Ida, if you remember, who lived outside of town, and our people didn't count them as Jewish women, although we knew one of them was the cobbler's own cousin. These women had no one and nothing and our women spat at them in the streets. Simcha invited these women to his Sabbaths too; and when they were sick, he sent his own wife to nurse them. He used to say, 'The poor should not be denied the blessing of giving,' and he sent money to Jerusalem in their name."

While Hester talked, I looked at Imah and saw her following with an intense look, her lips moving slightly with the words.

"Did you know this Simcha?" I asked her.

"Yes, yes," she said a little vaguely. "I heard of him as a very good man, a very saintly man." She seemed to be listening and answering to something else.

Aunt Ida had been gathering in silence. "Well, don't worry about a place in heaven for that man," she said. "If there is a heaven, he's too good for it altogether; but for the Sages of Zoromin, he was just right. Can you imagine"—and she waved at Aunt Hester—"a grandmother there, and still an innocent. Hester, you don't know any more now than you did when you were ten.

"*He* was the Saint, that Simcha, and his family, who weren't saints, were only cold, hungry, and a burden on the town. Watch out for saints, Hester, they eat more than you think. When the Saint decrees that his wealth be given to the poor, somebody has to stand baking all those little bread rolls that are given out of his great love. He says, 'Don't hand the beggar food at the door; ask him in, for he is your brother.' Someone has to clean the cups and the table and the floor after the visit of a hundred brothers. Someone has to fill the house of hungry stomachs with the smell of baking bread. The Saint's clothes are ragged, but he won't get new ones. Which is easier, I ask you—to darn a threadbare coat or to make a new one? Someone has to fix and fix again that saintly garment, and draw the Saint's frown when she curses old cloth that won't hold a needle!

"For heaven's sake, Hester, why do you think The Children of Joy were with us to eat that chicken? Reb Simcha knew he could be rich if he chose; he thought his children had the same choice he did. Those boys could hear a meat bone being dropped into soup half a mile away. If a man brushed a crumb from his beard, there was their knock on his door. . . . And why not? They were starving."

"What are you saying?" Hester looked scornfully at her sister. "That God should run to Zoromin to do the baking? The horror you speak of was that the saintly man drew his wife and children into his sanctity and caused them to do pious things—"

"Without the choice!" Ida cried.

"Aha!" Hester leaped up, her face glowing. Sixty of her years had fallen away, sixty pounds and all the chins and all the knotted veins that contended in her legs, and all the thousand compromises of a lifetime. "Where did that leave them then? Why, with all the rest of Zoromin! Without a choice, hungry and cold, and wondering if the prayer has always to be drowned by the rumbling in the belly. *But . . .*" (My God, she *had* been beautiful! The old, brown family photographs had missed it all, standing her up dead like an apple in a fruit dish; but she had been dancing with all those bright ribbons, and it was more than the ribbons her father had beaten her for. It had been the headlong, headstrong, passionate eagerness he must have seen in her.)

"With our Simcha, they had a look, Ida, a little minute's venture into the way people should be, the way the holy books tell them to be. Those men, the ordinary men of Zoromin—to them the Torah was only rules, and they never asked why: Wear *tefillin*, or God will strike you. Don't blow out a candle on the Sabbath or God will cripple you. In that poor place we had a holy man walking, alive, to show the people that a man is not an animal, that there is more than hunger and rules for what is forbidden!''

"And the people saw glory in this one-man Eden, this walking paradise in Zoromin? They did not. They were smarter than you think, Hester. They knew that a poor man gives less charity than a rich one, and that Simcha's children should have been his charity. They weren't exalted, Hester, they laughed at him and despised his wife and children. Children of Joy was a bitter title; as bitter as Chosen People in those days. We were all Children of Joy in Zoromin, singing in the synagogue and starving.''

"If the world knew virtue when it saw virtue, wouldn't *men* be Torah? Some didn't laugh at him, Ida. I didn't laugh. Didn't we have hard years after Zoromin? Didn't we need the memory of goodness? He was good, a saint.''

"A madman. If Zoromin had been rich enough to build a madhouse, he would have had the master bedroom.''

"A saint!''

"A madman!''

"Don't you see?'' Imah cried at them as they stood tight-faced, shouting against each other. "He's only mad in English, not in Yiddish. He . . . the *English* makes him mad; in Yiddish he's still a Saint!''

Their anger had overflowed their bodies, and suddenly, without reason, it found a home in me. I found myself grinding out words from a source I hadn't known was in me.

"What kind of people are you,'' I cried. "You had everything my friends and I admire, and you threw it away. You had all the security of the ceremonies and beliefs, lives full of meaning, dignity, and reality. That's what I came to Imah for, to find out how it was lost, the wonderful home life, when parents and children knew how to be loving and peaceful with one another; when there was the simple truth, not like today, all clouded and complicated. And now you've been so perverted by false values and materialism, you can't even remember what the old days were like!'' Then, impossibly, "Haven't you any respect for your elders?!''

Dead silence. . . . Then a first, small edge of sound from Hester. The edge broke, and then the others came laughing in behind and in the end they conquered me and took me with them, defeated and captive in laughter.

"At least," Ida gasped, "she can still make Jewish jokes." We laughed till tears ran down our faces.

"Zoromin was a poor village," Ida wept. "Maybe they were too poor to afford a real Saint."

"After all," Imah wept, "without some Saint or other, what would people do?"

"I want Saints," I wept, "but I want real ones."

"Who could afford it but Americans?" Hester was gasping. "Listen, when a woman can't have diamonds, she wears rhinestones; and when she can't have rhinestones, she wears glass and holds up her head."

"Is it true—did you mean it when you said that a man can be a Saint in Yiddish and a madman in English?"

"If not," Imah said, and got up to get a Kleenex, "wouldn't we all be Saints?"

"Then the dream of America was a fantasy—the hope was a lie!"

"American!" Aunt Hester said affectionately, and blew into her handkerchief. "Who would imagine, in so little time, our family would have such Americans?" She gazed at me with deep pride. "Look at her, she doesn't understand a single thing! . . . Oh, my knee aches so, I think I've been sitting in a draft!"

from

THE FACTS: A NOVELIST'S AUTOBIOGRAPHY

PHILIP ROTH

While World War II made America face the horror of anti-Semitism,
there was still an undercurrent of prejudice. It was more subtle than
out-and-out violence, but a part of the fabric of our country none-
theless. Second-generation Jews felt they were American first, Jewish
second. Still they found they were unable to work in certain industries
or attend certain universities. In this excerpt from his autobiography,
Philip Roth remembers how he first discovered discrimination. No
matter how American he felt, there were people who would always
look at him as a Jew.

  Philip Roth was born in Newark, New Jersey, and was educated
at Rutgers and Bucknell universities and the University of Chicago.
His books include Goodbye, Columbus *(1959), for which he won the*
1960 National Book Award in fiction; Letting Go; When She Was
Good; Portnoy's Complaint; The Breast; The Great American Novel;
My Life As a Man; The Professor of Desire; The Ghost Writer;
Zuckerman Unbound; The Counterlife; Deception; *and* Operation
Shylock.

The greatest menace while I was growing up came from abroad, from the
Germans and the Japanese, our enemies because we were American. I still
remember my terror as a nine-year-old when, running in from playing on
the street after school, I saw the banner headline CORREGIDOR FALLS on
the evening paper in our doorway and understood that the United States
actually could lose the war it had entered only months before. At home
the biggest threat came from the Americans who opposed or resisted us—
or condescended to us or rigorously excluded us—because we were Jews.
Though I knew that we were tolerated and accepted as well—in publicized
individual cases, even specially esteemed—and though I never doubted that
this country was mine (and New Jersey and Newark as well), I was not

unaware of the power to intimidate that emanated from the highest and lowest reaches of gentile America.

At the top were the gentile executives who ran my father's company, the Metropolitan Life, from the home office at Number One Madison Avenue (the first Manhattan street address I ever knew). When I was a small boy, my father, then in his early thirties, was still a new Metropolitan agent, working a six-day week, including most evenings, and grateful for the steady, if modest, living this job provided, even during the Depression; a family shoe store he'd opened after marrying my mother had gone bankrupt some years before, and in between he'd had to take a variety of low-paying, unpromising jobs. He proudly explained to his sons that the Metropolitan was "the largest financial institution in the world" and that as an agent he provided Metropolitan Life policyholders with "an umbrella for a rainy day." The company put out dozens of pamphlets to educate its policyholders about health and disease; I collected a new batch off the racks in the waiting room on Saturday mornings when he took me along with him to the narrow downtown street where the Essex district office of Newark occupied nearly a whole floor of a commercial office building. I read up on "Tuberculosis," "Pregnancy," and "Diabetes," while he labored over his ledger entries and his paperwork. Sometimes at his desk, impressing myself by sitting in his swivel chair, I practiced my penmanship on Metropolitan stationery; in one corner of the paper was my father's name and in the other a picture of the home-office tower, topped with the beacon that he described to me, in the Metropolitan's own phrase, as the light that never failed.

In our apartment a framed replica of the Declaration of Independence hung above the telephone table on the hallway wall—it had been awarded by the Metropolitan to the men of my father's district for a successful year in the field, and seeing it there daily during my first school years forged an association between the venerated champions of equality who signed that cherished document and our benefactors, the corporate fathers at Number One Madison Avenue, where the reigning president was, fortuitously, a Mr. Lincoln. If that wasn't enough, the home office executive whom my father would trek from New Jersey to see when his star began to rise slightly in the company was the superintendent of agencies, a Mr. Wright, whose good opinion my father valued inordinately all his life and whose height and imposing good looks he admired nearly as much as he did the man's easygoing diplomacy. As my father's son I felt no less respectful toward these awesomely named gentiles than he did, but I, like him, knew that they had to be the very officials who openly and guiltlessly conspired to prevent more than a few token Jews from assuming positions of anything approaching importance within the largest financial institution in the world.

One reason my father so admired the Jewish manager of his own district, Sam Peterfreund—aside, of course, from the devotion that Peterfreund inspired by recognizing my father's drive early on and making him an assistant manager—was that Peterfreund had climbed to the leadership of such a large, productive office despite the company's deep-rooted reluctance to allow a Jew to rise too high. When Mr. Peterfreund was to make one of his rare visits for dinner, the green felt protective pads came out of the hall closet and were laid by my brother and me on the dining room table, it was spread with a fresh linen cloth and linen napkins, water goblets appeared, and we ate off "the good dishes" in the dining room, where there hung a large oil painting of a floral arrangement, copied skillfully from the Louvre by my mother's brother, Mickey; on the sideboard were framed photographic portraits of the two dead men for whom I'd been named, my mother's father, Philip, and my father's younger brother, Milton. We ate in the dining room only on religious holidays, on special family occasions, and when Mr. Peterfreund came—and we all called him Mr. Peterfreund, even when he wasn't there; my father also addressed him directly as "Boss." "Want a drink, Boss?" Before dinner we sat unnaturally, like guests in our own living room, while Mr. Peterfreund sipped his schnapps and I was encouraged to listen to his wisdom. The esteem he inspired was a tribute to a gentile-sanctioned Jew managing a big Metropolitan office as much as to an immediate supervisor whose goodwill determined my father's occupational well-being and our family fate. A large, bald-headed man with a gold chain across his vest and a slightly mysterious German accent, whose family lived (in high style, I imagined) in New York (*and* on Long Island) while (no less glamorously to me) he slept during the week in a Newark hotel, the Boss was our family's Bernard Baruch.

Opposition more frightening than corporate discrimination came from the lowest reaches of the gentile world, from the gangs of *lumpen* kids who, one summer, swarmed out of Neptune, a ramshackle little town on the Jersey shore, and stampeded along the boardwalk into Bradley Beach, hollering "Kikes! Dirty Jews!" and beating up whoever hadn't run for cover. Bradley Beach, a couple of miles south of Asbury Park on the mid-Jersey coast, was the very modest little vacation resort where we and hundreds of other lower-middle-class Jews from humid, mosquito-ridden north Jersey cities rented rooms or shared small bungalows for several weeks during the summer. It was paradise for me, even though we lived three in a room, and four when my father drove down the old Cheesequake highway to see us on weekends or to stay for his two-week vacation. In all of my intensely secure and protected childhood, I don't believe I ever felt more exuberantly snug than I did in those mildly anarchic rooming houses, where—inevitably with more strain than valor—some ten or twelve women tried to share the shelves of a single large icebox, and to cook side by side, in a crowded communal kitchen, for children, visiting husbands, and elderly parents. Meals were eaten in the unruly, kibbutzlike atmosphere—so unlike the ambiance in my own orderly home—of the underventilated dining room.

The hot, unhomelike, homey hubbub of the Bradley Beach rooming house was somberly contrasted, in the early forties, by reminders all along the shore that the country was fighting in an enormous war: bleak, barbwired Coast Guard bunkers dotted the beaches, and scores of lonely, very young sailors played the amusement machines in the arcades at Asbury Park; the lights were blacked out along the boardwalk at night and the blackout shades on the rooming-house windows made it stifling indoors after dinner; there was even tarry refuse, alleged to be from torpedoed ships, that washed up and littered the beach—I sometimes had fears of wading gleefully with my friends into the surf and bumping against the body of someone killed at sea. Also—and most peculiarly, since we were all supposed to be pulling together to beat the Axis Powers—there were these "race riots," as we children called the hostile nighttime invasions by the boys from Neptune: violence directed against the Jews by youngsters who, as everyone said, could only have learned their hatred from what they heard at home.

Though the riots occurred just twice, for much of one July and August it was deemed unwise for a Jewish child to venture out after supper alone, or even with friends, though nighttime freedom in shorts and sandals was one of Bradley's greatest pleasures for a ten-year-old on vacation from homework and the school year's bedtime hours. The morning after the first riot, a story spread among the kids collecting Popsicle sticks and playing ring-a-lievo on the Lorraine Avenue beach; It was about somebody (whom nobody seemed to know personally) who had been caught before he could get away: the anti-Semites had held him down and pulled his face back and forth across the splintery surface of the boardwalk's weathered planks. This particular horrific detail, whether apocryphal or not—and it needn't necessarily have been—impressed upon me how barbaric was this irrational hatred of families who, as anyone could see, were simply finding in Bradley Beach a little inexpensive relief from the city heat, people just trying to have a quiet good time, bothering no one, except occasionally each other, as when one of the women purportedly expropriated from the icebox, for her family's corn on the cob, somebody else's quarter of a pound of salt butter. If that was as much harm as any of us could do, why make a bloody pulp of a Jewish child's face?

The home-office gentiles in executive positions at Number One Madison Avenue were hardly comparable to the kids swarming into Bradley screaming "Kike!"; and yet when I thought about it, I saw that they were no more reasonable or fair: they too were against Jews for no good reason. Small wonder that at twelve, when I was advised to begin to think seriously about what I would do when I grew up, I decided to oppose the injustices wreaked by the violent and the privileged by becoming a lawyer for the underdog.

When I entered high school, the menace shifted to School Stadium, then the only large football grounds in Newark, situated on alien Bloomfield Avenue, a forty-minute bus ride from Weequahic High. On Saturdays in the fall, four of the city's seven high schools would meet in a doubleheader, as many as two thousand kids pouring in for the first game, which began around noon, and then emptying en masse into the surrounding streets when the second game had ended in the falling shadows. It was inevitable after a hard-fought game that intense school rivalries would culminate in a brawl somewhere in the stands and that, in an industrial city of strongly divergent ethnic backgrounds and subtle, though pronounced, class gradations, fights would break out among volatile teenagers from four very different neighborhoods. Yet the violence provoked by the presence of a Weequahic crowd—particularly after a rare Weequahic victory—was unlike any other.

I remember being in the stands with my friends in my sophomore year, rooting uninhibitedly for the "Indians," as our Weequahic teams were known in the Newark sports pages; after never having beaten Barringer High in the fourteen years of Weequahic's existence, our team was leading them 6–0 in the waning minutes of the Columbus Day game. The Barringer backfield was Berry, Peloso, Short, and Thompson; in the Weequahic backfield were Weissman, Weiss, Gold, and fullback Fred Rosenberg, who'd led a sustained march down the field at the end of the first half and then, on a two-yard plunge, had scored what Fred, now a PR consultant in New Jersey, recently wrote to tell me was "one of the only touchdowns notched by the Indians that entire season, on a run that probably was one of the longer runs from scrimmage in 1947."

As the miraculous game was nearing its end—as Barringer, tied with Central for first place in the City League, was about to be upset by the weakest high school team in Newark—I suddenly noticed that the rival fans on the other side of the stadium bowl had begun to stream down the aisles, making their way around the far ends of the stadium toward us. Instead of waiting for the referee's final whistle, I bolted for an exit and, along with nearly everyone else who understood what was happening, ran down the stadium ramp in the direction of the buses waiting to take us back to our neighborhood. Though there were a number of policemen around, it was easy to see that once the rampage was under way, unless you were clinging to a cop with both arms and both legs, his protection wouldn't be much help; should you be caught on your own by a gang from one of the other three schools waiting to get their hands on a Weequahic Jew—our school was almost entirely Jewish—it was unlikely that you'd emerge from the stadium without serious injury.

The nearest bus was already almost full when I made it on board; as soon as the last few kids shoved their way in, the uniformed Public Service driver, fearful for his own safety as a transporter of Weequahic kids, drew the front door shut. By then there were easily ten or fifteen of the enemy, aged twelve to twenty, surrounding the bus and hammering their fists against its sides. Fred Rosenberg contends that "every able-bodied man from north Newark, his brother, and their offspring got into the act." When one of them, having worked his hands through a crevice under the window beside my seat, started forcing the window up with his fingers, I grabbed it from the top and brought it down as hard as I could. He howled and somebody took a swing at the window with a baseball bat, breaking the frame but miraculously not the glass. Before the others could join together to tear back the door, board the bus, and go straight for me—who would have been hard put to explain that the reprisal had been uncharacteristic and intended only in self-defense—the driver had pulled out from the curb and we were safely away from the postgame pogrom, which, for our adversaries, constituted perhaps the most enjoyable part of the day's entertainment.

That evening I fled again, not only because I was a fourteen-year-old weighing only a little over a hundred pounds but because I was never to be one of the few who stayed behind for a fight but always among the many whose impulse is to run to avoid it. A boy in our neighborhood might be expected to protect himself in a schoolyard confrontation with another boy his age and size, but no stigma attached to taking flight from a violent melee—by and large it was considered both shameful and stupid for a bright Jewish child to get caught up in something so dangerous to his physical safety, and so repugnant to Jewish instincts. The collective memory of Polish and Russian pogroms had fostered in most of our families the idea that our worth as human beings, even perhaps our distinction as a people, was embodied in the *incapacity* to perpetrate the sort of blood-letting visited upon our ancestors.

For a while during my adolescence I studiously followed prizefighting, could recite the names and weights of all the champions and contenders, and even subscribed briefly to *Ring*, Nat Fleischer's colorful boxing magazine. As kids my brother and I had been taken by our father to the local boxing arena, where invariably we all had a good time. From my father and his friends I heard about the prowess of Benny Leonard, Barney Ross, Max Baer, and the clownishly nicknamed Slapsie Maxie Rosenbloom. And yet Jewish boxers and boxing aficionados remained, like boxing itself, ''sport'' in the bizarre sense, a strange deviation from the norm and interesting largely for that reason: in the world whose values first formed me, unrestrained physical aggression was considered contemptible everywhere else. I could no more smash a nose with a fist than fire a pistol into someone's heart. And what imposed this restraint, if not on Slapsie Maxie Rosenbloom, then on me, was my being Jewish. In my scheme of things, Slapsie Maxie was a more miraculous Jewish phenomenon by far than Dr. Albert Einstein.

The evening following our escape from School Stadium the ritual victory bonfire was held on the dirt playing field on Chancellor Avenue, across from Syd's, a popular Weequahic hangout where my brother and I each did part-time stints selling hot dogs and french fries. I'd virtually evolved as a boy on that playing field; it was two blocks from my house and bordered on the grade school—''Chancellor Avenue''—that I'd attended for eight years, which itself stood next to Weequahic High. It was the field where I'd played pickup football and baseball, where my brother had competed in school track meets, where I'd shagged flies for hours with anybody who would fungo the ball out to me, where my friends and I hung around on Sunday mornings, watching with amusement as the local fathers—the plumbers, the electricians, the produce merchants—kibitzed their way through their weekly softball game. If ever I had been called on to express my love for my neighborhood in a single reverential act, I couldn't have done better than to get down on my hands and knees and kiss the ground behind home plate.

Yet upon this, the sacred heart of my inviolate homeland, our stadium attackers launched a nighttime raid, the conclusion to the violence begun that afternoon, their mopping-up exercise. A few hours after the big fire had been lit, as we happily sauntered around the dark field, joking among ourselves and looking for girls to impress, while in the distance the cart-wheeling cheerleaders led the chant of the crowd encircling the fire— ''And when you're up against Weequahic you're upside down!''—the cars pulled up swiftly on Chancellor Avenue, and the same guys who'd been pounding on the sides of my bus (or so I quickly assumed) were racing onto the field, some of them waving baseball bats. The field was set into the slope of the Chancellor Avenue hill; I ran through the dark to the nearest wall, jumped some six feet down into Hobson Street, and then just kept going, through alleyways, between garages, and over backyard fences, until I'd made it safely home in less than five minutes. One of my Leslie Street friends, the football team water boy, who'd been standing in the full glare of the fire wearing his Weequahic varsity jacket, was not so quick or lucky; his assailants—identified in the neighborhood the next day as "Italians"—picked him up and threw him bodily toward the flames. He landed just at the fire's edge and, though he wasn't burned, spent days in the hospital recovering from internal injuries.

But this was a unique calamity. Our lower-middle-class neighborhood of houses and shops—a few square miles of tree-lined streets at the corner of the city bordering on residential Hillside and semi-industrial Irvington—was as safe and peaceful a haven for me as his rural community would have been for an Indiana farm boy. Ordinarily nobody more disquieting ever appeared there than the bearded old Jew who sometimes tapped on our door around dinnertime; to me an unnerving specter from the harsh and distant European past, he stood silently in the dim hallway while I went to get a quarter to drop into his collection can for the Jewish National Fund (a name that never sank all the way in: the only nation for Jews, as I saw it, was the democracy to which I was so loyally—and lyrically—bound, regardless of the unjust bias of the so-called best and the violent hatred of some of the worst). Shapiro, the immigrant tailor who also did dry cleaning, had two thumbs on one hand, and that made bringing our clothes to him a little eerie for me when I was still small. And there was LeRoy "the moron," a somewhat gruesome but innocuous neighborhood dimwit who gave me the creeps when he sat down on the front stoop to listen to a bunch of us talking after school. On our street he was rarely teased but just sat looking at us stupidly with his hollow eyes and rhythmically tapping one foot—and that was about as frightening as things ever got.

A typical memory is of five or six of us energetically traversing the whole length of the neighborhood Friday nights on our way back from a double feature at the Roosevelt Theater. We would stop off at the Watson Bagel Company on Clinton Place to buy, for a few pennies each, a load of the first warm bagels out of the oven—and this was four decades before the bagel became a breakfast staple at Burger King. Devouring three and four apiece, we'd circuitously walk one another home, howling with laughter at our jokes and imitating our favorite baritones. When the weather was good we'd sometimes wind up back of Chancellor Avenue School, on the wooden bleachers along the sidelines of the asphalt playground adjacent to the big dirt playing field. Stretched on our backs in the open night air, we were as carefree as any kids anywhere in postwar America, and certainly we felt ourselves no less American. Discussions about Jewishness and being Jewish, which I was to hear so often among intellectual Jews once I was an adult in Chicago and New York, were altogether unknown; we talked about being misunderstood by our families, about movies and radio programs and sex and sports, we even argued about politics, though this was rare since our fathers were all ardent New Dealers and there was no disagreement among us about the sanctity of F.D.R. and the Democratic Party. About being Jewish there was nothing more to say than there was about having two arms and two legs. It would have seemed to us strange not to be Jewish—stranger still, to hear someone announce that he wished he weren't a Jew or that he intended not to be in the future.

Yet, simultaneously, this intense adolescent camaraderie was the primary means by which we were deepening our *Americanness*. Our parents were, with few exceptions, the first-generation offspring of poor turn-of-the-century immigrants from Galicia and Polish Russia, raised in predominantly Yiddish-speaking Newark households where religious Orthodoxy was only just beginning to be seriously eroded by American life. However unaccented and American-sounding their speech, however secularized their own beliefs, and adept and convincing their American style of lower-middle-class existence, they were influenced still by their childhood training and by strong parental ties to what often seemed to us antiquated, socially useless old-country mores and perceptions.

My larger boyhood society cohered around the most inherently American phenomenon at hand—the game of baseball, whose mystique was encapsulated in three relatively inexpensive fetishes that you could have always at your side in your room, not only while you did your homework but in bed with you while you slept if you were a worshiper as primitive as I was at ten and eleven: they were a ball, a bat, and a glove. The solace that my Orthodox grandfather doubtless took in the familiar leathery odor of the flesh-worn straps of the old phylacteries in which he wrapped himself each morning, I derived from the smell of my mitt, which I ritualistically donned every day to work a little on my pocket. I was an average playground player, and the mitt's enchantment had to do less with foolish dreams of becoming a major leaguer, or even a high school star, than with the bestowal of membership in a great secular nationalistic church from which nobody had ever seemed to suggest that Jews should be excluded.

(The blacks were another story, until 1947.) The softball and hardball teams we organized and reorganized obsessively throughout our grade-school years—teams we called by unarguably native names like the Seabees and the Mohawks and described as "social and athletic clubs"—aside from the opportunity they afforded to compete against one another in a game we loved, also operated as secret societies that separated us from the faint, residual foreignness still clinging to some of our parents' attitudes and that validated our own spotless credentials as American kids. Paradoxically, our remotely recent old-country Jewish origins may well have been a source of our especially intense devotion to a sport that, unlike boxing or even football, had nothing to do with the menace of brute force unleashed against flesh and bones.

The Weequahic neighborhood for over two decades now has been part of the vast black Newark slum. Visiting my father in Elizabeth, I'll occasionally take a roundabout route off the parkway into my old Newark and, to give myself an emotional workout, drive through the streets still entirely familiar to me despite the boarded-up shops and badly decaying houses, and the knowledge that my white face is not at all welcome. Recently, snaking back and forth in my car along the one-way streets of the Weequahic section, I began to imagine house plaques commemorating the achievements of the boys who'd once lived there, markers of the kind you see in London and Paris on the residences of the historically renowned. What I inscribed on those plaques, along with my friends' names and their years of birth and of local residence, wasn't the professional status they had attained in later life but the position each had played on those neighborhood teams of ours in the 1940s. I thought that if you knew that in this four-family Hobson Street house there once lived the third baseman Seymour Feldman and that down a few doors had lived Ronnie Rubin, who in his boyhood had been our catcher, you'd understand how and where the Feldman and the Rubin families had been naturalized irrevocably by their young sons.

In 1982, while I was visiting my widowered father in Miami Beach during his first season there on his own, I got him one night to walk over with me to Meyer Lansky's old base of operations, the Hotel Singapore on Collins Avenue; earlier in the day he'd told me that wintering at the Singapore were some of the last of his generation from our neighborhood— the ones, he mordantly added, "still aboveground." Among the faces I recognized in the lobby, where the elderly residents met to socialize each evening after dinner, was the mother of one of the boys who also used to play ball incessantly "up the field" and who hung around on the playground bleachers after dark back when we were Seabees together. As we sat talking at the edge of a gin-rummy game, she suddenly took hold of my hand and, smiling at me with deeply emotional eyes—with that special heart-filled look that *all* our mothers had—she said, ''Phil, the feeling there was among you boys—I've never seen anything like it again.'' I told her, altogether truthfully, that I haven't either.

from

AND THE BRIDGE IS LOVE

FAYE MOSKOWITZ

And the Bridge Is Love *is a collection of personal essays about family, growing up, and marriage. In this selection, Faye Moskowitz talks about how her older cousin Esther influenced her as a child. Esther, whose father was a rabbi, followed a strict Orthodox way of life, yet still managed to inspire the imaginations of those around her. From her red hair and polished fingernails to her belief in Orthodox traditions, Esther showed her younger cousins that you can carve your own way without compromising what you believe in.*

Faye Moskowitz is also the author of Whoever Finds This: I Love You *and* A Leak in the Heart: Personal Essays and Life Stories. *She teaches writing at George Washington University in Washington, D.C.*

I keep photographs in a large suitbox under my bed, certain the way people are that I will mount them someday in albums, classify them by date and place. Meanwhile, they curl and fade, the writing on their backs turns lilac, and I tell myself, when I think about it, that if I do not hurry, one day there will be no one to name the thousands of images, smiling or grave, staring out of the glossy paper.

I have one photograph of my cousin Esther. She faces the camera pensively, the sun making an aureole of the hair she bleached blond that year. For the picture she wears a white sweater and a single strand of pearls. Even in 1945, when she was sixteen, Esther had achieved a timeless elegance that makes people select the photo out of a welter of others and ask, "Who is she?"

Esther charted maps for me of exotic places my green imagination would take years to recognize. She taught me the cruel deception of appearances—how a treacherous undertow can wait under waters calm as the skin on a morning cup of cocoa, how toeholds can exist on seemingly unscalable rock. But by the time my mind and body were in sufficient

93

concord to follow her blazes, she was no longer there, no longer dancing just ahead of me.

I think I was always a little afraid of her; all of us cousins were. She had a temper that flared without warning like a phosphorus match that blows up and singes your thumbnail when you aren't expecting it. We attributed it to her red hair, so different from the ordinary shades of brown and black we all seemed to be stuck with. And she was skinny, too, and bit her nails like the girl in the ads did before the cartoon mother with the worry vees in her forehead found Ovaltine.

When Esther came to stay with us in Jackson during the summers we were little girls, the way all the Detroit cousins did at one time or another, I discovered that my mother was afraid of her, too. Esther held her nose when she was thirsty and said Jackson water stunk like rotten eggs. Of course, I had heard that one before; I told her Detroit water was full of clothes bleach, but my mother didn't say a word when Esther refused to eat strawberry Jell-O for dessert. "I'm not allowed to eat this stuff," Esther said. "Jell-O is made from unkosher cowbones." By that time I was not only ashamed of our water supply, but my mother and I both knew that Esther had found us out. She saw how we had let the ropes of religious ritual go slack, as people do sometimes when they move away from family, and experience tries belief. She saw how easy it is to compromise when observance becomes a matter of conscience rather than convention. She saw and, being Esther, she would tell.

At night we undressed quickly with our backs to one another, upstairs in my bake oven of a bedroom, the June bugs banging away against the screens, and I would already feel homesick in my very own room, thinking that Esther would want me to come visit her in Detroit; I hadn't the nerve to tell her I missed my mother when I hadn't even gone yet.

We'd lie in bed and giggle and talk until my dad yelled upstairs for us to go to sleep, and we'd be quiet for a moment and then laugh some more. We cousins disagreed about Esther; some of us called her swell, but the braver among us said she was a snot. Still, no one disputed her claim to second sight; somehow Esther always knew the exact moment my father would lose patience, put down his paper, and start for the stairs. Then all of a sudden she would yawn and tell me, "It's time for prayers." That was the part I hated most. She would declare in her redheaded authoritative tone, "The second we're done, we can't say another single word or it's a sin." She prayed out loud, continuing long after I had finished my one puny little prayer. As soon as she said "amen," she carefully pulled her nightgown down over the underpants she said it was a sin not to wear to bed. When she turned her back to me and left me alone, I could almost feel her stubborn lips clamped shut, could barely distinguish her heartbeat from mine.

Suddenly, in the dark silence, the outside world would enter my room: the death rattle of an old Ford, strangers murmuring on the street, an insistent mosquito, whining, waiting. That was the time when worry climbed in bed with me full of hindsight about the day, warnings for tomorrow. I was afraid to go to sleep, but there was no arguing with Esther about what was or was not a sin. Being a rabbi's daughter, she had a direct line to God, and I knew it, so she snookered me into terrified silence every time.

Esther had crazy eating habits, like so many scrawny kids. When we were allowed to go to the ice cream parlor for a malt, Esther carried an egg with her in a little brown paper bag blown up and twisted at the top so the egg would not break. You can imagine how she walked then, taking tiny mincing steps with the little sack held out in front of her. The soda jerk always made a production of cracking the egg one-handed, letting it drop into the frosty metal container from about a foot above it. My mother laughed when I asked for an egg for my malt. She pinched the back of my tree-trunk thighs and turned away without a further answer.

One summer Esther came with her own supply of Fleishmann's yeast, as if Jackson had no grocery stores and was truly the hick town the Detroit cousins all claimed it was. She was skinnier than ever, and my mother vowed to fatten her up, assuming the task was as easy as plumping the Thanksgiving turkey we penned in the coalbin and fed stale bread and cracked corn before the holiday. The brisket our family loved so much, so tender it fell into succulent strips before it could be cut, made Esther gag. She pushed the meat around on her plate and picked out bits of fat she pronounced disgusting when she and I were alone. Noodle kugel upset her stomach, she played with her mashed potatoes, and even my mother's feathery cinnamon rolls, still steaming, she pronounced "too rich." "It's that mooshed-up yeast she eats," my mother grumbled, looking with satisfaction at my potbelly. "Thank God, I don't have any trouble with you."

What did my mother know, with her accent so thick you could spread it like peanut butter and her Old Country ways? I became convinced that Esther's asceticism and strict adherence to Jewish law fostered her slender bones and redhead's milky skin. I loathed my plump body, over which I seemed to have lost all vestiges of control, and shut my eyes to the changes that were taking place in front of them until Esther told my mother one day, "For heaven's sake, Aunt Sophie, buy her a brassiere!"

I felt certain I had only to get closer to Esther and I would absorb her secret; perhaps there was still time to throw away the old design, shape my limbs to a different set of plans. Gentile Jackson had become my adversary, put perversely I found myself daily swallowing more of my Jewishness, hiding it, until the secret seemed to blow me up as with the tell-tale contours of an unwanted child. Expertly twirling on a round stool at Woolworth's, I ate forbidden BLTs, toasted, and when my classmates insisted that Chinese waiters were lepers who dropped finger bones into the chop suey, I turned up my nose the way Esther might have done and told bald-faced lies about how often my family ate at the Fairy Gardens.

As if breaking the Sabbath with Saturday matinees were not sin enough, I came home after the movies and cut, and tore, and pasted, and made a great show of sitting on my front porch embroidering in cross-stitch on small, stamped squares of linen. My most hideous secret I kept to myself, a cache of religious tracts picked up from store counters around town, New Testament readings I puzzled over at night by the light of a street lamp that lit a corner of my bedroom. Of course I hadn't the nerve to do any of these things in front of Esther; I could never admit how seductive "fitting in" had become or how convinced I was that the Jewish God I still so deeply believed in was going to strike me dead after He had tired of playing with me. That summer of the Fleishmann's yeast, my mother sent me to Detroit to stay with Esther until school started. And I was ready to go. For the first time in months, I began sleeping through the night again.

They came to Esther's house sometimes, the women, late Thursday afternoons or early Friday mornings, carrying their *Shabbos* chickens wrapped in liver-colored butcher paper and leaking newsprint. Then my uncle, whom even his brothers spoke of as the rabbi, wearing as always his stern black suit, would leave his study and solemnly escort the bewigged visitor into my aunt Celia's kitchen. There she, in the middle of her own Sabbath preparations, cleared a spot on the wooden work table and carefully protected it from possible contamination with thick layers of the *Jewish Daily Forward*.

The rabbi washed his hands while the visitor unwrapped the chicken for him to examine. "See, Rabbi, when I went to kosher the chicken, I saw this blemish on its heart," or, "What do you think, Rabbi? Look how the liver is so large and yellow." And my uncle, his tiny hooked nose slightly averted, would touch the organs with the tip of a carefully trimmed fingernail. Esther and I stood half hidden behind the pantry doorway, where I could catch underneath the scent of fresh dill and parsley from her mother's already simmering chicken soup, the visitor's rank sweat, the slightly sour stink of her yellow, waxy chicken. For a moment we were all caught in arrested motion, the woman calculating whether there was still time to get to the butcher again, anticipating the argument; Aunt Celia, dish towel or spoon in hand, stopping her work to await the decision.

I never had the courage to ask Esther if she sometimes wondered, as I did, whether her father took into account the shabbiness of a peeling handbag or a pair of shoes gone tipsy at the heels when he made his judgment. Even at twelve, I knew the purchase of another chicken would not hurt the rich women, but deep down I cheered for a positive verdict for them. I was always passionately arguing for fairness, yet I felt only disdain for the poor ones who might go without meat if the chicken were found to be unclean and therefore unkosher. Just as I worshiped Esther's power, though I couldn't define it, I was drawn to those who came in well-cut dresses and smart hats, eyes, and noses like crazed porcelain under their tiny veils. Their husbands could donate sterling candlesticks and gold-embroidered Torah covers to the synagogue, while the debt-ridden sat looking into their laps when the president of the shul made yet another appeal to the congregation for money. Perhaps it had nothing to do with fairness at all; perhaps I knew already that the world lined up on the side of the powerful, and I just didn't want to be caught in the wrong queue.

Like as not, the rabbi would find the chicken kosher and, tension broken, he, Esther's mother, and the woman would laugh and talk for a few moments, the visitor's eyes darting like little birds here and there in the spotless kitchen. Once, when Aunt Celia's back was turned, one of the women lifted the lid of a cooking pot, the steam clouding her glasses so that when she dropped the lid with an embarrassed clatter and said, "Excuse me, Rebbetzin," she appeared to have no eyes at all.

But they did have eyes, these women, and Esther used to tell me she knew they talked about her mother; she heard them sometimes in the U-shaped balcony of the synagogue, whispering to one another as they skillfully followed the prayers, sitting, standing, rocking back and forth, sitting again, turning the thin, red-rimmed pages of their prayer books with moistened fingers. Esther sat with her mother and sisters in the center of the U so they could look straight down to the *bemah* or slightly ahead to the altar where the rabbi stood.

Aunt Celia had red hair, too, the color of carrot *tzimmes* cooked in honey and darkened with cinnamon, shades deeper than Esther's; she refused to cover it with a wig the way many of the Orthodox women did, but wore it braided and twisted into a coronet like the beautiful queens pictured in books of fairy tales. I saw her one night in a thin white nightgown, seated at her dressing table brushing out that hair. Her head was bent over like a tulip after hard rain, and from the back of her white neck the red hair, catching sparks from a lamp, fell almost to the blue carpet.

I never told Esther about it, but whenever the women whispered, I remembered that scene of sparking hair and lamplight, and even then I felt they disapproved of Aunt Celia because anything so beautiful must surely be sinful.

And so the long hot days passed, Michigan summer, with an occasional breeze coming down from Canada to billow white window curtains as we slept. Though I missed my parents and my little brother, too, I didn't really think about them much. In my mind they shrank to manageable proportions so that they and my home and Jackson became to me like an idyllic scene in a glass globe with bits of fake snow swirling all around. I measured my life by Esther's rule, turned my energy to emulating her. Everything about her interested me: the way she tucked fragrant heart-shaped sachets in her underwear drawer, the drops of Tabu she touched to her pulse points before we went walking, the scarlet fingernail polish she applied, leaving white half moons at the cuticle and tips, the way her trim little figure bobbed and bent as she prayed.

On Friday nights and Saturday mornings, Esther and I went to the synagogue together, walking primly down Linwood Street, outwardly ignoring the boys who swarmed around her, their necks imprisoned in collars and ties, their wiry hair tamed by brilliantine. I fell in and out of love every five minutes. Seated in the balcony between Esther and Aunt Celia, I prayed so fervently and so noisily that Esther poked me in the side and said, "Cut it out. Everyone's looking at you."

The inchoate longing I was beset with, and the knife-blade of emotion that nicked me when I least expected it, I welcomed and even encouraged, bound as they were in my mind to Esther's spell and my desire for spiritual rebirth. The two of us lay in the sun on her back porch reading books from the Duffield branch library. We explored the stores up and down Linwood. In one dusty second-hand shop we found a small leathery bound volume of British poets; Esther bought it for my birthday. I had only to whisper, "Maid of Athens, ere we part, /Give, oh give me back my heart!" and I was reduced to weeping into a little handkerchief I carried now always at the ready. The cantor's wail, quivering past the balcony to the gold-leafed ceilings of Blaine Shul, seemed both an elegy for Jewish suffering through the ages and a validation of my own hunger.

Esther's parents slept in chaste twin beds, as did my Orthodox grandparents, a lamp table between like a bundling board. Esther told me it was a sin for husbands and wives to sleep in double beds because there were times when women were unclean and their husbands were forbidden to go unto them. That's how she put it: "go unto them." The biblical language and the knowledge of my own parents' wickedly narrow double bed, the one I had thrown tantrums to get into only short years before, tied religion and sex together in a knot I had difficulty picking apart. That and the Yeshiva boys who had begun to put their hands in front of their eyes, palms out like startled starfish, when I passed near them. Esther said they weren't allowed to look at women because it was a sin, and all the while I was trying to purge my own self of sin, I felt vaguely elated at being old enough to be the potential cause of it.

I entered West Intermediate that fall, and Esther went away to school, an Orthodox seminary for girls in Brooklyn. She didn't write, and we lost track of one another for a while. My adolescence progressed normally: enough misery to keep the death wish my usual state, an occasional high to keep me from actually taking the gas-pipe. During one Passover holiday break I spent the night with Esther. My family had moved back to Detroit by then and, surrounded by other Jews, I had finally found a religious balance that didn't have me constantly falling on my face.

That was the year Esther became a blonde. (I sat on the toilet lid and watched her dab on peroxide and ammonia with an old toothbrush.) Without her red hair, she seemed almost a black-and-white version of herself, instead of a study in Technicolor. We laughed about the old days, and I called the rabbi "Uncle David," and even gave him a cool peck on the cheek the way I did my other uncles.

Esther and I lay in bed and bragged about boys, trying to top one another's stories of how far we'd gone with each one. For a little while I thought maybe I had caught up with her at last, but then she told me about some of the crazy girls at her school and how many of them were lesbians. She laughed in an old, high-pitched way I didn't remember, and grabbed my hand and said, "Lesbian love! Get it?" Oh, I got it, all right. *The Well of Loneliness* had gone through Durfee like the flu that spring, but like most of the books we passed from locker to locker, it raised more questions than it answered.

Esther graduated from the seminary and began attending Wayne University. She smoked cigarettes in the Cass/Warren Drugs with other students from the English department and mooned over the popular professors. It wasn't long before word was bruited around the family of one particular boy who was after Esther, not a goy, but in the rabbi's eyes he might as well have been. My Aunt Ida said that was what they got for letting Esther go to Wayne with all the communists. She knew someone who knew the boy's family. The rumor was they didn't go to shul, even on Yom Kippur. Esther said her friend was an agnostic and told me that she didn't care, and I believed her.

Esther and Ben took to meeting at my house, and once again her life had me in thrall. Ben gave her books to read: *The Sorrows of Werther* and Rilke's *Duino Elegies*. Once Esther showed me something Ben had enclosed in a letter he sent her, a little poem by James Joyce that began, "Lean out of the window, Golden Hair . . ." I envied her that poem as I had once envied her slenderness and the certainty of her prayers. I memorized it, sang it in my bones, a kind of leitmotif, my secular prayer to ward off images of my own fevered and, to me, quite ordinary gropings.

I kept out of the way, discreetly disappearing when Esther and Ben arrived at my house hand in hand, reappearing when Ben left so Esther could lie on my bed and sigh about the hopelessness of it all. She told me they were thinking of running away to Toledo where you could get married without your parents' consent if you were underage. It was all so romantic to me: Romeo and Juliet with a Jewish accent.

One day we headed for Rouge Park in Ben's car, Esther beside him. I remember clearly the old streetcar tracks on Linwood under our wheels, the car lurching from side to side so we slid around on the seats like wrapped packages. "Okay, this is it," Ben said as if he had just thought of it. "We're going to Toledo and get married, and when we come back, no one will be able to do anything about it." He turned around and looked straight at me. "You," he said, "will be our witness."

For a moment it all came crashing in on me: what everyone would say, the cousins, the women. How much of all our lives was wrapped in the cord of their expectations and approval, how much of that cord was wound on the spool of ritual and observance. And I still didn't really know how I felt about it all; I needed a sign from Esther to guide me. We didn't end up in Toledo; Esther got so hysterical that Ben had to turn the car around and take her back to our house.

Later Ben said, "I'm tired of sneaking around like a thief in the night." He told Esther he was going to approach the rabbi man to man and explain that nothing as reactionary as religion was going to come between him and Esther. He wanted the rabbi's blessing . . . or else. Esther cried and said all this would kill her father, that he would never forgive her for forsaking her orthodoxy. Ben said, "What century are you people living in anyway?"

One Saturday in October, Ben drove down La Salle and parked directly in front of Esther's house. Hatless and smoking a cigarette, he walked up the winding path to the front door and rang the bell, thereby committing three more sins at once. When he demanded to talk to Esther, smoke trailing out of his mouth, the shocked rabbi ordered him never to see Esther again. That story spread around our family like a kitchen grease fire.

Not long after that, Esther went to live with her sister in New York, and we went back to our old lives, a little shaken, as if for a short time we had been mesmerized by flames we had allowed to go unchecked and then, only with difficulty, managed to smother. When I thought about Esther, I spun fanciful tales about renunciation and romance, at once disappointed with her for giving up, and at the same time relieved that she hadn't made my own growing choices more difficult. I imagined that the women finally got to her, that the whispering became too loud for her to ignore.

But now, years later, I wonder about the random nature of choice, the impulsive dart around one corner rather than another, the obscured vision beyond each making the outcome simply one more gamble. Perhaps I have it all wrong. It may be that for Esther being Jewish went far deeper than the shallow surfaces I had been dazzled and fooled by for so long. It may be that in the end she could no more compromise her beliefs than she could change her redheaded nature by bleaching her hair.

I only know that some months later a cousin said she'd heard Esther was engaged to a young rabbi from Queens. I saw her once after she was married. The past stretched between us like a line of flapping wash; we talked about wedding presents and new furniture. And then she went back to New York, and I didn't see her again.

Esther died in childbirth one stone-gray day in winter; she was twenty-one. We brought her home so she could be buried in the cemetery next to her mother. My grandmother, shrunken in her sorrow, skin hanging on her frame like a wrinkled dress, spared me the funeral, for I was married myself by then, and pregnant.

At the rabbi's house, I wandered from room to empty room, looking for Esther, feeling my childhood crumbling like stale bread. Neighbors and friends had filled the kitchen with food. The table on which we once watched women place their *Shabbos* chickens was covered with bagels and kaiser rolls, strudel and mandel bread, baskets of fruit so perfect each piece might have been made out of wax. I broke off a cluster of heavy green grapes and carried it up the wide, carpeted stairway to Esther's old room. I could hear the low murmur of voices as the mourners returning from the cemetery rinsed their fingers at an outside faucet before they entered the house.

In front of Esther's vanity, I sat on a bench and stared into the shrouded mirror. With a tiny pair of gold scissors she once used to trim her nails, I cut a slash in the collar of my dress, and then I ate the green grapes slowly, one by one. When I finished, I closed my eyes and said a made-up prayer for Esther. ''Lean out of the window,'' I whispered, tasting the sweet flesh of green grapes. ''Lean out of the window, Golden Hair.''

from

GENERATION WITHOUT MEMORY

ANNE ROIPHE

This autobiographical excerpt from Generation Without Memory: A Jewish Journey in Christian America *examines what it is to be an American Jew in the age of assimilation. From the eyes of a twelve-year-old, Anne Roiphe explores how important it is to hold on to your individuality, despite pressure to act like everyone else.*

A journalist and novelist, Anne Roiphe has written Digging Out *(as Anne Richardson),* Up the Sandbox, Long Division, *and* Torch Song Out *(as Anne Richardson). She lives in New York.*

I am twelve years old at a girls' camp in Maine. I love camp. I love field hockey, tennis, and baseball. I love the tall pines and the canoes and the ice-cold morning air and the oil lamps that glow at night under the stars on the bunkhouse steps. I love the counselors, who are tall and athletic, who go to physical education schools in Boston and don't ever wear makeup or high heels. They smell clean and honest. They talk about sportsmanship and integrity and trying harder and doing your best. They talk about independence in the woods and survival in the water. They don't talk about money or men. I would give anything in the world for them to approve of me. I make plans to grow up and become a gym teacher too. I love archery, hiking, and learning the names of the birds and the trees. My fellow campers are all Jewish children from prosperous suburbs and the older established Jewish enclaves in Atlanta, Nashville, and Cleveland. There are many from Elkins Park, Pennsylvania, Scarsdale and Great Neck, New York. The counselors are all Methodists, Presbyterians, Yankees. The owners of the camp are two older German-Jewish women named Aunt Caroline and Miss Kitty.

One morning the whole camp is summoned to a meeting after the raising of the flag on the flagpole that stands inside the circle of tents around which the bugle plays at the appropriate hours. We are all looking forward to overnight camping trips to the mountains and lakes of Maine. We will be driven by bus to starting points on the Rangeley Lakes and to the base of Mount Washington. At this meeting we are told what to pack and who is going in which group. Then Aunt Caroline asked all the counselors to please leave the meeting. This was an unusual procedure. When the last of them had gone into their bunks or up to the main house, she told us that Jewish people tended to be very loud and aggressively noisy and that the people of Maine would hear us and make remarks about Jews and so we should try to be very quiet and dignified when going through towns or stopping in public places where natives might hear us.

"You must not give them reason to dislike you. You must control your loud Jewish voices."

There was silence among the campers. The meeting was dismissed. I went back to my bunk and wrote and asked my mother to come and get me and take me home. I went to Aunt Caroline and Miss Kitty and told them that those remarks were prejudiced. Jews were not louder than anyone else, I said. Aunt Caroline pointed out that I was the only camper who did not see complete justice in her words. She said I was too young to understand that there were real ethnic differences among people, and that Jews did indeed tend to be loud and emotional and noisy. I tried to explain my point of view to my friends and counselors. No one seemed to understand why I was so upset. Everyone tried to jolly me out of my bad mood. A few days later we went out of camp on our trips. Whenever I saw Maine people in candy stores by the side of roads or on the lake, I yelled and screamed my loudest. I felt I owed that noise to someone.

"The Middle Classes"

LYNNE SHARON SCHWARTZ

Moving away from the theme of Jews as the minority, "The Middle Classes" is an intriguing look at prejudice against blacks. In the same way Philip Roth looked at the subtle discrimination of Jews in the excerpt from The Facts, *Lynne Sharon Schwartz explores the unknowing bigotry of a Jewish family in Brooklyn.*

The narrator of the story watches her parents react to her piano teacher, Mr. Simmons. Her father says, "Even though he is a colored man I can talk to him just like a friend. I mean I don't feel any difference. It's a very strange thing." Every Wednesday for six years her father repeats the same thought "as if he newly discovered it." Many years later, at her wedding, the narrator's mother feels compelled to parade the Simmonses around as if they are on display. In the end, the daughter refuses to see the difference between the two families—after all, they are both middle class.

Lynne Sharon Schwartz grew up in Brooklyn and has written four novels. Leaving Brooklyn, Disturbances in the Field, Rough Strife, *and* Balancing Acts. *She is also the author of two collections of short stories:* Acquainted with the Night *and* The Melting Pot and Other Subversive Stories. *She lives in New York with her husband and two children.*

They say memory enhances places, but my childhood block of small brick row houses grows smaller every year, till there is barely room for me to stand upright in my own recollections. The broad avenue on our corner, gateway to the rest of the world, an avenue so broad that for a long time I was not permitted to cross it alone, has narrowed to a strait, and its row of tiny shops—dry cleaners, candy store, beauty parlor, grocery store— has dwindled to a row of cells. On my little block itself the hedges, once staunch walls guarding the approach to every house, are shrunken, their sharp dark leaves stunted. The hydrangea bush—what we called a snowball bush—in front of the house next to mine has shrunk; its snowballs have melted down. And the ledges from each front walk to each driveway, against whose once-great stone walls we played King, a kind of inverse handball, and from whose tops we jumped with delectable agonies of fear—ah, those ledges have sunk, those leaps are nothing. Small.

In actuality, of course, my Brooklyn neighborhood has not shrunk but it has changed. Among the people I grew up with, that is understood as a euphemism meaning black people have moved in. They moved in family by family, and one by one the old white families moved out, outwards, that is, in an outward direction (Long Island, Rockaway, Queens), the direction of water—it seems not to have occurred to them that soon there would be nowhere to go unless back into the surf where we all began— except for two of the old white families who bravely remained and sent reports in the outward directions that living with the black people was fine, they were nice people, good neighbors, and so these two white families came to be regarded by the departed as sacrificial heroes of sorts; everyone admired them but no one would have wished to emulate them.

The changes the black families brought to the uniform block were mostly in the way of adornment. Colorful shutters affixed to the front casement windows, flagstones on the walkways leading to the porch steps, flowers on the bordering patches of grass, and quantities of ornamental wrought iron; a few of the brick porch walls have even been replaced by wrought-iron ones. (Those adjacent porches with their low dividing walls linked our lives. We girls visited back and forth climbing from porch to porch to porch, peeking into living room windows as we darted by.) But for all these proprietary changes, my block looks not so very different, in essence. It has remained middle class.

Black people appeared on the block when I lived there too, but they were maids, and very few at that. Those few came once a week, except for the three families where the mothers were schoolteachers; their maids came every day and were like one of the family, or so the families boasted, overlooking the fact that the maids had families of their own. One other exception: the family next door to mine who had the snowball bush also had a live-in maid who did appear to live like one of the family. It was easy to forget that she cleaned and cooked while the family took their ease, because when her labors were done she ate with them and then sat on the porch and contributed her opinions to the neighborhood gossip. They had gotten her from the South when she was seventeen, they said with pride, and when her grandmother came up to visit her the grandmother slept and ate and gossiped with the family too, but whether she too was expected to clean and cook I do not know.

It was less a city block than a village, where of a hot summer evening the men sat out on the front porches in shirtsleeves smoking cigars and reading newspapers under yellow lanterns (there were seven New York City newspapers) while the wives brought out bowls of cherries and trays of watermelon slices and gossiped porch to porch, and we girls listened huddled together on the steps, hoping the parents would forget us and not send us to bed, and where one lambent starry summer evening the singular fighting couple on the block had one of their famous battles in the master bedroom—shrieks and blows and crashing furniture; in what was to become known in local legend as the balcony scene, Mrs. Hochman leaned out of the open second-floor casement window in a flowing white nightgown like a mythological bird and shouted to the assembled throng, "Neighbors, neighbors, help me, I'm trapped up here with a madman" (she was an elocution teacher), and my mother rose to her feet to go and help but my father, a tax lawyer, restrained her and said, "Leave them alone, they're both crazy. Tomorrow they'll be out on the street holding hands as usual." And soon, indeed, the fighting stopped, and I wondered, *What is love, what is marriage? What is reality in the rest of the world?*

The daughters of families of our station in life took piano lessons and I took the piano lessons seriously. Besides books, music was the only experience capable of levitating me away from Brooklyn without the risk of crossing bridges or tunneling my way out. When I was about eleven I said I wanted a new and good piano teacher, for the lady on Eastern Parkway to whose antimacassared apartment I went for my lessons was pixilated. She trilled a greeting when she opened the door and wore pastel colored satin ribbons in her curly gray hair and served tea and excellent shortbread cookies, but of teaching she did very little. So my mother got me Mr. Simmons.

He was a black man of around thirty-five or forty recommended by a business acquaintance of my father's with a son allegedly possessed of musical genius, the development of which was being entrusted to Mr. Simmons. If he was good enough for that boy, the logic ran, then he was good enough for me. I was alleged to be unusually gifted too, but not quite that gifted. I thought it very advanced of my parents to hire a black piano teacher for their nearly nubile daughter; somewhere in the vast landscape of what I had yet to learn, I must have glimpsed the springs of fear. I was proud of my parents, though I never said so. I had known they were not bigoted but rather instinctively decent; I had known that when and if called upon they would instinctively practice what was then urged as "tolerance," but I hadn't known to what degree. As children do, I underestimated them, partly because I was just discovering that they were the middle class.

Mr. Simmons was a dark-skinned man of moderate height and moderate build, clean-shaven but with an extremely rough beard that might have been a trial to him, given his overall neatness. A schoolteacher, married, the father of two young children, he dressed in the style of the day, suit and tie, with impeccable conventionality. His manners were also impeccably conventional. Nice but dull was how I classified him on first acquaintance, and I assumed from his demeanor that moderation in all things was his hallmark. I was mistaken: he was a blatant romantic. His teaching style was a somber intensity streaked by delicious flashes of joviality. He had a broad smile, big teeth, a thunderous laugh, and a willing capacity to be amused, especially by me. To be found amusing was an inspiration. I saved my most sophisticated attitudes and phraseology for Mr. Simmons. Elsewhere, I felt, they were as pearls cast before swine. He was not dull after all, if he could appreciate me. And yet unlike my past teachers he could proclaim ''Awful!'' with as much intrepidity as ''Beautiful!'' ''No, no, no, *this* is how it should sound,'' in a pained voice, shunting me off the piano bench and launching out at the passage. I was easily offended and found his bluntness immodest at first. Gradually, through Mr. Simmons, I learned that false modesty is useless and that true devotion to skill is impersonal.

Early in our acquaintance he told me that during the summers when school was out his great pleasure was to play the piano eight hours in a row, stripped to the waist and sweating. It was January when he said this, and he grinned with a kind of patient longing. I recognized it as an image of passion and dedication, and forever after, in my eyes, he was surrounded by a steady, luminous aura of fervor. I wished I were one of his children, for the glory of living in his house and seeing that image in the flesh and basking in the luxuriant music. He would be playing Brahms, naturally; he had told me even earlier on that Brahms was his favorite composer. ''Ah, Brahms,'' he would sigh, leaning back in his chair near the piano bench and tilting his head in a dreamy way. I did not share his love for Brahms but Brahms definitely fit in with the entire picture—the hot day, the long hours, the bare chest, and the sweat.

Mr. Simmons had enormous beautiful pianist's hands—they made me ashamed of my own, small and stubby. Tragicomically, he would lift one of my hands from the keyboard and stare at it ruefully. ''Ah, if only these were bigger!'' A joke, but he meant it. He played well but a bit too romantically for my tastes. Of course he grasped my tastes thoroughly and would sometimes exaggerate his playing to tease me, and exaggerate also the way he swayed back and forth at the piano, crooning along with the melody, bending picturesquely over a delicate phrase, clattering at a turbulent passage, his whole upper body tense and filled with the music. "You think that's too schmaltzy, don't you?" laughing his thunderous laugh. The way he pronounced *schmaltzy,* our word, not his, I found very droll. To admonish me when I was lazy he would say, "*Play* the notes, *play* the notes," and for a long time I had no idea what he meant. Listening to him play, I came to understand. He meant play them rather than simply touch them. Press them down and make contact. Give them their full value. Give them yourself.

It seemed quite natural that Mr. Simmons and I should come to be such appreciative friends—we were part of a vague, nameless elite—but I was surprised and even slightly irked that my parents appreciated him so. With the other two piano teachers who had come to the house my mother had been unfailingly polite, offering coffee and cake but no real access. About one of them, the wild-eyebrowed musician with the flowing scarves and black coat and beret and the mock-European accent, who claimed to derive from Columbia University as though it were a birthplace, she commented that he might call himself an artist but in addition he was a slob who could eat a whole cake and leave crumbs all over the fringed tapestry covering her piano. But with Mr. Simmons she behaved the way she did with her friends; I should say, with her friends' husbands, or her husband's friends, since at that time women like my mother did not have men friends of their own, at least in Brooklyn. When Mr. Simmons arrived at about three forty-five every Wednesday, she offered him coffee—he was coming straight from teaching, and a man's labor must always be respected—and invited him to sit down on the couch. There she joined him and inquired how his wife and children were, which he told her in some detail. That was truly dull. I didn't care to hear anecdotes illustrating the virtues and charms of his children, who were younger than I. Then, with an interest that didn't seem at all feigned, he asked my mother reciprocally how her family was. They exchanged such trivia on my time, till suddenly he would look at his watch, pull himself up, and with a swift, broad smile, say, "Well then, shall we get started?" At last.

But my father! Sometimes my father would come home early on Wednesdays, just as the lesson was ending. He would greet Mr. Simmons like an old friend; they would clap each other on the shoulder and shake hands in that hearty way men do and which I found ridiculous. And my father would take off his hat and coat and put down his *New York Times* and insist that Mr. Simmons have a drink or at least a cup of coffee, and they would talk enthusiastically about—of all things—business and politics. Boring, boring! How could he? Fathers were supposed to be interested in those boring things, but not Mr. Simmons. After a while Mr. Simmons would put on his hat and coat, which were remarkably like the hat and coat my father had recently taken off, pick up his *New York Times*, and head for his home and family.

And my father would say, "What a nice fellow that Mr. Simmons is! What a really fine person!" For six years he said it, as if he had newly discovered it, or was newly astonished that it could be so. "It's so strange," he might add, shaking his head in a puzzled way. "Even though he's a colored man I can talk to him just like a friend. I mean, I don't feel any difference. It's a very strange thing." When I tried, with my advanced notions, to relieve my father of the sense of strangeness, he said, "I know, I know all that"; yet he persisted in finding it a very strange thing. Sometimes he boasted about Mr. Simmons to his friends with wonder in his voice: "I talk to him just as if he were a friend of mine. A very intelligent man. A really fine person." To the very end, he marveled; I would groan and laugh every time I heard it coming.

Mr. Simmons told things to my father in my presence, important and serious things that I knew he would not tell to me alone. This man-to-man selectivity of his pained me. He told my father that he was deeply injured by the racial prejudice existing in this country; that it hurt his life and the lives of his wife and children; and that he resented it greatly. All these phrases he spoke in his calm, conventional way, wearing his suit and tie and sipping coffee. And my father nodded his head and agreed that it was terribly unfair. Mr. Simmons hinted that his career as a classical pianist had been thwarted by his color, and again my father shook his head with regret. Mr. Simmons told my father that he had a brother who could not abide the racial prejudice in this country and so he lived in France. "Is that so?" said my mother in dismay, hovering nearby, slicing cake. To her, that anyone might have to leave this country, to which her parents had fled for asylum, was unwelcome, almost incredible, news. But yes, it was so, and when he spoke about his brother Mr. Simmons's resonant low voice was sad and angry, and I, sitting on the sidelines, felt a flash of what I had felt when the neighbor woman being beaten shrieked out of the window on that hot summer night—ah, here is reality at last. For I believed that reality must be cruel and harsh and densely complex. It would never have occurred to me that reality could also be my mother serving Mr. Simmons home-baked layer cake or my father asking him if he had to go so soon, couldn't he stay and have a bite to eat, and my mother saying, "Let the man go home to his own family, for heaven's sake, he's just done a full day's work." I also felt afraid at the anger in Mr. Simmons' voice; I thought he might be angry at me. I thought that if I were he I would at least have been angry at my parents and possibly even refused their coffee and cake, but Mr. Simmons didn't.

When I was nearing graduation from junior high school my mother suggested that I go to the High School of Music and Art in Manhattan. I said no, I wanted to stay with my friends and didn't want to travel for over an hour each way on the subway. I imagined I would be isolated up there. I imagined that the High School of Music and Art, by virtue of being in Manhattan, would be far too sophisticated, even for me. In a word, I was afraid. My mother wasn't the type to press the issue but she must have enlisted Mr. Simmons to press it for her. I told him the same thing, about traveling for over an hour each way on the subway. Then, in a very grave manner, he asked if I had ever seriously considered a musical career. I said instantly, "Oh, no, that sounds like a man's sort of career." I added that I wouldn't want to go traveling all over the country giving concerts. He told me the names of some women pianists, and when that didn't sway me, he said he was surprised that an intelligent girl could give such a foolish answer without even thinking it over. I was insulted and behaved coolly towards him for a few weeks. He behaved with the same equanimity as ever and waited for my mood to pass. Every year or so after that he would ask the same question in the same grave manner, and I would give the same answer. Once I overheard him telling my mother, "And she says it's a man's career!" "Ridiculous," said my mother disgustedly. "Ridiculous," Mr. Simmons agreed.

Towards the end of my senior year in high school (the local high school, inferior in every way to the High School of Music and Art in Manhattan), my parents announced that they would like to buy me a new piano as a graduation present. A baby grand, and I could pick it out myself. We went to a few piano showrooms in Brooklyn so I could acquaint myself with the varieties of piano. I spent hours pondering the differences between Baldwin and Steinway, the two pianos most used by professional musicians, for in the matter of a piano—unlike a high school—I had to have the best. Steinways were sharp-edged, Baldwins more mellow; Steinways classic and traditional, Baldwins romantically timeless; Steinways austere, Baldwins responsive to the touch. On the other hand, Steinways were crisp compared to Baldwins' pliancy; Steinways were sturdy and dependable, while Baldwins sounded a disquieting tone of mutability. I liked making classifications. At last I decided that a Baldwin was the piano for me— rich, lush, and mysterious, not at all like my playing, but now that I think of it, rather like Mr. Simmons's.

I had progressed some since the days when I refused to consider going to the High School of Music and Art in Manhattan. If it was to be a

Baldwin I insisted that it come from the source, the Baldwin showroom in midtown Manhattan. My mother suggested that maybe Mr. Simmons might be asked to come along, to offer us expert advice on so massive an investment. I thought that was a fine idea, only my parents were superfluous; the two of us, Mr. Simmons and I, could manage alone. My parents showed a slight, hedging reluctance. Perhaps it was not quite fair, my mother suggested, to ask Mr. Simmons to give up a Saturday afternoon for this favor. It did not take an expert logician to point out her inconsistency. I was vexed by their reluctance and would not even condescend to think about it. I knew it could have nothing to do with trusting him: over the years they had come to regard him as an exemplar of moral probity. Evidently the combination of his being so reliable and decent, so charming, and so black set him off in a class by himself.

I asked the favor of Mr. Simmons and he agreed, although in his tone too was a slight, hedging reluctance; I couldn't deny it. But again, I could ignore it. I had a fantasy of Mr. Simmons and myself ambling through the Baldwin showroom, communing in a rarefied manner about the nuances of difference between one Baldwin and another, and I wanted to make this fantasy come true.

The Saturday afternoon arrived. I was excited. I had walked along the streets of Manhattan before, alone and with my friends. But the thought of walking down Fifty-seventh Street with an older man, clearly not a relative, chatting like close friends for all the sophisticated world to see, made my spirits as buoyant and iridescent as a bubble. Mr. Simmons came to pick me up in his car. I had the thrill of sliding into the front seat companionably, chatting like close friends with an older man. I wondered whether he would come around and open the door for me when we arrived. That was done in those days, for ladies. I was almost seventeen. But he only stood waiting while I climbed out and slammed it shut, as he must have done with his own children, as my father did with me.

We walked down broad Fifty-seventh Street, where the glamour was so pervasive I could smell it: cool fur and leather and smoky perfume. People looked at us with interest. How wondrous that was! I was ready to fly with elation. It didn't matter that Mr. Simmons had known me since I was eleven and seen me lose my temper like an infant and heard my mother order me about; surely he must see me as the delightful adult creature I had suddenly become, and surely he must be delighted to be escorting me down Fifty-seventh Street. I would have liked to take his arm to complete the picture for all the sophisticated world to see, but some things were still beyond me. I felt ready to fly but in fact I could barely keep up with Mr. Simmons's long and hurried stride. He was talking as companionably as ever, but he seemed ill at ease. Lots of people looked at us. Even though it was early April he had his overcoat buttoned and his hat brim turned down.

We reached the Baldwin showroom. Gorgeous, burnished pianos glistened in the display windows. We passed through the portals; it was like entering a palace. Inside it was thickly carpeted. We were shown upstairs. To Paradise! Not small! Immensely high ceilings and so much space, a vista of lustrous pianos floating on a rich sea of green carpet. Here in this grand room full of grand pianos Mr. Simmons knew what he was about. He began to relax and smile, and he talked knowledgeably with the salesman, who was politely helpful, evidently a sophisticated person.

"Well, go ahead," Mr. Simmons urged me. "Try them out."

"You mean play them?" I looked around at the huge space. The only people in it were two idle salesmen and far off at the other end a small family of customers, father, mother, and little boy.

"Of course." He laughed. "How else will you know which one you like?"

I finally sat down at one and played a few timid scales and arpeggios. I crept from one piano to another, doing the same, trying to discern subtle differences between them.

"Play," Mr. Simmons commanded.

At the sternness in his voice I cast away timidity. I played Chopin's "Revolutionary Etude," which I had played the year before at a recital Mr. Simmons held for his students in Carl Fischer Hall—nowadays called Cami Hall—on Fifty-seventh Street, not far from the Baldwin showroom. (I had been the star student. The other boy, the musical genius, had gone off to college or otherwise vanished. I had even done a Mozart sonata for four hands with Mr. Simmons himself.) Sustained by his command, I moved dauntlessly from Baldwin to Baldwin, playing passages from the "Revolutionary Etude." Mr. Simmons flashed his broad smile and I smiled back.

"Now you play," I said.

I thought he might have to be coaxed, but I was forgetting that Mr. Simmons was never one to withhold, or to hide his light. Besides, he was a professional, though I didn't understand yet what that meant. He looked around as if to select the worthiest piano, then sat down, spread his great hands, and played something by Brahms. As always, he *played* the notes. He pressed them down and made contact. He gave them their full value. He gave them himself. The salesmen gathered round. The small family drew near to listen. And I imagined that I could hear, transmogrified into musical notes, everything I knew of him—his thwarted career, his school-

113

teaching, his impeccable manners, his fervor, and his wit; his pride in his wife and children; his faraway brother; his anger, his melancholy, and his acceptance; and I also imagined him stripped to the waist and sweating. When it was over he kept his hands and body poised in position, briefly, as performers do, as if to prolong the echo, to keep the spell in force till the last drawn-out attenuation of the instant. The hushed little audience didn't clap, they stood looking awed. My Mr. Simmons! I think I felt at that moment almost as if he were my protégé, almost as if I owned him.

We didn't say much on the way home. I had had my experience, grand as in fantasy, which experiences rarely are, and I was sublimely content. As we walked down my block nobody looked at us with any special interest. Everyone knew me and by this time everyone knew Mr. Simmons too. An unremarkable couple. At home, after we reported on the choice of a piano, Mr. Simmons left without even having a cup of coffee. He was tired, he said, and wanted to get home to his family.

Later my mother asked me again how our expedition had been.

"Fine. I told you already. We picked out a really great piano. Oh, and he played. He was fantastic, everyone stopped to listen."

My mother said nothing. She was slicing tomatoes for a salad.

"I bet they never heard any customer just sit down and play like that."

Again no response. She merely puttered over her salad, but with a look that was familiar to me: a concentrated, patient waiting for the proper words and the proper tone to offer themselves to her. I enjoyed feeling I was always a step ahead.

"I know what you're thinking," I said nastily.

"You do?" She raised her eyes to mine. "I'd be surprised."

"Yes. I bet you're thinking we looked as if he was going to abduct me or something."

The glance she gave in response was more injured than disapproving. She set water to boil and tore open a net bag of potatoes.

"Well, listen, I'll tell you something. The world has changed since your day." I was growing more and more agitated, while she just peeled potatoes. Her muteness had a maddening way of making my words seem frivolous. She knew what she knew. "The world has changed! Not everyone is as provincial as they are here in Brooklyn!" I spit out that last word. I was nearly shouting now. "Since when can't two people walk down the street in broad daylight? We're both free—" I stopped suddenly. I was going to say free, white, and over twenty-one, an expression I had found loathsome when I heard my father use it.

"Calm down," my mother said gently. "All I'm thinking is I hope it didn't embarrass him. It's him I was thinking about, not you."

I stalked from the room, my face aflame.

I went to college in Manhattan and lived in a women's residence near school. For several months I took the subway into Brooklyn every Wednesday so I could have a piano lesson with Mr. Simmons, it being tacitly understood that I was too gifted simply to give up "my music," as it was called; I slept at home on my old block, then went back up to school on Thursday morning. This became arduous. I became involved with other, newer things. I went home for a lesson every other Wednesday, and soon no Wednesdays at all. But I assured Mr. Simmons I would keep renting the small practice room at school and work on my own. I did for a while, but the practice room was very small and very cold, and the piano, a Steinway, didn't sound as lush as my new Baldwin back home; there was an emptiness to my efforts without the spur of a teacher; and then there were so many other things claiming my time. I had met and made friends with kindred spirits from the High School of Music and Art, and realized that had I listened to my mother I might have known them three years sooner. The next year I got married, impulsively if not inexplicably; to tell why, though, would take another story.

Naturally my parents invited Mr. and Mrs. Simmons to the wedding. They were the only black people there, among some hundred and fifty guests. I had long been curious to meet Mrs. Simmons but regrettably I could not get to know her that afternoon since I had to be a bride. Flitting about, I could see that she was the kind of woman my mother and her friends would call "lovely." And did, later. She was pretty, she was dressed stylishly, she was what they would call "well-spoken." She spoke the appropriately gracious words for a young bride and one of her husband's long-time students. In contrast to Mr. Simmons' straightforward earnestness, she seemed less immediately engaged, more of a clever observer, and though she smiled readily I could not imagine her having a thunderous laugh. But she fit very well with Mr. Simmons, and they both fit with all the other middle-aged and middle-class couples present, except of course for their color.

Mrs. Simmons did not know a soul at the wedding and Mr. Simmons knew only the parents of the boy genius and a few of our close neighbors. My mother graciously took them around, introducing them to friends and family, lots of friends and lots of family, so they would not feel isolated. I thought she overdid it—she seemed to have them in tow, or on display, for a good while. I longed to take her aside and whisper, "Enough already, Ma. Leave them alone." But there was no chance for that. And I knew how she would have responded. She would have responded silently, with a look that meant, "You can talk, but I know what is right to do," which

I could not deny. And in truth she was quite proud of knowing a man as talented as Mr. Simmons. And had she not introduced them they certainly would have felt isolated, while this way they were amicably received. (Any bigots present successfully concealed their bigotry.) My mother was only trying to behave well, with grace, and relatively, she succeeded. There was no way of behaving with absolute grace. You had to choose among the various modes of constraint.

For all I know, though, the Simmonses went home and remarked to each other about what lovely, fine people my parents and their friends were, and how strange it was that they could spend a pleasant afternoon talking just as they would to friends, even though they were all white. How very strange, Mr. Simmons might have said, shaking his head in a puzzled way, taking off his tie and settling down behind his newspaper. It is a soothing way to imagine them, but probably false.

I had always hoped to resume my piano lessons someday, but never did. And so after the wedding Mr. Simmons disappeared from my life. Why should it still astonish me, like a scrape from a hidden thorn? There were no clear terms on which he could be in my life, without the piano lessons. Could I have invited the Simmonses to our fifth-floor walk-up apartment in a dilapidated part of Manhattan for a couples evening? Or asked him to meet me somewhere alone for a cup of coffee? At what time of day? Could my parents, maybe, have invited the Simmonses over on a Sunday afternoon with their now teen-aged children and with my husband and me? Or for one of their Saturday night parties of mah-jongg for the women and gin rummy for the men and bagels and lox for all? Could Mr. Simmons, too, have made some such gesture? Possibly. For I refuse to see this as a case of *noblesse oblige:* we were all the middle classes.

But given the place and the time and the dense circumambient air, such invitations would have required people of large social imagination, and none of us, including Mr. and Mrs. Simmons, had that. We had only enough vision for piano lessons and cups of coffee and brief warm conversations about families, business, politics, and race relations, and maybe I should be content with that, and accept that because we were small, we lost each other, and never really had each other, either. Nonetheless, so many years later, I don't accept it. I find I miss him and I brood and wonder about him: where is he and does he still, on summer days, play the piano for eight hours at a stretch, stripped to the waist and sweating?

"THE HIGH HOLY DAYS"

from

DEBORAH, GOLDA, AND ME: BEING FEMALE AND JEWISH IN AMERICA

LETTY COTTIN POGREBIN

Letty Cottin Pogrebin provides an abbreviated tour of the Jewish holiday calendar as she remembers her childhood High Holy Days, Hanukkah, and Passover. These holidays provide a cultural and spiritual link with Jews past and future, and provide a way for her to celebrate her Judaism. As an adult, she had difficulty reconciling the Judaism of her childhood with her feminist views, but the pull of her youthful memories of religion proved too strong. She found a way to observe her faith and her feminist beliefs and to share a new, thoroughly American Judaism with others.

A founding editor of Ms. magazine, Pogrebin is a well-known writer about feminism, women and the workplace, children, and politics. She lives with her husband in New York.

Although I think of Rosh Hashanah and Yom Kippur as my father's holidays (Hanukkah and Passover were my mother's), I still have some warm and positive associations with the High Holy Days of my childhood. First, they embodied the very essence of new beginnings, for autumn, not spring, was when everything was new: my clothes, my classroom, books, pencil box, teachers—and Jewish chronology, which decreed a fresh start, a clean slate, a chance to improve on the past.

Second, the High Holy Days were special to me because the last two digits of the new year always corresponded to my age. In 1949, for example, when the Jewish year was 5710, I was ten years old. This annual coincidence made me feel some small connection to the incomprehensible notion of five millennia having passed since the creation of the world.

Third, the High Holies, as I called them, was the time when I consciously

117

recommitted myself to aspire to my mother's character and my father's achievements. However Pollyannaish it sounds, that's the sort of child I was. I wanted to be his kind of Jew and her kind of human being. I wanted to think like him and act like her. Speaking from my doubled perspective, his example was a constant reminder of my intellectual shortcomings, but the heavier burden was my failure to measure up to her kindness: I had been selfish where she was self-sacrificing, vain where she was effortlessly modest. Next year I would be better.

I recognize the stirrings of those long-ago High Holy Day feelings whenever I buy new fall clothes. According to the Talmud, on the Days of Judgment, Jews are not supposed to appear serious and dowdy the way we might dress to appear before a human judge. For God, we are instructed to dress festively, in bright new garments that symbolize our cheerful confidence in spiritual regeneration. So each fall, my mother and I went shopping together, hoping to find something I would be willing to wear to services. It wasn't a pleasant process. For most of my youth, I hated my scrawny body and stick-straight legs. Long after my friends had blossomed into puberty and graduated to Junior and Misses sizes, I was still skulking into the Preteen department with my mother at my side murmuring reassurances that next year I'd finally "develop."

Patiently, she sat on a bench in my dressing room bucking up my spirits as I tried on one outfit after another until I made a few grudging selections: a taffeta dress with a lace collar, a blue corduroy jumper and white eyelet blouse, a plaid pleated skirt with a wool sweater set. When it was her turn to try on clothes, I sat in her dressing room but never patiently. I was overheated. I was irritable. I hated department stores. I wanted to go home.

We went home by subway—forty minutes on the E or F train to Jamaica—weighted down with boxes from S. Klein on The Square, or Ohrbach's or Macy's, with me fussing and squirming—until I could collapse on the living room sofa. Nothing perked me up faster than my father's inevitable demand for a fashion show. He wanted to see his "girls" dressed up to do him proud. So, after an exhausting day, we unwrapped our new purchases and modeled them for him. He always raved about how we looked and what we had bought. Whether he truly approved, I will never know. It didn't matter anyway; his praise was my reward for enduring a day in the stores.

On Rosh Hashanah, I got dressed early and walked the mile to synagogue with my father. Mommy would come later, after she had made the beds and prepared the lunch we would expect when we came home from services, or the dinner—always dairy—that we would devour after the twenty-four-hour fast of Yom Kippur. I did not stay home to help. On the High

Holies, I was my father's daughter. I went to shul with him, running to keep up with his rapid strides, swinging my little-girl purse, with a Chap Stick and a linen hanky tucked inside.

My father carried his tallit in a blue velvet pouch with a Star of David embroidered on it in gold threads. He never turned the pouch toward his body or hid it in a paper bag as other men did but carried it openly, inviting the gaze of our Gentile neighbors, advertising his Jewish star the way men flaunt their designer labels today. His confidence established my comfort level. Of course I had no tallit, but around my neck, I wore a slender gold chain on which hung my Jewish star.

Inside the sanctuary, my father blessed his tallit, kissed it, and flung it around his shoulders with the unconscious grace of one who had performed the gesture countless times before. When I sat beside him, I would drape one end of the silky shawl across my shoulders, enjoying the swing of its fringe against my arm. Maybe I did it to feel closer to him. Maybe I did it to wrap myself in the comfort of his Judaism. All I remember is wanting to have a tallit of my own.

IT'S NOT JUST TALLIT ENVY proclaimed a button circulated at a long-ago Jewish feminist conference. But for me, it *was* tallit envy. What I wished for was not a boy's sex but his tallit and tefillin and his significance in Jewish life—especially life at the Jamaica Jewish Center.

The Center was my second home. I saw it the way we "see" any familiar environment, noticing nothing in particular until something in it has changed. On the High Holy Days, the grand ballroom was changed, from an all-purpose space where we danced Israeli dances and watched Jewish National Fund films, into a lustrous sanctuary big enough to hold all the congregants who showed up at this time of year if no other. How well I remember that room: The Holy Ark was set in the center of the stage with huge vases of gladioli on either side. On that very stage I had played in the school Purim production; now it was hallowed ground. Also flanking the Ark were two ornate candelabra taller than I was. There were throne chairs for the VIPs (where my father sat during the years when he was president of the shul). And standing like sentries at the borders of the stage were two flags, the stars and stripes, and the white flag with the blue Star of David which we called "the Jewish flag" before there was an Israel. In the auditorium, rows of gilt chairs with red velvet seats were lined up neatly. Balconies swept around three sides of the room—not for women's separatism (we were a Conservative synagogue with mixed seating) but for come-lately members of our huge congregation.

I remember the people too: the rabbi and cantor, looking as pink as popes in their special-occasion white robes and satin crowns; the ushers (all men), who seemed so important because they dispensed prayer books, mediated children's disputes, and controlled our coming in and going out like the guards at the gates of Oz.

My Hebrew School friends, who made their way to the seat locations their families reserved year after year—the way society families reserve a box at the opera—signaled to me when they were going to take a bathroom break and wanted me to meet them outside. Most of the time, I stayed put and followed the service. I had learned very young to daven in Hebrew, rocking back and forth on my heels as my father did and as I sometimes do today, no matter how much it bemuses the synagogue elders. I took the High Holy Days seriously. They were my time of reckoning. During the silent devotion, I began my soul-searching, concentrating all my thoughts on my behavior over the previous year. I enumerated my sins. I resolved to remedy my faults and prayed hard that I might be written in the Book of Life for the coming year.

But the hours were long and sometimes my eyes led my mind astray: to Bobby Rabin or Bobby Malkin or whichever boy had set my heart aflame that year. To counting the light bulbs in the ceiling fixtures. To imagining how I would look in Marsha Smilen's bangs or Dena Pinsky's bottle curls. To the fur stole draped around my mother's chair, skinny foxes joined head to tail, their beady eyes intact. Then, ashamed of my meanderings, I would return to my meditation and repentance.

The audio portion of these memories contains two tracks: one carries the deep chorus of a thousand congregants praying aloud, the other the rustling murmur of them whispering to each other so loudly that the rabbi had to interrupt the service to ask them to stop. Both kinds of clamor sound Jewish to me: the monologue addressed to God and the dialogue between Jews. Both provided the background music of my introspection, a mix as comforting to me as the sound of my parents' voices in the next room at home.

My *kavvanah* (spiritual concentration) was at its best not during private prayer, the province of children at bedtime, but during the public litany of confession whose text could have been written today. In this prayer, every member of the congregation—woman and man, child and adult—admits to collective wrongdoing, in unison, in the first person plural. *We* had sinned. (The discovery that adults had been bad was both unnerving and reassuring.) *We* were imperfect. There was no room for individual disclaimers. All of us had committed these infractions: we were stubborn, spiteful, and jealous; we were liars and talebearers. We had broken our promises. We had been greedy and mean-spirited. We were in this together, supplicants at the same well of mercy.

After my mother's death and despite my many spiritual detours, I never failed to attend shul on Rosh Hashanah and Yom Kippur. The Jewish New Year was the real new year; January First some pagan imitation.

So every autumn—even though these were my father's holidays, even when I felt angriest at him and at patriarchy, even when I lived alone in New York and answered to no one, even when I married my nonbeliever husband—I paid for a single ticket and went to stand with other Jews on the Days of Awe. Any synagogue would do, as long as it did not have a *mehitzah.* All I needed was a Jewish space in which I could give strict account of my deeds, ask forgiveness from a God I felt owed me a favor, and say Kaddish for my mother. Every Rosh Hashanah, I put on my new fall clothes and took my place in some overflow service in some synagogue basement and ten days later, after Yom Kippur, this wandering worshiper disappeared from the Jewish community until the same time next year. . . .

I wasn't one of those Jewish kids who envied Christians their Christmas. I never even wished for a Christmas tree—and not because I didn't know what I was missing. Every Christmas Eve, my Irish-Catholic friend Sue, who lived across the street in a semidetached brick house identical to mine, invited me over to help her family trim their tree and share in the frenzy of present wrapping before the family went to midnight Mass. We sang Christmas carols and nibbled Christmas cookies, and the grown-ups drank beer and eggnog as we worked for hours stringing the colored lights and garlands of tinsel around the pine branches, and hooking shiny ornaments and candy canes onto the limbs. When we finished, Sue's father climbed the kitchen stepladder and placed a sequined star on top, and then, around the base of the tree, we spread Ivory Flakes ''snow'' and on it set a manger scene that reminded me of my dollhouse. I was never too sure of the events it symbolized but I knew a baby named Jesus was the hero, and I knew he was a Jew.

Never having read the New Testament, I got my information about Christianity straight from Sue. She told me her priest said Jesus was born a Jew and died at the hands of Jews, which made me vaguely uncomfortable although it didn't seem to affect her or her family's feelings about me one way or the other. There was always a little something for me tucked into one of the fuzzy red stockings hanging from the mirror.

All this hoopla made me feel excited and happy but never jealous. I had my Hanukkah, Sue had her Christmas, and all seemed right with the world. And when she came over to my house to share in my family's festivities, I felt I was offering her not a second-rate Christmas, but a holiday with its own magic and its own glow. In fact, if I remember correctly, I felt a little sorry for Sue: her holiday was over in twenty-four hours while mine lasted for eight glorious days.

In our house, the antique silver menorah gleamed at the center of a table covered in white damask and placed in front of a window. The candelabrum had eight little silver cups for oil lined up along its base, and a ninth little cup hooked onto the top of a hammered-silver backplate. Rather than oil, we used candles the color of orange peel; we lit one for each night plus the *shamash*, or caretaker candle, which we used to kindle each of the tapers and then placed in the topmost cup. Tiny lead dreidels (spinning tops) were scattered on the table along with Hanukkah *gelt*, chocolate coins wrapped in gold foil, the prizes for our dreidel game. From the ceiling, my mother and I had hung dreidels, menorahs, wine goblets, and six-pointed Jewish stars that we'd cut out of construction paper. My crayon drawings of the Maccabee soldiers, whose heroism the holiday commemorates, decorated the walls and my HAPPY HANUKKAH poster was tacked out front on our entrance door.

In the living room, a mountain of presents accumulated for weeks before the holiday, each gift-wrapped by my mother in blue and white, the colors of the Jewish flag. Along with surprises for everyone in our extended family, there were eight presents just for me. This wasn't like a birthday when you blew out your candles and got a nice gift. At Hanukkah, you *didn't* blow out the candles and you got a present every night for a week and a day. . . .

As I leap from the High Holy Days to Hanukkah and now to Passover, you may be wondering if my spirituality is to the topography of Judaism what the famous *New Yorker* map is to the standard globe. Saul Steinberg's cartoon shows the Hudson River nearly abutting the West Coast to create a graphic representation of the parochialism of Manhattanites. My spiritual map reveals a similar truncation of Jewish tradition. But I know what I'm leaving out, and why.

I'm short-changing all the other holidays because they are way stations for me, not major stops on memory's route. They have synagogue resonances but not deeply personal ones. I remember waving my apple-topped Jewish flag on Simchat Torah when we completed the Torah reading for the year and began again at the beginning. I remember ratcheting my noisemaker to drown out Haman's name during the reading of the Megillah on Purim, the Festival of Queen Esther. On Sukkot, I helped to erect the temporary dwelling in which Jews are supposed to live for a week under the stars. We built our sukkah up on the roof of the Jamaica Jewish Center, and though no one slept in it, my parents and I came there after dinner for wine and cake.

One year, on the open porch over the garage behind our house, we built our own sukkah with a latticed roof woven out of maple branches and walls decorated with gourds, dried flowers, and paper chains. Eating meals there with my parents was like playing house with grown-ups. Why we did that once and never again I have no idea—and there is no one left to ask.

These holidays get short shrift here not for lack of respect but due to a shortage of deposits in my memory bank. This is not the case with Passover, where the memories are earning interest. I have described my mother's marathon of preparations—how she scoured away the *chametz* and cooked for days—and my father's star turn as leader of the seder wearing his white *kittel* and reclining in his chair at the head of the table. But what about *my* Passover?

I must confess that as a child I hated the interminable hours we spent at the seder table reading every word of the Haggadah, the story of the Exodus which is rendered in legends, rabbinic discussions, prayers, parables, blessings, and songs. Our seder began after the family, maybe twenty-five of us, had settled ourselves at a long, pieced-together table and each of the males above Bar Mitzvah age had stood up one by one to recite the kiddush over the first cup of wine. The wives of the married men rose with them, standing silently at their sides like ladies-in-waiting—and they waited, like well behaved ladies, for their husbands to speak to God on their behalf. When one of the men faltered or mispronounced a word, I had to hold myself back from correcting him. But no female, not even a yeshiva girl, imagined it was her right to say the kiddush.

After the men finished, my father held up the matzah and spoke the opening line of the seder: "This is the bread of affliction that our forefathers ate in the land of Egypt," and as the tale began unfolding yet again, I felt like shouting, "We know this already! What's the point of going through it all over again!?"

It took me a long time to understand that going through it all over again *is* the point: that an event has no meaning until human beings invest it with meaning. Retelling the Exodus story year after year is what has turned event into symbol, and symbol into a liberation ethos that invests the Jewish people with a clear sense of purpose. I had to learn why we are instructed not to merely recall those four hundred years of slavery but to feel as if we *ourselves* had been slaves in Egypt. In the 125 generations since Moses led the children of Israel to Mount Sinai, Jews have been reiterating that we are descended from a slave people, not from kings and queens or gods and goddesses. Remembering our oppression helps us identify with the oppressed. Recalling that "we were strangers in Egypt," we are enjoined to care for the stranger in our midst.

Long after I knew the story by heart, I kept uncovering layers of its meaning until I now see the Exodus as a radical paradigm—the first "master story" that renders spiritual issues political. The revelation of Jewish law at Sinai brought the covenant into history, as Michael Walzer puts it in his book *Exodus and Revolution*. In other words, the contract between God and the Jewish people requires Jews to imitate God, and since God intervened with Pharaoh to liberate the Hebrew slaves, Jews are expected to intervene in the political world to free the oppressed. Exodus teaches us that history is not incorrigible. For as long as Jews take our mandate seriously and imitate God's liberation model, we can affect events. We can be the vehicle for social progress and world redemption.

Lately, I have also become quite taken with the Exodus as a framework for black-Jewish understanding. Both blacks and Jews have known Egypt. Jews have known it as certain death (the killing of the firstborn, then the ovens and gas chambers). Blacks have known it as death and terror by bondage (the Middle Passage, Gory Island, Jim Crow, and the lash). As a rule, blacks try to forget their slavery because enduring it *obliterated* their identity as a free people; Jews choose to remember our slavery because escaping it *gave* us our identity as a free people.

Our experiences differ most profoundly once our peoples left bondage behind. Blacks of both sexes escaped from their Egypt but have not yet crossed the Red Sea. The pharaoh's soldiers are still at their heels. Their Moses has been murdered. They are still awaiting their miracles. As for Jews, the men heard the revelation at Sinai, and entered the Promised Land where they are now living less than perfect lives. But Jewish women are still wandering in the desert, awaiting inclusion in the covenant, awaiting their Sinai.

It took me a long time to notice that when Moses spoke to the Israelites to prepare them to receive the Law at Sinai, he addressed only the men: "Be ready on the third day and do not go near a woman" (Exodus 19: 15). Why not "Husbands and wives do not go near each other?" Weren't women there? If we were not addressed when God's contract with the Jews was forged, and if we cannot undergo circumcision, the physical sign of the covenant, then we must ask whether we are included in the arrangement. And if not, was the original oversight God's or man's? And how long must we keep wandering?

When I was growing up, the seder elicited none of these thoughts; it was simply hours of nonstop davening and too much food. My cousins and I passed the time at the children's table giggling, or sitting among our elders complaining and fidgeting. Happily, our misery was relieved by several beloved rituals which, mercifully, are well distributed throughout the Haggadah, maybe for just that reason—to keep the children interested.

My seder was made endurable by the Four Questions, the Four Sons, the Ten Plagues, Elijah's visit, "Dayenu," the *haroset* and hard-boiled egg; the ransoming of the *afikoman* (the broken half of matzah hidden early in the evening by the seder leader), and finally, the after-dinner songfest.

I loved the Four Questions and the *afikoman* because these rituals were explicitly reserved to us kids and they were the most consequential events of the evening. Without the Four Questions, the seder could not begin, since the Haggadah provides the answers (and how could one have answers before questions?). And the seder could not end unless the children who had "stolen" the *afikoman* were willing to return it for a suitable ransom (in my family, the price was one silver dollar per child), since everyone had to eat a piece of this special "dessert" matzah before the final grace could be said.

I asked the Four Questions for an inordinate number of years, not because I was always the youngest at the table—a criterion dictated by tradition—but because for a long time I remained the youngest child who could chant the Hebrew. The English translation was recited by my junior cousins as soon as each one learned to read.

I was also the ringleader of the *afikoman* thieves because I had made it my business never to let my father out of my sight. I watched where he put the piece of matzah that he had wrapped in his napkin and tucked away while trying to distract us with jokes, funny faces, and other diversionary tactics. The instant he left the dining room for the ritual hand-washing, I sprang into action, retrieved the special matzah, and after a quick and raucous consultation with my cousins, rehid it in a new location.

The story of the Four Sons was of no interest to me except as a kind of lottery: Which of us kids would be dealt the worst parts? We roared when my father called on one of us to read the passage about the Simple Son who asks stupid questions, or the Wicked Son who ridicules Passover, or the Son Who Does Not Know How to Ask anything. Each of us wanted to be the Wise Son with the right questions. I don't remember noticing that there were no daughters, wise or simple.

Reciting the Ten Plagues had the appeal of a good horror movie. It gave me the chills but at a comfortable distance. *Blood. Frogs. Lice. Noxious beasts.* Each ominous word, which the whole group uttered portentously in unison, was accompanied by the dipping of the pinky finger into one's wine and tapping the tainted drop onto one's plate. *Pestilence. Boils. Hail. Locusts. Darkness. The slaying of firstborn boys.* Some did their dipping left, right, and center but I liked to be neat about it. My Plagues, ten little fingerprints of red wine, circled my plate like a Limoges border design. The trick was *not* to absentmindedly lick your pinky when you finished, thereby ingesting locusts and lice. We kids thought that idea was hilarious. My father squelched our laughter by reminding us that the reason Jewish people recite the Plagues is to remember the Egyptians' suffering, not to revel in their punishment. This was a powerful mandate to put at the tip of a child's pinky, especially one who, at eight or nine years old, failed to see the merits of sympathizing with her enemies.

It was also a powerful ritual—and always a child's honor—to open the door for Elijah, the prophet who was said to visit every Jewish home to sip from the goblet reserved for him in the center of the seder table. Legend has it that Elijah would be the forerunner of the Messiah, so the wine was there to signify every Jew's readiness for redemption.

At the proper moment, one child went to open the outside door while the rest of us remained in our seats, eyes glued to Elijah's cup, straining to see the wine stir as his spirit took a sip—a special effect I later learned was accomplished by an adult yanking discreetly on the tablecloth.

Singing was another thing that made the long seders tolerable. I particularly loved "Dayenu," whose chorus wound around itself like a hooked rug, and whose verses rested on a seductive literary device. If God only had given us the Torah, *dayenu*, it would have sufficed. And if God only had given us the Sabbath, *dayenu*, each gift would have been enough for anyone. And still, there were more. Secretly, I rewrote the song and dedicated it to my cousin Pris. "If Pris was only pretty, *dayenu*. And if she was only a good jacks player, *dayenu*." And so on into infinity—with choruses in between.

The eating of the *haroset*, a sublime combination of chopped apples, walnuts, cinnamon, and Manischewitz Concord grape wine, carried me through another stretch of boredom. The mixture, which we spread on pieces of matzah, was a dual symbol: first, of the mortar made by Jewish slaves under the Egyptian lash, and second, of the sweetness of God who remembered the Jewish people and put an end to such labors. The bitter/sweet contradiction confounded me. When I asked my father how one thing could represent such opposites, he answered that it typified Jewish experience and I'd better get used to it. Being the Chosen People didn't mean we were chosen for the best.

I loved my father's exegeses; his wisecracks and midrashim reminded me of the elucidations of the great rabbis. When I was very small and my grandfather ran the seder, we weren't supposed to interrupt. But my father encouraged questions, so I asked him whatever popped into my mind— even though my cousins gave me dirty looks because his answers lengthened the service considerably. I accepted his view of the *haroset*, but later, when I helped myself to extra servings, I willed it to be all sweetness and no mortar.

The arrival at the table of a bowl full of hard-boiled eggs signaled the end of the first part of the service and the beginning of the seder meal. Although not officially prescribed, dipping the egg (symbol of rebirth) into a small bowl of salt water (the tears of our enslaved ancestors) is a common practice and one that I took to heart. I used to dip my egg into the water with a quick and gingerly flourish so as not to let it absorb too much sadness. My father, on the other hand, always mashed his egg with his fork, making a soup of life and tears, clouding his salt water with white and yellow lumps. The sight disgusted me—so much so that I had to look away. At the same time, it reaffirmed my childhood view of my father as a man who tempted the fates but came up lucky. His egg seemed to conquer suffering, incorporating it into an earthy stew, while my egg was afraid of the brine.

After a belt-bursting meal, when waves of adult conversation threatened to inundate us children, my mother—always aware of everyone's needs—would come to the rescue. She would excuse us from the table, and send us up to the bedrooms or down to the rumpus room until it was time to negotiate for the retrieval of the *afikoman*. This transaction accomplished, most of my cousins wanted to take their silver dollars and run. I wanted to sing, and sing, and sing: "Chad Gadya," "Eliyahu Hanavi," "Addir Hu," "Echad Me Yodayah," "Ki Lo Noeh"—everything in the book.

Those exuberant hymns and story-songs seemed to express what the seder had been driving at all night; they made the whole evening worth the price of endurance. I was grateful to the men who stayed at the table bellowing every last word with me. I had no use for the women. Why were they puttering around when they could be singing? Why hadn't they learned the words after all these years? I never considered the mountains of dirty dishes in the kitchen. I was too busy speed-singing the intricate lyrics in competition with my uncles and male cousins. I was too busy feeling like an honorary son.

from

An Orphan in History

PAUL COWAN

Like thousands of other American Jews, Paul Cowan's parents chose to ignore their Jewish roots. When they died unexpectedly, Cowan started a search for his own past and found that he was the descendant of rabbis. This excerpt from Cowan's highly acclaimed memoir, An Orphan in History, *is a fascinating and inspiring account of the strength of tradition and heritage which, although long ignored, can be easily revitalized.*

Because he nearly lost his personal link to the history of Judaism, Paul Cowan made sure his children had the opportunity to know their past, and he was instrumental in reviving Ansche Chesed, a Conservative synagogue.

Paul Cowan, who died in 1988, was a New York journalist and a staff writer for The Village Voice. *He authored three other books:* The Tribes of America, The Making of an Un-american, *and* Mixed Blessings: Jews, Christians, and Intermarriage, *which was written with his wife, Rachel. He was a Peace Corps volunteer and a civil rights and antiwar activist.*

I entered Choate when I was thirteen, bar mitzvah age. If I didn't know much about synagogue life, I knew even less about church life. I remember the first few times I attended the mandatory nightly chapel services. All the worshipers knew what hymns to sing. Was there a sort of spiritual telepathy that united them? I was a very scared young boy—awed by the easy suburban grace of my classmates, who seemed far more self-assured than the wealthiest assimilated Jews I had known in New York. I certainly didn't want to betray my ignorance by asking dumb questions. So it took me a very bewildered week to realize that the numbers tacked onto the church's pillars referred to the little red hymnal in front of me.

Sometimes for me that Choate chapel was a magic place. I loved the musty smell of the old wooden pews, especially on rainy days. The hymns became so important to me that I memorized dozens of them. Perhaps some, like "Onward, Christian Soldiers" and "Glorious Things of Thee Are Spoken" (which had the same melody as "Deutschland Über Alles") should have bothered me. They didn't. They awed me. So did the sight of my classmates receiving confirmation from the bishop of Connecticut, who looked majestic in his white robe and deep purple stole, with a miter in his right hand. Once in a while, usually as exams approached, I would go down to chapel for morning services, which weren't mandatory. I'd drink the grape juice and eat the wafer that symbolized communion. In a way it was superstitious. Choate's God was the only one I knew, and I figured that if I appeased Him I'd get good grades on my exams. But I knew I was also a very lonely boy, who needed to believe in a Supreme Being to ease my relentless fear.

There were about twenty-five Jewish kids out of the five hundred students at Choate. Most of them had more religious training than I, and they experienced flashes of guilt, not moments of exhilaration, during the high points of the Episcopalian ritual. On Holy Days like Rosh Hashana and Yom Kippur—whose meaning I knew, but never connected to my own life—some of them would disappear from chapel—and often from school—to participate in ceremonies I couldn't quite imagine.

One of them, Joel Cassel, had spent his first thirteen years in a Jewish community in Waterbury, Connecticut. We were friends, but we never once discussed our backgrounds or our feelings while we were at Choate. Long after we had graduated he told me that his family had kept kosher back in Waterbury, that he had had a Conservative bar mitzvah, that he'd been president of his synagogue's youth group. His father, like mine, had sent him to Choate because the school seemed like the gateway to the American dream, but his father's ambition didn't ease Joel's sense of displacement. Outwardly, he was a tough, funny kid. I envied him his ability to win friends by making our classmates laugh. But inwardly he must have hurt terribly.

The chapel services were the focus of his pain. My favorite hymns, like "Onward, Christian Soldiers," offended him so much, he told me in later years, that every single night, while the rest of us were reciting the Lord's Prayer or the Episcopalian litany, he would ask God to forgive him for being in chapel at all. He'd promise God that "If I say Christ, I don't mean it—believe me."

Every night, as the service ended, the school's headmaster would bid us to pray "through Jesus Christ, our Lord." After Yom Kippur in our junior year, the Christian words seemed so offensive to Joel that he decided to push his mood of repentance into action and defy the blessing directly. He

129

refused to bow his head in prayer. The small symbolic revolt excited all the Jews at Choate. We met once, decided that none of us would bow our heads, and called ourselves "the Wallingford Jew Boys." It was the kind of act that would have appealed to my mother—and did appeal to the moralistic, wrathful Polly Cowan in me. I remember holding my head high those nights, feeling an incredibly strong surge of tribal loyalty that I'd never before experienced.

Our action clearly threatened the Reverend Seymour St. John, the head-master. One night he gave a sermon insisting that if he went to a mosque he'd take off his shoes; if he went to a synagogue he'd wear a skullcap. "When in Rome, do as the Romans do," he admonished us. (None of us had the knowledge or the wit to point out that his Anglican forebears hadn't exactly followed that advice.) In only slightly veiled terms, he threatened to expel anyone who insisted on keeping his head upright. Our revolt collapsed instantly. We were isolated and vulnerable once again. Since none of us had the courage to exchange stories of the anti-Semitism we had experienced, each of us felt we were being tormented because we were personally deficient.

Wade Pearson lived next door to me during my first year at Choate. Night after night he would come into my room and lecture me about how pushy and avaricious Jews are. Did I think the character Shylock came out of Shakespeare's imagination? Did I think Fagin was a pure invention of Dickens'? No, they were generic types. I—and my kind—were just like those forebears. During those sessions, Wade's friend Chip Thornton, a fat kid who was reputed to be a great wit, would add mirth to our literary talk by calling me "the traveling muzzy" because of my acne, or making jokes about "the mockies"—a term for Jews I had never heard before.

Lester Atkins, a loutish kid who sat behind me in junior year math class, used to clamp his feet so tightly against my jacket that if I leaned forward to answer a question I'd wind up with an unmendable rip. One day he snatched my geometry book. He gave it back to me at the end of class, though he didn't tell me he'd written me a message. That night I went to my teacher's apartment to ask for help with homework. The teacher pointed to a carefully-lettered sign that had been inscribed on the upper-right-hand corner of the page we had been working on that day. Had I written it myself? he asked. FUCK YOU, YOU KIKE, it said.

Then there was Ned the Gimp, as he called himself, who used to limp into the common room of the dorm where we all lived one summer, and greet me with the thick, mocking Yiddish accent he had lifted from Mr. Kitzel on the old Jack Benny show. The other kids thought the routine was a riot. I know that Joel Cassel, who had been toughened by the years he had spent as one of the few Jews in the public schools of Waterbury, Connecticut, would have found some way to neutralize the Gimp with banter. I couldn't do that. Usually I'd laugh nervously, hoping that my acquiescence would allow me to blend into the gang that seemed so menacing—until the next day when the Gimp's onslaught would resume. By then, I'd read *The Sun Also Rises*. I had the terrible feeling that I was the reincarnation of the long-suffering Robert Cohn. That was reinforced when a friend of mine asked me why I was so passive when the Gimp was around. Oddly, my friend's well-meaning question hurt me even more than the Gimp's insults. For it convinced me that all the kids at Choate saw me as Robert Cohn: helpless and weak-willed: a prototypical defenseless Jew.

I never told my parents about the anti-Semitism I experienced at Choate. I never told anyone. I felt guilty about it, as if I were personally responsible for my plight. Each autumn they had a Fathers' Weekend at the school. Lou, still rising in the media world, was his usual *shmeicheling* self, charming the teachers with his personality, trying to cement our relationship to the school by donating a complete set of Modern Library books. I felt very much in the shadow of this energetic, self-made, successful man. I didn't want to take the risk of describing my problems, for that might make him feel that his oldest son was a failure. Besides, what could he—or Polly—do about the anti-Semitism? Complain to the headmaster? I didn't want them—or anyone—to wage my fights for me. I was very impressionable back then. In sermon after sermon, the Reverend St. John told us that Choate was a place where you took responsibility for yourself. You went "the extra mile" if you had a problem. I accepted that view. It seemed unmanly to complain.

For nearly three years, I'd lie awake every night, fantasizing about ways to escape from the school. Then I realized I didn't want to leave in what I considered disgrace. So I'd fantasize ways to impress the bigots, ways to leave with dignity.

I actually did impress them. By senior year, I was a big shot on the newspaper, the literary magazine, the debate society. I'd found a special motley substratum of bright, wacky friends—my working-class Italian roommate, who was there on a science scholarship; the son of Spanish immigrants who lived in Wallingford, where Choate was located; a very poetic jazz musician; a brilliant, worldly exchange student from Switzerland. We created a fantasy world for ourselves which mocked the real world in which our classmates lived. For example, after vacations, dozens of kids would boast about visiting two New York whores, Gussie and Sally. My roommate and I named our goldfish Gussie and Sally. In New York we'd crash the society dances, and puzzle the serious preppy girls with questions about where we could stable the polo ponies we had just brought up from Panama. At Choate, one dance weekend, we organized a folk sing where my date—about whom I'd written a very romantic story in the school literary magazine—was the star. Our classmates flocked to that, not to the formal events which the school had organized. By senior year we were bright enough and lively enough to seem quite glamorous. We had succeeded on our own terms.

But those successes created a new set of problems. Now kids who wanted to befriend me often made a conscious effort to disassociate me from other Jews. Hans Peterson, a bookish lacrosse player, came from Long Island. The Jews were taking over his home town, he would inform me, and I should know their true nature. They were loud and money-minded, bad-mannered, and aggressively sarcastic. Of course, I was different: I was soft-spoken, well-read, with a taste for parody and fantasy. At least, that was his explicit message. His implicit message was that I bore direct responsibility for his new neighbors.

In my senior year, Sidney Konig, a younger Jewish kid on my corridor, was the new target of abuse. I didn't really like him. He was so whiny, so defensive, so obviously Jewish-looking, that I secretly believed he deserved the treatment he was receiving. Still, I became his ally. As seniors, my Italian roommate and I wielded power over the other kids. We'd punish anyone who mistreated Sidney.

Why, I wonder now, could I debate Hans or defend Sidney with a degree of aggressiveness I could never display when the Gimp was teasing me? My answer makes me a little uncomfortable.

It stems from my mother's insistence that in the presence of anti-Semitism I should always announce I was a Jew. What a curiously mixed message that was! For years, I thought it simply contained the willed bravery of her *noblesse oblige*. But now I realize that there was an unmistakable, slightly disdainful pride in her sense that, with my Welsh name, my brown hair, my thin nose, I could "pass" for whatever I wanted. I could be free in America, not wed to any ghetto.

So, in her opinion, as a totally assimilated Jew—or, rather, as a Jew who could escape whenever I wanted—I was supposed to remember the Holocaust and defend my less fortunate kinsmen, the Sidneys, the Jews who were moving into Hans's town on Long Island, in just the same way as I was supposed to defend the blacks.

In grade school, it never occurred to Polly—or to me—that *I* might be the Jew who needed defending. I wasn't prepared for personal abuse. When it came I was paralyzed with confusion and surprise. And I was paralyzed with the feeling that it was both self-demeaning and gauche to fight back.

My four years at Choate shattered the illusion Polly had helped implant. And they reinforced her equally strong, completely contradictory assertion that a Jew in any profession, under any name, was subject to attack.

After the four years at Choate, I could never pretend that I was and wasn't Jewish: that I could be part of a family which fought oppression in the name of the six million, and yet remain personally unscarred by anti-Semitism. I couldn't hide, except by surrendering my Jewish identity completely. Neither Wade nor Lester the Lout nor Ned the Gimp cared at all whether my name was Paul or Saul, Cowan or Cohen; whether I went to chapel or synagogue on Yom Kippur; whether I bowed my head and said an Episcopalian litany or held it high and recited the Shema. Either way, I was a Shylock, a Mr. Kitzel, a kike.

Once I'd been through that experience, my mother's message about the six million became, perhaps, the single most important fact of my life. For, though I didn't begin to understand the consequences of my feelings for decades, I knew from then on that it was unthinkable that anyone would ever separate me from my tribe.

"The Grandfather
Without a Memory"

ARTHUR MAGIDA

Describing his childhood growing up in the Bronx, Arthur Magida talks about being "raised on egg creams and comic books," enduring innumerable seders, few of which he understood, watching yarmulkes fall off his head because they never fit properly, and never being able to tolerate the woolen suit he had to wear to synagogue because it always itched. "And so," he says, "now you understand what it means to have been raised Jewish in America: forever suffering, forever itching. . . ."

In this essay, which originally appeared in the Baltimore Jewish Times, *Arthur Magida talks about coming to terms with his grandfather, a man who believed in silence and respect, but who never shared the sage wisdom that is somehow expected from our elders.*

Arthur Magida is an editor and writer who is currently working on his first book. In 1994, he was among the top ten finalists for the Pulitzer Prize in feature writing. He is also editorial director of Jewish Lights, a publisher of books on spirituality. He lives in Baltimore with his wife and three children.

For almost a year, there had been an extra place at our table. Everyone sat as they usually did: my father, of course, at the head with my mother opposite him; my sister next to the refrigerator; I across from her with my back to the cupboards. And next to me sat the newcomer, an old man whom I hardly knew: my Grandfather, my mother's father.

My Grandfather had come to live with us. For a fairly independent and private man, it had always seemed paradoxical that he had lived with others for as long as I could remember. Mostly, he and Grandma had shared a cramped, two-bedroom apartment in the Bronx with my mother's older sister and her husband and two sons. When Grandma died, he stayed on and when his son-in-law died at a sad young age of the last of many heart attacks, he stayed on.

There came a time, though, when he became a burden and was not just a fixture. That came when he was no longer aging and was—quite simply and finally—aged. Then, he could no longer give himself insulin shots. Then, he pounded the floors with a rhythmical limp. Then, he came our way.

I was sure that Grandpa came to live with us because everyone knew he was dying. But I never inquired. The news was simply given to my sister and myself that Grandpa was coming and we took it with few questions, but some puzzlement.

There was a dull sense of disappointment when I heard who our guest would be. I had never really understood this old man and I had never really felt close to him. Quite the contrary, in fact. He was of the age when he could not work and, more to the point, when he could not enjoy himself. There were hints of a lift that his shoulders had once had; they suggested that he had once been a strong man, maybe even an imposing man. But now he had a sagging pallor that said that he knew that his time was coming, that he had heard the echo of his own end and that he was not ready for it.

But the end of a man—even of my own Grandfather—meant little to me, a slight ten-year-old who preferred making model planes and ships to running around with my few friends and going to dances at the Community Center that were given for us much too prematurely since no one knew what to do during the slow dances other than sway clumsily in place or try not to sweat on your partner or step on her toes.

I was a fairly shy, uncertain boy and Grandpa's presence did not help. I had always been intimidated, almost cowed by him and generally lapsed into a protective silence when he was around. The silence seemed to be the only thing that made either of us halfway comfortable, so it was a handy and easy device.

My gagging of myself had gotten to be almost a reflex when Grandpa was around because it seemed that's what he generally wanted; silence at each year's Seder as we kids giggled at the torrent of Hebrew flowing to our dumb, uncomprehending ears; silence whenever I joined my grandparents for their peculiar dinners of borscht and kasha and black bread; silence as he davened in the dim morning light with a box spectrally perched on his forehead and an arm straited in black ribbons. My world, when he was around, was a hushed one: tongues lay still and silent; my ears grew hungry for ordinary chatter and babble.

We lived in a town in northeastern Pennsylvania about 125 miles from New York City. My father drove to the city one day and came back that evening with Grandpa and the trunk full of two brown-striped suitcases, three paper bags full of clothes and one suit. My Grandfather's second suit was on his back.

There was no fanfare on his arrival and everything was quite proper. Dinner was served—quietly, of course. There were some feeble efforts at conversation and then respite was found, in that most American way, the metallic glare of TV. His bed was made in the den and we all went to our separate rooms. My mother probably felt that she was a dutiful daughter, my father who also had never been overly comfortable with Grandpa, probably felt imposed upon; and my sister and I chafed at our obligatory silence.

For the months that he stayed with us, there was a new and jarring rhythm in our house. Doors which had always been open were now shut for privacy; dinners which had always been leisurely were now slightly hurried. The den turned into Grandpa's room and the rest of us were either exiled or felt like we were trespassing when entering.

For the first few months of Grandpa's stay, I shared with him what had always been my side of the kitchen table. The table was built to easily fit four and, in a pinch, maybe five. To make room for Grandpa, I was miserably crammed against a tableleg. But it seemed like a necessary—and expected—inconvenience.

One night, though, I had enough of submissively courting tablelegs and bolting down my dinner. I asked my sister to permanently change places with me and spuriously explained that I was tired of squeezing into the thin space between the table and the cupboard.

We switched and I never sat next to Grandpa again. I never wanted to. Everyone knew—but never said—the real reason why I had wanted to move.

I'm not sure why this relatively minor incident is virtually the only event that I can remember from Grandpa's stay with us. Surely, other more momentous and important things happened. And yet, this carefully meditated slight—which took all my temerity—is all that stands out and, maybe from my vantage, all that matters.

Throughout all this, I had a rough, juvenile hunch that something was amiss. I felt that some vague cultural, genetic, ethnic link had never been soldered. Everything that I had ever read or seen about grandfathers was not what was happening. Every grandfather painted by the thoroughly New England brush of Norman Rockwell for *Saturday Evening Post* covers had rosy cheeks, a hearty smile and a cherubic grandchild snuggled on his lap; every grandfather described by Sholem Aleichem gave sage, untutored advice to his grandchildren, wisdom gleaned from years of hunching over the Torah and over one's own tsuras.

But no wisdom came my way. No hearty smiles for me. Not even lollipops, as far as I can remember. What I got instead was endless admonitions to be quiet, to be still, to be—most of all—respectful. Respect—and not love or, at the very least, endearment—was what this old man wanted and he somehow mistook obedience for esteem.

I may have inwardly cringed at all this, but it was not then my nature to protest. So while I yearned for a sage or a semitic Santa Claus, I kept my ten-year-old mouth shut and was resentfully mute.

What made this all the more painful was that Grandpa was the last of my four grandparents. And that none of them had ever truly touched me. Grandpa's wife had died when I was about seven. About all that I can recall of her is that she taught me how to tie my shoes; behind that pragmatism, there was, perhaps, great love. And my father's parents had both died by the time I was two.

Now, the only living connection with the land and the times of my ancestors was an old man who gave me no pats on the head and no treats, not even from the world which had once been his. There were no tales of dybbuks, no accounts of long hours in candlelit shuls on Friday nights or of December winds whipping across Polish hills and into finely cracked walls as children courted sleep, weighed against the cold by the warm heaviness of goosedown. There were no memories of delight and none of sorrow; none of joy and none of sadness. Perhaps the many injunctions for silence were a much more contemporary and immediate forsaking of the past; maybe Grandpa's holding of his yesterdays at bay was meant to deny, also, his present, maybe even his future.

At that time, I was entranced with history, with the majesty and ferocity of what had gone on before me. I saved Sunday afternoons for Walter Cronkite and "You Are There"; I spent many a school hour furtively skimming through history texts when I was supposed to be mastering multiplication (with which I still have troubles). The days before my coming into the world often had more meaning and power for me than the relative few that had passed since my birth, history was not just dates and battles and economic theories gone awry—it gave meaning and purpose and direction to my own flimsy life. And here was a history—my *own* history—watching Lucy and Desi in the den.

Grandpa was not, I believe, trying to forget Eastern Europe; he had left before the Continent reeked of the Fuhrer and there had somehow been no pogroms in his part of Poland. He just saw no use for the place he had come from; the old country had vanished, he was in America now.

Grandpa's condition worsened about a half-year after he moved in with us. His limp so burdened him that he could barely walk and he resented the cane that his doctor insisted he use. He preferred to hobble his way through the house, so favoring his one good leg that he virtually ignored the other.

One day, he left our house for the hospital. When he came out a week later, he didn't return to stay with us. Instead, he went to a nursing home that my father happened to own.

Surprisingly, the house was a bit empty. Nothing, I thought, had been gained by Grandpa's arrival, but something had been lost by his departure. Maybe it was his own imminent death that we felt, maybe it was the passing of the last of those who had come before us.

My school was around the corner from the nursing home and I usually went there on Wednesdays for lunch. I can't say that the food was particularly tasty, but the kitchen help always managed to sneak me a treat like ice cream or chocolate cake.

As I opened the main door to the nursing home on the first Wednesday after Grandpa's admission, I caught the usual semi-choking odor of Lysol and lurking death, a heady brew for a boy. A few paces down the hall, I stood in front of the room Grandpa shared with three other men, uncertain whether to go in. I was torn because Grandpa and I were of the same flesh—and I had been taught to be polite to my elders. And, yet, I knew that if I went in there would be many silences and nothing to say.

I finally opened the door. The room was bright with sunlight, its quiet broken every few minutes by one man's formless, hopeless moaning. The other men made no sounds and no moves. I went over to Grandpa's bed, where he lay looking a bit more thin than usual. I leaned over until he saw me and he blinked his eyes several times in surprise, in appreciation.

As usual, there was not much to say. We passed a few minutes in the usual small talk—school, my family, the weather. The topics were familiar, but even more so was the lack of anything to say about them. When I couldn't think of anything else to say, I made up some excuse about being late for lunch and turned for the door. As I turned, I saw for the first time the place where the blanket flattened where his right leg had been before he went to the hospital. I wanted to say something, but couldn't think of anything so I left the room as if nothing had changed or ever would.

For the next three months, I went—as usual—to the nursing home for Wednesday lunches; I visited Grandpa maybe four times over all those Wednesdays. We always talked about the same things and I always looked covertly at that flat, smooth blanket just below his hip and never said a word about the missing limb.

The visits soon came to be pointless since I spent most of my time standing in silence in front of his bed, shifting my weight from leg to leg or mentally going over some notes for a test that coming afternoon. Often, I could simply walk by his room since the door was mostly closed. But once, the door was wide open and Grandpa was lying flat on his back watching the languorous traffic in the hall. He looked right at me and I at him. But neither of us gave any sign that he had seen the other. There was only the subtle, still acknowledgement of two generations which had never really known each other. Two generations that had never really tried.

For the rest of the day, I felt naughty and tainted and furtive; for a ten-year-old, I had been terribly nasty and bold. And yet, for once, I had saluted my Grandfather in the one way he had always urged me to behave— silently—and there was a perverse bit of pride and contrary satisfaction amid all the damning recriminations.

That was the last time I saw Grandpa. I didn't go to the funeral; kids in my family didn't go to that kind of thing. I don't remember anyone grieving; there were no tears, no remembrances. I suppose that was kept for the funeral home and the cemetery. There was nothing that indicated that he had once been here and was no longer other than collecting into a big paper bag some of his clothes that had remained in our house and giving them to Goodwill. For the few days that they stayed at the front door before being picked up, they were the only testimony—for me—that he had once passed our way.

from

THE SEARCH FOR GOD AT HARVARD

ARI GOLDMAN

*When Goldman's parents divorced, he and his brothers split their
time between their parents' homes. Perhaps to make up for their home
lives, their parents decided they would be best educated in a Conservative yeshiva, Conservative in the Jewish sense, which means taking little interest in secular concerns like Zionism or world events.*

In this excerpt from The Search for God at Harvard, *Goldman
illustrates how well Orthodox Jews function in the secular world, even
though they tend to separate themselves from mainstream events.*

A religion reporter with The New York Times, *Ari Goldman spent
a year at Harvard Divinity School to enhance his reporting skills.
Out of his experiences came* The Search for God at Harvard, *a fascinating look both at world religions and into Goldman's heart.*

My classmates at the Div School, I was soon to find, were different from
those at the other professional schools at Harvard. While there were many
bright and thoughtful students at the Law School or the Business School,
there were few for whom the law or business was at the core of their lives.
These were disciplines they did and did well, but the disciplines didn't
define them. The more I got to know my fellow Div School students, the
more I found that, for them, religion was at the center. My encounter with
my classmates drew me to examine my own life and try to find just where
religion fit.

More than any other event in my life, my parents' divorce in 1955, when
I was six years old, shaped me into the person I am, professionally, emo-
tionally, and religiously.

My earliest memories center on the place where, before the divorce, we
briefly called ourselves a family, a three-story house on Westbourne Parkway in Hartford. Our family—my mother, father, older brother, Shalom,
and younger brother, Dov—lived on the top floor, and to get there we
would walk up an open wooden staircase in the rear that took us through

the toy-strewn porches of our downstairs neighbors. We had a clothesline that stretched from our porch across the backyard to another three-family house.

My favorite diversion was hunting in the backyard for bugs and worms and, after a rain, maybe a frog, and playing with them on the back porch. In those days, dry-cleaning stores and drugstores used to run promotions giving away goldfish, turtles, and salamanders. These became my greatest treasures. And once my father brought home a baby chick whose feathers had been dyed kelly green—a St. Patrick's Day promotion. The chick ran wildly around the house until my mother shooed it out the back door and it lived out its brief, green life in a shoe box on my porch.

The St. Patrick's Day chick incident might sound like an amusing vignette out of *I Love Lucy*, but in our house it was the trigger for a fight between my parents. Loud verbal confrontations in the house were often followed by a door slammed in anger and an eerie, tension-laden silence.

I loved that back porch. It was my playground, my menagerie, my stage, my tree house, and my refuge from family turbulence. My mother said that she knew I was back from nursery school when she heard me singing as I climbed up the back stairs to the porch.

There was another element of that life that I loved, Friday night. It was a time when, by the magic of the Sabbath candles, we were transformed into a happy, picture-book family. The recriminations and bickering would cease and the music would begin. Dov was just a baby at the time, but Shalom and I would sit at the gleaming white table in our "Shabbat outfits," dark blue pants and white cotton shirts open at the collar. Our hair was still wet from our pre-Sabbath baths, and it was combed neatly across our foreheads. Yarmulkes were bobby-pinned to our heads. My mother waved her hands over the lighted candles and covered her eyes as she stood in a silent moment of meditation. Afterwards, she took us into her arms and kissed us, lingering an extra moment to drink in our freshness. She told us that we looked like the two angels that tradition says accompany the men home from the Friday-night synagogue service.

When, a little while later, my father returned from the synagogue, we lined up in front of him for the Sabbath blessing, the eldest, Shalom, first and then me. "May God make you like Ephraim and Menashe," he said, invoking the two grandsons of Jacob who, as Joseph's children, were especially beloved. Bending down to reach us, my father cradled our heads between his strong hands as he recited the blessing. "May He bless you and keep you . . . and give you peace."

My father, who worked hard all week managing and selling real estate, became our rabbi and cantor on Friday night. He took us through the meal singing the joyous melodies of the Hasidim and the resolute songs of the Chalutzim, the Israeli pioneers who, we were told, were singing the same songs as they worked to turn the desert green. My mother, a confirmed ''listener'' rather than singer, hummed along with a smile of contentment on her face.

On one such Friday night, I sensed the perfect opportunity. ''I want a dog,'' I announced between songs.

''Not again,'' my mother said. ''Sweetheart, I already told you, no dogs. Anyway, I think you're allergic to dogs.''

''Judy,'' my father interrupted. ''You don't know that for sure and besides, I don't see the harm—''

''Marvin.'' Her voice was rising. ''Don't contradict me in front of the children.'' And that was the end of the singing. The music stopped and the candles went out.

Not long after, my parents were divorced. The fight over the dog, of course, had nothing to do with it. It was just another in a series and, no doubt, one of the more benign of their tortured nine-year marriage. But try telling that to a five-year-old boy.

All sons and daughters of divorce blame themselves. In their minds, the only way to expiate the guilt is to re-create what was lost. That is why each of us harbors a dream, the dream of bringing our parents back together again. On a subconscious level, this becomes our life's work. For me, the mission was to re-create the serenity and harmony of the Sabbath table. That was all I needed to do to restore our fall from Paradise.

For a move so fraught with consequences, the act ending my parents' marriage was a starkly simple one. One morning after my father left for work, my mother gathered up the three of us and boarded a New York–bound train. From Grand Central Station, we took a taxi to Jackson Heights, a working-class neighborhood in New York's borough of Queens where my mother's twin sister, Jean, lived with her husband, Herb, a doctor. With a young family of their own, they lived in an apartment on the ground floor of a private house, using the front of the apartment for Herb's medical practice and the rear as their living quarters. My mother, Shalom, Dov, and I moved in. Shalom and I slept on couches in Herb's waiting room and had to clear our bedclothes out of the way before the first patients arrived in the morning. After a few months, my mother found a place of our own, a cramped one-bedroom apartment a few blocks away.

Despite the turmoil, however, there was one constant in my life that proved critical—the practice of Orthodox Judaism. Whether I was in my mother's apartment in Jackson Heights or in the Hartford home of my father, I knew that on Friday night we would gather around a table covered in white. For twenty-five hours, from sundown Friday until the stars came out Saturday night, we observed a kind of limbo time, where, in effect, everyday life came to a halt. The same set of rules in both homes: no watching television, no turning on electric lights, no talking on the telephone, no riding in cars, and no writing anything down, not even homework assignments. The Sabbath was instead a time for attending synagogue, reading a novel, taking a leisurely walk to the park, or reflecting on the week past.

To someone not brought up with these rules, all the Sabbath restrictions might sound onerous. But, for me, the faithful practice of Orthodox Judaism proved to be the one comfort in my childhood, the one act that was filled with the possibility of redemption. I clung—and I continue to cling—to it like a raft in a turbulent sea.

Am I devoted to Orthodox observance then for the wrong reasons? Am I still mired in a juvenile fantasy that the Sabbath table will bring my parents together? Do I still need so desperately to find a common bond between my two very different parents?

One of the lessons of Div School was that there are no wrong reasons. When, in our conversation after class, Rabbi Jacobs picked up the acorn, he was saying that origins aren't everything. There is the tree, and the tree exists in and of itself. Enjoy the tree. Knowing that it was once an acorn doesn't make it any less sturdy or any less shady. Likewise, in the observance of Judaism, the origins of the laws—whether made by God or fabricated by man—are not the factors that determine validity. Neither is the Sabbath diminished because it sustains me with a comfort that my parents could not.

As wrenching as divorce was, and continues to be, for me, it did provide great job training. What better place, after all, to learn to be a journalist? Divorce made me a specialist in entertaining different points of view without having to make judgments about them. Take a simple thing like packing clothes for a weekend trip, something I did often while shuttling between my mother in New York and my father in Connecticut. Since I would always be attending synagogue when I visited my father, I had to pack a sport jacket. My mother believed that in packing jackets, the buttons should be fastened and the arms folded back, like a shirt from the laundry. My father, however, insisted on turning the jacket inside out, punching in the shoulder pads and folding it inside out into the suitcase. So, when I headed north to Hartford, my jacket was packed Mom's way; when I headed south, it was packed Dad's way.

After the divorce, my father, then in his early thirties, moved back to the home of his parents. By today's standards, it seems like an odd move, but then it made perfect sense, especially since his mother, Grandma Nettie, was there to help take care of "Marvin's boys" on our frequent visits. Grandpa Sam, recently retired from the clothing business after the city built a highway through his store, was the world's greatest devotee of newspapers. Each morning after breakfast—as Grandma cleaned up the kitchen and geared up for lunch—Grandpa would sit in a big high-backed, embroidered chair near the front door and read the morning paper, *The Hartford Courant*. When he finished, he would begin on the Yiddish paper, *The Tag-Morning Journal* (which he read with fluency, despite the fact that he, like all my grandparents, was American-born). Then he moved on to the *Connecticut Jewish Ledger*. The smell of one of Grandma's soups would soon fill the house, and Grandpa would yell, "Nettie, I'm getting hungry." After lunch, Grandpa would sit in his chair by the door waiting for the afternoon paper, the *Hartford Times*, to drop.

He was a simple man, this lover of newspapers. I never saw him read a book, except for a prayer book, which he followed without passion every Saturday morning in the synagogue. At home, he was stern and impatient and would peer over his paper to mete out verbal discipline when we got too noisy or into fights. And he played favorites. My brothers and I, the products of divorce (in his mind, the products of failure), were something of an embarrassment. What he took pride in were his other grandchildren, the offspring of his son-in-law the rabbi, the one who'd married his eldest daughter, Ruth, and led the big Orthodox synagogue in the Bronx. When friends came over, Grandpa would put down his newspaper and proudly talk about "Ruth and the Rabbi"—out of deference, he wouldn't even use his first name—and their kids. It made no difference to my grandfather that "Marvin's boys" were playing in the next room.

My father was my refuge, especially on Saturday mornings. He insisted on being among the first men in the synagogue, and I eagerly joined him because I loved our walks together. The streets were quiet; we had them all to ourselves. I put my hand in his, and we began to sing. I must have been seven or eight years old, but already we were preparing for my bar mitzvah. We sang the traditional songs of the synagogue and sometimes improvised by putting the words to more modern Israeli and Hasidic melodies. Everyone told me I had a good voice, a sweet voice, a voice so high that it could touch the heavens. In the synagogue, I sang the solos that could be performed before one reaches the age of maturity, and I looked forward eagerly to my bar mitzvah.

The bar mitzvah service was held in 1962 at the Orthodox synagogue near my mother's house in Jackson Heights. My father and several of his relatives, who, like us, do not drive on the Sabbath, stayed in a motel about a mile away on Queens Boulevard. Using the traditional singsong chant, I read the Torah portion of the week. It was *B'raishis*, In the Beginning, and took in the first five and a half chapters of Genesis, the Creation, the Fall of Man, and the birth of Noah. I read it from the Torah scroll, but I knew every word and detail without looking. The earth was emptiness and void and from it God fashioned the world. He created the sun and the moon, light and darkness, oceans and streams, and all manner of vegetation. God made the creatures that crawl on the earth and that fly in the heavens. And finally, in His crowning act, God breathed life into a pile of clay and created Adam. But Adam was unhappy, so God caused a heavy sleep to come upon him and He took Adam's rib and created from it a "helpmate" for Adam. Adam was pleased and called her Eve, "because she is the mother of all living things."

The happiness of creation was only to be followed by the tragedy of the first sin and the banishment of Adam and Eve—Mother and Father—from the Garden of Eden. For Christians the story of the first sin—Original Sin—is replete with meaning. It represents the Fall of Man, a fall that could be redeemed only through the coming of Jesus. For Jews, however, there is no belief that a Savior is necessary for redemption; instead, the individual has the power to redeem himself or herself through good works and repentance.

Long before I knew of the Christian approach, the Fall of Man had a special meaning in my own life. The story harked back to a time when my parents were together, gathered with their children around the Sabbath table, a state of grace that was to be only short-lived. At my bar mitzvah, the fall was played all over again. No sooner had I read the Genesis story from the Torah to my family—assembled as one unit in the synagogue—than I saw them split again into different factions. After the service, my mother and father made two separate bar mitzvah parties for me. My mother's family went off to one catering hall, my father's to another. I was shuttled back and forth like some exhibit animal in the circus. I wish I could suggest that this was just a lapse in judgment by otherwise well-meaning parents, but the same dual celebration (if you can call it that) was held for both my brothers. Six bar mitzvahs for three boys.

A few years later, when I could see the absurdity of this—how family animosities could not be set aside for the moment of our individual joy—I harbored a fantasy. I dreamed that someday I would get married and invite all of my relatives, on both my mother's and father's sides, to a festive wedding banquet. I would have them all together in one room, and it would be up to me to make the seating arrangement. My mother and father would be at the same table. My aunt who filled my ears with ugly gossip about my grandmother would be seated next to her. The people who disliked each other the most, that is, would be forced to smile and be polite. The main course would be rib steak, and the table would be set with steak knives so sharp that they would catch the glimmer of the chandeliers. In the middle of the meal, just as all the family, exercising the greatest politeness, would be lifting their knives to cut into the steak, I would sneak outside and pull the main power switch so that the hall would be cast in total darkness.

Would anyone survive, I wondered, or would it be like the last scene in *Hamlet*, where hatred triumphs and no one lives?

So much for fantasy. The wedding Shira and I had on Labor Day 1983 was considerably different. For one thing, the food was vegetarian, so there was no need for razor-sharp knives. Family members on both sides had mellowed considerably. The wedding was held on the well-groomed grounds of the Connecticut home of my mother and her second husband. Despite his refusal to walk down the aisle since the wedding was at my mother's house, my father graciously attended with his new wife. The old fights, if not the old animosities, had subsided.

But the old scars remained.

from

THE CHOSE

CHAIM POTO

Until Chaim Potok artfully explained the worl... *Hasidic Jews in his classic novel* The Chosen, *published in 1967, few people understood them.*

Set in Brooklyn during World War II, The Chosen *is the story of how Reuven, the son of an Orthodox scholar, befriends Danny, son of a famous Hasidic rabbi. Their worlds couldn't have been more different, though both boys are Jewish. During a neighborhood softball game, Danny Saunders hits Reuven in the eye with the ball, sending Reuven to the hospital. As Reuven's eyes heals, he and Danny become friends. In this excerpt, Reuven visits Danny's shul, and meets Danny's father, Reb Saunders.*

Chaim Potok is a graduate of Yeshiva University, with rabbinical ordination (Conservative) from the Jewish Theological Seminary of America. A skilled novelist and essayist, his novels include The Promise, My Name Is Asher Lev, *and* Davita's Harp. *His articles have appeared in national periodicals such as* The New York Times Book Review; American Judaism; *and* Saturday Review.

It was a light, dreamless sleep, a kind of half-sleep that refreshes but does not shut off the world completely. I felt the warm wind and smelled newly cut grass, and a bird perched on a branch of the ailanthus and sang for a long time before it flew away. Somehow I knew where that bird was, though I did not open my eyes. There were children playing on the street, and once a dog barked and a car's brakes screeched. Someone was playing a piano nearby, and the music drifted slowly in and out of my mind like the ebb and flow of ocean surf. I almost recognized the melody, but I could not be sure; it slipped like a cool and silken wind from my grasp. I heard a door open and close and there were footsteps against wood, and then silence, and I knew someone had come onto the porch, but I would not open my eyes. I did not want to lose that twilight sleep, with its odors and

147

whispered flow of music. Someone was on the porch, looking
felt him looking at me. I felt him slowly push away the sleep,
finally, I opened my eyes, and there was Danny, standing at the foot
the lounge chair, with his arms folded across his chest, clicking his
tongue and shaking his head.

"You sleep like a baby," he said. "I feel guilty waking you."

I yawned, stretched, and sat up on the edge of the lounge chair. "That
was delicious," I added, yawning again. "What time is it?"

"It's after five, sleepyhead. I've been waiting here ten minutes for you
to wake up."

"I slept almost three hours," I said. "That was some sleep."

He clicked his tongue again and shook his head. "What kind of infield
is that?" He was imitating Mr. Galanter. "How can we keep that infield
solid if you're asleep there, Malter?"

I laughed and got to my feet.

"Where do you want to go?" he asked.

"I don't care."

"I thought we'd go over to my father's shul. He wants to meet you."

"Where is it?" I asked him.

"It's five blocks from here."

"Is my father inside?"

"I didn't see him. Your maid let me in. Don't you want to go?"

"Sure," I said. "Let me wash up and put a tie and jacket on. I don't
have a caftan, you know."

He grinned at me. "The uniform is a requirement for members of the
fold only," he said.

"Okay, member of the fold. Come on inside with me."

I washed, dressed, told Manya that when my father came in she should
let him know where I had gone, and we went out.

"What does your father want to see me about?" I asked Danny as we
went down the stone stairway of the house.

"He wants to meet you. I told him we were friends."

We turned up the street, heading toward Lee Avenue.

"He always has to approve of my friends," Danny said. "Especially if
they're outside the fold. Do you mind my telling him that we're friends?"

"No."

"Because I really think we are," Danny said.

I didn't say anything. We walked to the corner, then turned right on Lee
Avenue. The street was busy with traffic and crowded with people. I wondered what any of my classmates would think if they saw me walking with

Danny. It would become quite a topic of conversation in the neighborhood. Well, they would see me with him sooner or later.

Danny was looking at me, his sculptured face wearing a serious expression. "Don't you have any brothers or sisters?" he asked.

"No. My mother died soon after I was born."

"I'm sorry to hear that."

"How about you?"

"I have a brother and a sister. My sister's fourteen and my brother is eight. I'm going on sixteen."

"So am I," I said.

We discovered that we had been born in the same year, two days apart.

"You've been living five blocks away from me all these years, and I never knew who you were," I said.

"We stick pretty close together. My father doesn't like us to mix with outsiders."

"I hope you don't mind my saying this, but your father sounds like a tyrant."

Danny didn't disagree. "He's a very strong-willed person. When he makes up his mind about something, that's it, finished."

"Doesn't he object to your going around with an apikoros like me?"

"That's why he wants to meet you."

"I thought you said your father never talks to you."

"He doesn't. Except when we study Talmud. But he did this time. I got up enough courage to tell him about you, and he said to bring you over today. That's the longest sentence he's said to me in years. Except for the time I had to convince him to let us have a ball team."

"I'd hate to have my father not talk to me."

"It isn't pleasant," Danny said very quietly. "But he's a great man. You'll see when you meet him."

"Is your brother going to be a rabbi, too?"

Danny gave me a queer look. "Why do you ask that?"

"No special reason. Is he?"

"I don't know. Probably he will." His voice had a strange, almost wistful quality to it. I decided not to press the point. He went back to talking about his father.

"He's really a great man, my father. He saved his community. He brought them all over to America after the First World War."

"I never heard about that," I told him.

"That's right," he said, and told me about his father's early years in Russia. I listened in growing astonishment.

Danny's grandfather had been a well-known Hasidic rabbi in a small town in southern Russia, and his father had been the second of two sons. The firstborn son had been in line to inherit his father's rabbinic position, but during a period of study in Odessa he suddenly vanished. Some said he had been murdered by Cossacks; for a time there was even a rumor that he had been converted to Christianity and had gone to live in France. The second son was ordained at the age of seventeen, and by the time he was twenty had achieved an awesome reputation as a Talmudist. When his father died, he automatically inherited the position of rabbinic leadership. He was twenty-one years old at the time.

He remained the rabbi of his community throughout the years of Russia's participation in the First World War. One week before the Bolshevist Revolution, in the autumn of 1917, his young wife bore him a second child, a son. Two months later, his wife, his son, and his eighteen-month-old daughter were shot to death by a band of marauding Cossacks, one of the many bandit gangs that roamed through Russia during the period of chaos that followed the revolution. He himself was left for dead, with a pistol bullet in his chest and a saber wound in his pelvis. He lay unconscious for half a day near the bodies of his wife and children, and then the Russian peasant who tended the stove in the synagogue and swept its floor found him and carried him to his hut, where he extracted the bullet, bathed the wounds, and tied him to the bed so he would not fall out during the days and nights he shivered and screamed with the fever and delirium that followed.

The synagogue had been burned to the ground. Its Ark was a gutted mass of charred wood, its four Torah scrolls were seared black, its holy books were piles of gray ash blown about by the wind. Of the one hundred eighteen Jewish families in the community only forty-three survived.

When it was discovered that the rabbi was not dead but was being cared for by the Russian peasant, he was brought into the still-intact home of a Jewish family and nursed back to health. He spent the winter recovering from his wounds. During that winter the Bolshevists signed the treaty of Brest-Litovsk with Germany, and Russia withdrew from the war. The chaos inside the country intensified, and the village was raided four times by Cossacks. But each of those times the Jews were warned by friendly peasants and were concealed in the woods or in huts. In the spring, the rabbi announced to his people that they were done with Russia, Russia was Esav and Edom, the land of Satan and the Angel of Death. They would travel together to America and rebuild their community.

Eight days later, they left. They bribed and bargained their way through Russia, Austria, France, Belgium, and England. Five months later, they arrived in New York City. At Ellis Island the rabbi was asked his name, and he gave it as Senders. On the official forms, Senders became Saunders. After the customary period of quarantine, they were permitted to leave the island, and Jewish welfare workers helped them settle in the Williamsburg section of Brooklyn. Three years later the rabbi married once again, and in 1929, two days before the stock market crash, Danny was born in the Brooklyn Memorial Hospital. Eighteen months later his sister was born, and five and a half years after the birth of his sister, his brother was born by Caesarean section, both in that same hospital.

"They all followed him?" I asked. "Just like that?"

"Of course. They would have followed him anywhere."

"I don't understand that. I didn't know a rabbi had that kind of power."

"He's more than a rabbi," Danny said. "He's a tzaddik."

"My father told me about Hasidism last night. He said it was a fine idea until some of the tzaddikim began to take advantage of their followers. He wasn't very complimentary."

"It depends upon your point of view," Danny said quietly.

"I can't understand how Jews can follow another human being so blindly."

"He's not just another human being."

"Is he like God?"

"Something like that. He's a kind of messenger of God, a bridge between his followers and God."

"I don't understand it. It almost sounds like Catholicism."

"That's the way it is," Danny said, "whether you understand it or not."

"I'm not offending you or anything. I just want to be honest."

"I want you to be honest," Danny said.

We walked on in silence.

A block beyond the synagogue where my father and I prayed, we made a right turn into a narrow street crowded with brownstones and sycamores. It was a duplicate of the street on which I lived, but a good deal older and less neatly kept. Many of the houses were unkempt, and there were very few hydrangea bushes or morning glories on the front lawns. The sycamores formed a solid, tangled bower that kept out the sunlight. The stone banisters on the outside stairways were chipped, their surfaces blotched with dirt, and the edges of the stone steps were round and smooth from years of use. Cats scrambled through the garbage cans that stood in front of some of the houses, and the sidewalks were strewn with old newspapers, ice cream and candy wrappers, worn cardboard cartons, and torn paper bags. Women in long-sleeved dresses, with kerchiefs covering their heads, many with infants in their arms, others heavily pregnant, sat on the stone steps of the stairways, talking loudly in Yiddish. The street throbbed with the noise of playing children who seemed in constant motion, dodging around cars, racing up and down steps, chasing after cats, climbing trees, balancing themselves as they tried walking on top of the banisters, pursuing one another in furious games of tag—all with their fringes and earlocks dancing wildly in the air and trailing out behind them. We were walking quickly now under the dark ceiling of sycamores, and a tall, heavily built man in a black beard and black caftan came alongside me, bumped me roughly to avoid running into a woman, and passed me without a word. The liquid streams of racing children, the noisy chatter of long-sleeved women, the worn buildings and blotched banisters, the garbage cans and the scrambling cats all gave me the feeling of having slid silently across a strange threshold, and for a long moment I regretted having let Danny take me into his world.

We were approaching a group of about thirty black-caftaned men who were standing in front of the three-story brownstone at the end of the street. They formed a solid wall, and I did not want to push through them so I slowed my steps, but Danny took my arm with one hand and tapped his other hand upon the shoulder of a man on the outer rim of the crowd. The man turned, pivoting the upper portion of his body—a middle-aged man, his dark beard streaked with gray, his thick brows edging into a frown of annoyance—and I saw his eyes go wide. He bowed slightly and pushed back, and a whisper went through the crowd like a wind, and it parted, and Danny and I walked through, Danny holding me by the arm and nodding his head at the greetings in Yiddish that came in quiet murmurs from the people he passed. It was as if a black-waved, frozen sea had been sliced by a scythe, forming black, solid walls along a jelled path. I saw black-and gray-bearded heads bow toward Danny and dark brows arch sharply over eyes that stared questions at me and at the way Danny was holding me by the arm. We were almost halfway through the crowd now, walking slowly together, Danny's fingers on the part of my arm just over the elbow. I felt myself naked and fragile, an intruder, and my eyes, searching for anything but the bearded faces to look at, settled, finally, upon the sidewalk at my feet. Then, because I wanted something other than the murmured greetings in Yiddish to listen to, I began to hear, distinctly, the tapping sounds of Danny's metal-capped shoes against the cement pavement. It seemed a sharp, unnaturally loud sound, and my ears fixed on it, and I could hear it clearly as we went along. I listened to it intently—the soft scrape of the shoe and the sharp tap-tap of the metal caps—as we went up the stone steps of the stairway that led into the brownstone in front of which the crowd stood. The caps tapped against the stone of the steps, then against the stone of the top landing in front of the double door—and

152

I remembered the old man I often saw walking along Lee Avenue, moving carefully through the busy street and tapping, tapping, his metal-capped cane, which served him for the eyes he had lost in a First World War trench during a German gas attack.

The hallway of the brownstone was crowded with black-caftaned men, and there was suddenly a path there, too, and more murmured greetings and questioning eyes, and then Danny and I went through a door that stood open to our right, and we were in the synagogue.

It was a large room and looked to be the exact size of the apartment in which my father and I lived. What was my father's bedroom was here the section of the synagogue that contained the Ark, the Eternal Light, an eight-branched candelabrum, a small podium to the right of the Ark, and a large podium about ten feet in front of the Ark. The two podiums and the Ark were covered with red velvet. What was our kitchen, hallway, bathroom, my bedroom, my father's study and our front room, was here the portion of the synagogue where the worshipers sat. Each seat consisted of a chair set before a stand with a sloping top, the bottom edge of which was braced with a jutting strip of wood to prevent what was on the stand from sliding to the floor. The seats extended back to about twenty feet from the rear wall of the synagogue, the wall opposite the Ark. A small portion of the synagogue near the upper door of the hallway had been curtained off with white cheesecloth. This was the women's section. It contained a few rows of wooden chairs. The remaining section of the synagogue, the section without chairs, was crowded with long tables and benches. Through the middle of the synagogue ran a narrow aisle that ended at the large podium. The walls were painted white. The wooden floor was a dark brown. The three rear windows were curtained in black velvet. The ceiling was white, and naked bulbs hung from it on dark wires, flooding the room with harsh light.

We stood for a moment just inside the door near one of the tables. Men passed constantly in and out of the room. Some remained in the hallway to chat, others took seats. Some of the seats were occupied by men studying Talmud, reading from the Book of Psalms, or talking among themselves in Yiddish. The benches at the tables stood empty, and on the white cloths that covered the tables were paper cups, wooden forks and spoons, and paper plates filled with pickled herring and onion, lettuce, tomatoes, gefülte fish, Shabbat loaves—the braided bread called chalah—tuna fish, salmon, and hard-boiled eggs. At the edge of the table near the window was a brown leather chair. On the table in front of the chair was a pitcher, a towel, a saucer, and a large plate covered with a Shabbat cloth—a white satin cloth, with the Hebrew word for the Shabbat embroidered upon it in gold. A long serrated silver knife lay alongside the plate.

A tall, heavyset boy came in the door, nodded at Danny, then noticed me, and stared. I recognized him immediately as Dov Shlomowitz, the player on Danny's team who had run into me at second base and knocked me down. He seemed about to say something to Danny, then changed his mind, turned stiffly, went up the narrow aisle, and found a seat. Sitting in the seat, he glanced at us once over his shoulder, then opened a book on his stand, and began to sway back and forth. I looked at Danny and managed what must have been a sick smile. "I feel like a cowboy surrounded by Indians," I told him in a whisper.

Danny grinned at me reassuringly and let go of my arm. "You're in the holy halls," he said. "It takes getting used to."

"That was like the parting of the Red Sea out there," I said. "How did you do it?"

"I'm my father's son, remember? I'm the inheritor of the dynasty. Number one on our catechism: Treat the son as you would the father, because one day the son will be the father."

"You sound like a Mitnaged," I told him, managing another weak smile.

"No, I don't," he said. "I sound like someone who reads too much. Come on. We sit up front. My father will be down soon."

"You live in this house?"

"We have the upper two floors. It's a fine arrangement. Come on. They're beginning to come in."

The crowd in the hallway and in front of the building had begun coming through the door. Danny and I went up the aisle. He led me to the front row of seats that stood at the right of the large podium and just behind the small podium. Danny sat down in the second seat and I sat in the third. I assumed that the first seat was for his father.

The crowd came in quickly, and the synagogue was soon filled with the sounds of shuffling shoes, scraping chairs, and loud voices talking Yiddish. I heard no English, only Yiddish. Sitting in the chair, I glanced over at Dov Shlomowitz, and found him staring at me, his heavy face wearing an expression of surprise and hostility, and I suddenly realized that Danny was probably going to have as much trouble with his friends over our friendship as I would have with mine. Maybe less, I thought. I'm not the son of a tzaddik. No one steps aside for me in a crowd. Dov Shlomowitz looked away but I saw others in the crowded synagogue staring at me too, and I looked down at the worn prayer book on my stand, feeling exposed and naked again, and very alone.

Two gray-bearded old men came over to Danny, and he got respectfully to his feet. They had had an argument over a passage of Talmud, they told him, each of them interpreting it in a different way, and they wondered who had been correct. They mentioned the passage, and Danny nodded, immediately identified the tractate and the page, then coldly and mechanically repeated the passage word for word, giving his interpretation of it, and quoting at the same time the interpretations of a number of medieval commentators like the Me'iri, the Rashba, and the Maharsha. The passage was a difficult one, he said, gesticulating with his hands as he spoke, the thumb of his right hand describing wide circles as he emphasized certain key points of interpretation, and both men had been correct; one had unknowingly adopted the interpretation of the Me'iri, the other of the Rashba. The men smiled and went away satisfied. Danny sat down.

"That's a tough passage," he said. "I can't make head or tail out of it. Your father would probably say the text was all wrong." He was talking quietly and grinning broadly. "I read some of your father's articles. Sneaked them off my father's desk. The one on that passage in *Kiddushin* about the business with the king is very good. It's full of real apikorsische stuff."

I nodded, and tried another smile. My father had read that article to me before he had sent it off to his publisher. He had begun reading his articles to me during the past year, and spent a lot of time explaining them.

The noise in the synagogue had become very loud, almost a din, and the room seemed to throb and swell with the scraping chairs and the talking men. Some children were running up and down the aisle, laughing and shouting, and a number of younger men lounged near the door, talking loudly and gesticulating with their hands. I had the feeling for a moment I was in the carnival I had seen recently in a movie, with its pushing, shoving, noisy throng, and its shouting, arm-waving vendors and pitchmen.

I sat quietly, staring down at the prayer book on my stand. I opened the book and turned to the Afternoon Service. Its pages were yellow and old, with ragged edges and worn corners. I sat there, staring at the first psalm of the service and thinking of the almost new prayer book I had held in my hands that morning. I felt Danny nudge me with his elbow, and I looked up.

"My father's coming," he said. His voice was quiet and, I thought, a little strained.

The noise inside the synagogue ceased so abruptly that I felt its absence as one would a sudden lack of air. It stopped in swift waves, beginning at the rear of the synagogue and ending at the chairs near the podium. I heard no signal and no call for silence; it simply stopped, cut off, as if a door had slammed shut on a playroom filled with children. The silence that followed had a strange quality to it: expectation, eagerness, love, awe.

A man was coming slowly up the narrow aisle, followed by a child. He was a tall man, and he wore a black satin caftan and a fur-trimmed black hat. As he passed each row of seats, men rose, bowed slightly, and sat again. Some leaned over to touch him. He nodded his head at the murmur of greetings directed to him from the seats, and his long black beard moved back and forth against his chest, and his earlocks swayed. He walked slowly, his hands clasped behind his back, and as he came closer to me I could see that the part of his face not hidden by the beard looked cut from stone, the nose sharp and pointed, the cheekbones ridged, the lips full, the brow like marble etched with lines, the sockets deep, the eyebrows thick with black hair and separated by a single wedge like a furrow plowed into a naked field, the eyes dark, with pinpoints of white light playing in them as they do in black stones in the sun. Danny's face mirrored his exactly—except for the hair and the color of the eyes. The child who followed him, holding on to the caftan with his right hand, was a delicate miniature of the man, with the same caftan, the same fur-trimmed hat, the same face, the same color hair, though beardless, and I realized he was Danny's brother. I glanced at Danny and saw him staring down at his stand, his face without expression. I saw the eyes of the congregants follow the man as he came slowly up the aisle, his hands clasped behind his back, his head nodding, and then I saw them on Danny and me as he came up to us. Danny rose quickly to his feet, and I followed, and we stood there, waiting, as the man's dark eyes moved across my face—I could feel them moving across my face like a hand—and fixed upon my left eye. I had a sudden vision of my father's gentle eyes behind their steel-rimmed spectacles, but it vanished swiftly, because Danny was introducing me to Reb Saunders.

"This is Reuven Malter," he said quietly in Yiddish.

Reb Saunders continued to stare at my left eye. I felt naked under his gaze, and he must have sensed my discomfort, because quite suddenly he offered me his hand. I raised my hand to take it, then realized, as my hand was going up, that he was not offering me his hand but his fingers, and I held them for a moment—they were dry and limp—then let my hand drop.

"You are the son of David Malter?" Reb Saunders asked me in Yiddish. His voice was deep and nasal, like Danny's, and the words came out almost like an accusation.

I nodded my head. I had a moment of panic, trying to decide whether to answer him in Yiddish or English. I wondered if he knew English. My Yiddish was very poor. I decided to answer in English.

"Your eye," Reb Saunders said in Yiddish. "It is healed?"

"It's fine," I said in English. My voice came out a little hoarse, and I swallowed. I glanced at the congregants. They were staring at us intently, in complete silence.

Reb Saunders looked at me for a moment, and I saw the dark eyes blink, the lids going up and down like shades. When he spoke again it was still in Yiddish.

"The doctor, the professor who operated, he said your eye is healed?"

"He wants to see me again in a few days. But he said the eye is fine."

I saw his head nod slightly and the beard go up and down against his chest. The lights from the naked bulb on the ceiling gleamed off his satin caftan.

"Tell me, you know mathematics? My son tells me you are very good in mathematics."

I nodded.

"So. We will see. And you know Hebrew. A son of David Malter surely knows Hebrew."

I nodded again.

"We will see," Reb Saunders said.

I glanced out of the sides of my eyes and saw Danny looking down at the floor, his face expressionless. The child stood a little behind Reb Saunders and stared up at us, his mouth open.

"*Nu*," Reb Saunders said, "later we will talk more. I want to know my son's friend. Especially the son of David Malter." Then he went past us and stood in front of the little podium, his back to the congregation, the little boy still holding on to his caftan.

from

ROOMMATES:

MY GRANDFATHER'S STORY

MAX APPLE

Roommates *is the extraordinary story of Max Apple and his grand-father, Herman "Rocky" Goodstein and their lifelong connection. From the time he is seven and moves into Rocky's room, Max Apple is guided by this incredible man, who teaches him always to be strong.*

In this excerpt, Rocky gets his grandson a job at the Rexall drug-store so he can learn to be a professional man. "You'll never have to work nights," Rocky says. Working at the Rexall, Max learns about Einstein and science, 3-D comic books, and the power of penicillin. But most important, he comes to understand generational differences and how to benefit from them.

Max Apple grew up in Michigan. His books include The Oranging of America and Other Stories, Zip, Free Agents, *and* The Propheteers. *He teaches writing at Rice University in Houston.*

When I was twelve Rocky gave up on my intellect. My approaching bar mitzvah made him face reality. I would become a man, but not a rabbi.

Tenderly, he gave me the news that was not news to me. "Not everyone can do it," he said. "In Europe you would have had a chance."

"In Europe," I reminded him, "I would have been dead."

He had an alternate plan. He believed in apprenticeships. "You can be a professional man," he said. "You'll never have to work nights."

He walked with me to the Rexall drugstore a block from our house. I waited at the soda fountain while Rocky talked to the pharmacist, a man I knew only as Doc. Doc had two gold teeth like fangs when he opened his mouth wide, warning us not to read the comic books.

A tall man on level ground, Doc was a giant when he stood in the elevated pharmacist's booth and looked out at his goods, his eyes more observant than today's electronic cameras.

He stepped down from his perch—he and Rocky walked toward me. I sat on a round stool, staring straight at a tube of Unguentine, trying to look as professional as I could.

"Your grandpa tells me," Doc said, "that you want to be a druggist."

Rocky had coached me in advance. I had a line. "If he asks you something," Rocky had said, "just say, 'I'm ready to work.' That's all."

I nodded.

"Can I trust you around the comic books?"

"I'm ready to work," I said.

"A lot of sick people come in here, you know that," Doc said. "You'll be exposed."

"I'm ready to work."

"You may be ready," he said, "but you're too young. It's against the law."

"Sonofabeetches," Rocky said. "The unions are ruining him, too. Give the boy a chance, Doc. I want him to be something."

"I told you, Rocky, I can't hire him, but . . . maybe . . ." He stared at me.

"I'm ready to work," I said.

"You can hang around," Doc said. "You can learn the ropes."

He walked behind the soda fountain to the stainless-steel surface where the soda flavorings and the milk shake machines were. He handed me a damp red rag.

I held it in two hands as if it were a money belt.

While I wiped the sticky surface of the soda fountain, Doc went back to his druggist's perch and Rocky, accepting my failure and my limitations, walked to the American Bakery satisfied that he had done what had to be done. I would be a professional man.

At the Rexall store I also swept the floor, straightened the shelves, and stayed alert for learning the secrets of the druggist's trade.

"If you're a good worker," Rocky had told me, "he'll take you in the back and show you how he makes the medicines. Once you know that, you'll understand science."

I waited, but science eluded me. Doc didn't fill that many prescriptions. Most of the time he worked crossword puzzles from some of the magazines on the rack. After tearing out the puzzle pages he'd put the magazine back for sale.

"Nobody'll miss it," he said. Though I was careful not to risk my job by reading the comic books, Doc didn't seem to mind if I read the newspaper or the magazines. Since I was about to become a scientist myself, I began to notice how often Albert Einstein appeared in the news. I read everything I could about him in *Life* and *Look* and *Collier's* and the *Grand Rapids Press* and reading about the great physicist whetted my appetite to understand prescriptions.

One day I finally asked Doc when he was going to show me the compounds.

"Okay," he said. "You wanna know medicine—I'm gonna show you."

He told Jerry, the fountain worker, to watch the entire store. He led me, not just behind the counter, but into the back room, where there were boxes full of cigarettes and candy and toothpaste and Vaseline alongside the glass bottles of medicine.

"There's two big things wrong with the world," Doc said. "One is war, the other is the clap."

He opened a bottle and put a blue-and-orange capsule into my hand. "Look at that," he said. "Know what you're holding?"

I didn't know. "Penicillin," Doc said.

He took the capsule out of my hand and dropped it back in the bottle. "I've seen you reading about Einstein in *Life*."

I nodded.

"It's all baloney. I mean, he might have invented the atomic bomb all right, but it wasn't the bomb that saved us—it was penicillin.

"The Germans had a plot to give everybody the clap. You're too young—I'm not gonna tell you how, but once they knew we had penicillin they called it off. So what do you think is more important, the bomb or penicillin?"

"Penicillin," I said.

"Don't forget it," Doc said.

I tried not to, but all the magazines had pictures of the flash of light and the mushroom cloud. Doc's blue-and-orange capsules couldn't compete with all that power.

When I read that Einstein didn't believe in God and never went to synagogue, it strengthened my own resolve. I became absolutely certain, in spite of Doc, that I liked Einstein even more than penicillin. The great scientist gave me confidence. One Saturday when Rocky was hurrying me to get ready for synagogue, I dropped my own atom bomb. I refused to go.

He left without me, and that afternoon we had it out. With Einstein in my corner I denounced religion.

Rocky called me an *apikoros*, the Hebrew version of the Greek *epicurean*, and he stopped talking to me. He didn't wake me, he didn't take me to the bakery with him, he didn't bring pastries home. When I came into the living room to watch baseball or wrestling with him, he left.

The rest of the family wisely stayed out of it. It complicated matters that at this time I was actively preparing for my bar mitzvah. Whatever I believed, I certainly intended to go through with that. I wanted the presents.

"Call off the bar mitzvah," he said. "An *apikoros* doesn't need a bar mitzvah."

I refused, and my family backed me up.

"Go ahead," Rocky said, "have a bar mitzvah, but I won't be there."

We went down to the wire. My parents, the rabbi, nobody could convince either of us to give in. I said it was science versus faith, a phrase I read in *Life* magazine. More likely I was getting even for all the years of stale tutoring. Ten days before I became a man, the drugstore got its first shipment of 3-D comic books. There had been rumors that they were coming for months, and other than the bar mitzvah nothing excited me more. Sharkey, who distributed magazines and tobacco, whetted my appetite. He had seen one. "Superman looks like he's flying off the page to punish you," he said. "You've never seen anything like it."

There were already 3-D movies. I had seen ads for *Bwana Devil*, but it was downtown at the Majestic and too expensive. I had to wait until it came to the Town on Bridge Street as part of a triple feature.

In the weeks of my apprenticeship at the Rexall store, I had never, while on duty, opened a comic book. The day the 3-Ds arrived, I couldn't resist. I bought one for a dollar, ten times the price of a regular comic. There were five 3-D titles, but Mighty Mouse did me in. I wanted to see the red line that signified his speed in three dimensions.

When Doc caught me, I had opened the cellophane packet that contained the red-and-blue three-dimensional glasses and I was sitting on a pile of *Police Gazette* issues, holding the comic at an angle to feel the full force of Mighty Mouse coming off the page.

Doc yanked the comic out of my hands. I held on so tightly that one of the pages ripped in half. He pulled the glasses off my face.

"Get out," he said. "You know the rules."

I ran home and went to my bedroom before I started to cry. When Rocky came in I was really sobbing. He still wasn't talking to me. He left the room, but in a minute he came back. He sat down beside me.

"What happened?" he asked.

"Doc kicked me out," I said. "I'll never be a druggist." I told him why.

Later, Jerry, who worked at the fountain, told me what happened. Rocky walked to the back, into the employees only area, where Doc was mixing a prescription.

"He went at Doc with his fists," Jerry said. "It was the funniest thing I ever saw. The old guy wanted to fight. Doc didn't want to hit him, so he just kept running around the Hallmark card display and finally he yelled for me to watch the store and he ran out the door."

I was still crying when Rocky came home.

"It was his fault," Rocky said. "The druggist put Einstein into your head. I'm glad you won't be a druggist."

He rubbed my back until I stopped crying.

At my bar mitzvah he sat in the first row and motioned for me to sing louder. He corrected my four mistakes in the Hebrew reading. I gave my speech in Yiddish, a language that only my family and a few of the old people understood. I spoke about what was on my mind, the atomic bomb. I compared it to the Flood in Noah's time and reminded my audience that nobody promised rainbows after bombs.

After the bar mitzvah, I didn't flaunt Einstein and Rocky was equally discreet about God. For prescriptions we went to the Cut-Rate store on Leonard Street.

"Battles and Celebrations"

from

Bronx Primitive

KATE SIMON

Kate Simon's remembrances of her childhood on New York's Lower East Side are perhaps the quintessential Jewish immigrant story: eastern European Jews making their way in the New World. Simon provides a glimpse into the lives of a family of nonobservant Jews, and interestingly, also into the lives of immigrant Italians of the time. Though her mother abruptly announces that she no longer believes in Judaism, the holiday rituals in Simon's home continued.

Just as the First World War was ending, four-year-old Kaila left Warsaw with her mother and baby brother and traveled across the ocean to America to join her father. At Ellis Island, Kaila became Caroline (later nicknamed Kate by her mother), and in the neighborhood around 178th Street and Lafontaine Avenue in the Bronx, she became thoroughly American.

Her father was a skilled cobbler who created sample shoes that were taken to Fifth Avenue stores. Her mother stayed home with the children, although she was a talented seamstress and took in sewing jobs.

Kate Simon is a travel writer and lives in New York. Her books are regarded as classics and have been used as sociology texts at universities. Bronx Primitive: Portraits in a Childhood *was nominated for a National Book Critics Circle Award.*

In the fall, shapes became brisk, as sharp as the folds on new book covers. The hat factory smoke gathered itself together like long horses to ride the wind. The pale, weak forearms of our summer fathers disappeared under stiff dark cloth. Buildings began again to look like precise cutouts. The leaves fell from my tree and dried and turned in the gutter, making sounds like funeral veils. The jingling wagon of the ices man and its colored bottles disappeared. The icebox iceman put on his wool beanie with the pompom. Mrs. Katz closed the front window of her candy store and one could no longer buy from the sidewalk or hang out there as if one were going to buy, any minute. The gardeners in Crotona Park pulled out the red spikey flowers and gave them to us in big bunches. The *goyish* butchers hung the gray stretched-out bodies of hares in their windows. The kosher butchers heaped mounds of chicken fat to be rendered for use in Rosh Hashanah meals that celebrated the Hebrew New Year. Warm-skinned fruits gave way to cool apples and round purple Concord grapes appeared in slatted baskets in every greenstore, and Jews and Italians on the block began to make wine. In a corner of every kitchen was a purple mess to which sugar was added and, I think, alcohol; it was watched and fed, attended to as if each family had a new baby. And, like a monstrous new baby, the wine stank up the street; it was a fleshy acrid smell, dark and dusty, and the end product that we sipped never seemed worth the trouble, the worried care. (Was I jealous of a small vat of spoiled grapes? Quite possibly. At times there seemed to be no limit to the greed for feeling jealous.)

Among the fall fashions that swept in on us from inventive Arthur Avenue, like making rings of dried peach pits, decorating the backs of our hands with cockamamies, soaking bubble gum in a glass of water overnight—as Joey's father did his false teeth—to make it hard and resistantly chewy the next morning, was that of embroidering, part of a *Little Women* phase, a time of maidenly dignity and refinement. We girls had small embroidery hoops, a few hanks of colored thread, and a stamped bit of cloth to work on. In for the sociability rather than the craft, a number of us settled for fast cross-stitching. When confronted with a leaf or flower, some would make a loop, catch it with a stitch at the end, and there it was, a petal. Those of us who, like myself, came from houses of dexterous, admired hands filled in the leaves and petals laboriously and with satisfaction as the spaces became shape and color, the cloth stippled with French knots and its edges tastefully tassled.

Ranged at the sides of the stoop stairs, six or eight of us sat like Old Country village women tatting or knitting in gossiping twilights. We let the gossiping go and sang and sang even when the light was too dim for sewing, outsinging the calls of our parents. We sang loudly at first, each voice outstriding the other. Shortly, an esthetic emerged; sad parts were sung heartbreakingly softly, jolly parts were sung jauntily but never coarsely shouted. We became divas, operatic actresses like Geraldine Farrar and Rosa Raisa, capable of melting the cement sidewalk with "Because I love you, I've tried so hard but can't forget," with "Not for just an hour, not for just a day, not for just a year, But Always." We were seductive minxes, spit-curled soubrettes in "Does your mother know you're out, Cecilia? Does she know that I'm about to steal ya," a felicity of rhyme matched only by Henry Wadsworth Longfellow. We were quivering, freezing, starving old ladies when we whimpered "Over the hill, over the hill" on our way to the poorhouse. One of our most satisfying songs was a ballad that had wandered with pioneers and immigrants to settle, with small local variations, into many cities (one version, more recently heard as sung by Westchester girls, placed the action in Tarrytown; another *mise en scène* was Buffalo). Our version, sung with dreamy rue and gentle defiance, ran, as ballads do, to length. The truncated matter left by memory holds the bare bones of the story:

> *In Jersey City where I did dwell*
> *A butcher's boy I loved so well.*
> *He stole my heart away from me*
> *And sat another on his knee.*
>
> *He sat another on his knee*
> *Because she had more gold than me.*
> *Her gold will fade, her silver fly*
> *And then she'll be as poor as I.*

We were, of course, repeating the joy of singing in the school auditorium and, more remotely, repeating traditions of which we had no conscious awareness, echoing the group singing on the evening streets of villages in Russia, in Poland, in Hungary, in Italy, to which we were still intimately linked.

The fights of autumn in Apartment 5B, 2029 Lafontaine, started with pencil boxes and rulers and went on to clothing for the New Year holidays. My brother didn't care; a new pair of pants meant staying clean and untorn, no marble shooting on his knees, no stickball and sliding to home base, a manhole cover in the middle of the horse-shit street. He would just as soon not, but he got them and suffered mildly. My growth was more erratic than his, all finished by the time I was eleven, a leaps-and-bounds development that left me bewildered and with clothing that never fit. To allow for lengthenings and broadening like Alice in Wonderland, a new coat was bought two sizes too large, the sleeves covering my hands to the fingernails, the skirt almost to my ankles, and as poisonous as the cloak Medea sent her doomed rival Creusa. By the next year's holidays, the coat was tight across my back, the sleeves bared my wrists, the skirt was high above my knees, and the whole confection was as hideous as it had been the year before. I wore the coat when it was long, I wore it when it was short; I had no choice. But my mother and father had some sharp words on "humiliating" a growing girl, and what the devil did she mean by "humiliating"; wasn't the coat new or like new? Anyhow, she had no business indulging my "*pianovi chasto*" sensibilities. There were millions of children all over the world who didn't have a rag for their behinds, who were freezing in the streets of Russia or working, at my age, in the coal mines of Pennsylvania. They were off! And I took my misery to the fire escape, hoping I would catch double pneumonia in the wind and became as pale and thin as Bessie Love and almost die in a clean white hospital, my life saved by Wallace Reid, who told my father, straight out, not to be such a stingy louse and made him promise to reform. Otherwise, he, Wallace Reid, would go to the police and arrange to adopt me.

After the "Ohlly Nohly" sung by our black neighbors on Ninety-eighth Street came other religious experiences on Lafontaine, one on a Friday evening in November. The cookies baked that afternoon were in a covered dish on a high kitchen shelf beyond a child's reach, the kitchen smelled of gefilte fish and the rest of the house of lemon oil furniture polish, forever the smell of cleanliness. The wooden floors were slick and shining; there were freshly washed and starched curtains on the dining-living room windows. My mother had put two candlesticks on the big round dining table, lit them, and placed a white cloth on her head. She began to talk at them in the same singsong that Uncle David murmured when he bound his arm with black leather strips and swayed back and forth. It was talking to God, we had been told, and women did it only on Friday night, the only time God had for women. In the middle of a phrase my mother took off her headcloth, blew out the candles, and, turning to my astonished father, said—in Polish, which we still spoke sometimes—"No more. I never believed it, I don't now. And I don't have to do it to please my mother, or anyone, here." She never lit candles again, although Friday night kept its usual smells, shines, and crispness appropriate to the Eve of Wonderful Saturday the day of the movies, and later reenactment of our favorite bits, the girls snaking like vamps, the boys leaping up and down the stairs, thrusting and jabbing the air with sticks like the swords of Douglas Fairbanks.

Nor did our mother ever go to the synagogue on Arthur Avenue, except once or twice to hear my brother sing in the choir when she dragged me to join the women's section where the grandmothers held lemonlike fruits to their noses, meant to revive them should the Yom Kippur fast cause them faintness. It was insufferable to know that he earned two dollars for Passover and two dollars for the ten days of Rosh Hashanah–Yom Kippur.

I could sing as true and loudly as he and could learn to make the Hebrew sounds as quickly, but they didn't—*ever*—take girls. It would be gratifying to suggest feminist passion in the resentment, but it dealt only with the stinker amassing two dollars and two dollars more, a fair advance toward a two-wheeler bike, while I earned nothing. Arithmetic, an abomination too, helped feed the angry fires: you could go to the movies twenty times for two dollars, or buy forty big five-cent ice-cream cones. I could be distracted now and then from my brother's pile of gold on Yom Kippur. I liked Yom Kippur; there was something extreme, outrageous, about it, especially when the old men got angry with God. Passover was fun, seders with funny things on the table: baked bones, baked egg, a bitter mash, a sweet mash whose significance we were told and forgot in sipping wine and hunting for the hidden matzo. After we all sang "*Chad Gad Yoh*," something about a little goat in one of those songs that got bigger and bigger (like "Old MacDonald Had a Farm"), we were dumped on a pile of coats in the bedroom to lie in a nest, like birds, to sleep on warm clouds like Wynken, Blynken, and Nod. Passover meant *bubeluch*, plump matzo meal pancakes covered with sugar, and it meant, on rainy days when we took lunch to school, matzo smeared with chicken fat or, best of all, a cold scrambled egg between two slabs of buttered matzo. And then there was the great classic, *matzo brei*, pieces of matzo soaked in milk, squeezed into a delectable mess, and fried to golden curls and flakes—one of the dishes that evokes piercing darts of nostalgia in every Jewish breast and stories of childhood Passovers complete with lightly drunken uncles.

But with all its pleasures, Passover was only nice. Yom Kippur was weird, monumental. Imagine not eating for a whole day to prove something or other to God, or yelling at God in the synagogue as the bearded old men did in their white shawls, their heads thrown back, their Adam's apples tearing at their skinny throats. They made animal noises as their bodies whipped back and forth almost to the ground, their open mouths jerking their beards as they sang wildly of atonement and complaint. With a towel over my head, I practiced the urgent bending back and forth and making Hebrew sounds, but didn't get any feeling into it, or out of it, and no understanding. When I turned down oatmeal one Yom Kippur morning, announcing I was going to fast, my father said that in that case I shouldn't have had barley soup and boiled beef last night, the time to have started fasting. Anyhow, it doesn't count until you're thirteen and a boy, and anyhow, don't be crazy. Eat.

There was a certain enjoyable distinction and shame in being among the few Jews on the block who used the same utensil for both butter and meat dishes, blithely denying the Bible's injunction, as my father explained it, not to seethe lambs in the milk of their mothers. Why? He didn't know exactly. We never saw the forbidden shrimp and lobster; too expensive for anyone we knew, they presented no problem. Ham and pork were surrounded by trembling auras: the absolutely forbidden, made more repulsive by slabs of white lard like dead flesh and the smooth pink piglets like skinned babies grinning from the windows of butcher shops. Neither of my parents ate pork or bacon—my mother tried once when she was frying bacon for my sick sister and couldn't force the first bite into her mouth—simply because their upbringing and the millennia of ancestors, including Moses and the Prophets, thundered against the violation and paralyzed their mouths and throats.

Pretty, springy Miss Torrence asked me to buy a sandwich for her one rainy day; it was to be ham and cheese with lettuce and mayonnaise on white bread. I carried it back to school from the German delicatessen on 180th Street as if it were an explosive thing, away from my body, the bag held only by my thumb and forefinger, proud to have been given such a distinguished commission by one of the goddesses, heroic because I was risking God's displeasure. Carrying ham, its abominableness enhanced by being stuck to cheese, a milk dish, the forbidden esoterica folded together on elegant, neatly cut Tip-Top white bread, infinitely high-class compared to our thick slabs of rye or cornbread, made buying and delivering the sandwich just frightening enough, just forbidden enough, just confusing enough to be a glorious adventure.

While the fall and the Jewish New Year belonged to us, the winter belonged to the *goyim* and Christ, their closest relative, now only remotely ours because we had treated him so badly; stuck him on a pole with nails and cut open his side and made him drink vinegar. The customary American symbols of Christmas—the elaborately wrapped toys brought by Santa Claus and laid under a glittering tree, the green wreaths and red ribbons—were absent from the Italian houses. Instead of Christmas trees, the De Santises, the Silvestris, the Bianchis arranged little country scenes of farm animals and shepherds with crooks all looking up in admiration at the pretty blond lady with the new baby in her lap. The Bianchis also had beautiful little angels with long fingers like Good Fairies. They came all the way from Naples, Carla told me, brought by her silent grandmother, thin, austere, always dressed in black. No one, not even Carla, was allowed to touch them. The only house festivities, Maria Silvestri told me, was a lot of eating of fish on Christmas Eve and card playing and wine drinking when the men grabbed and pinched the women. Early in the morning, the women and the old men went to church to greet the newborn Christ, leaving the men and children who had come up from Mulberry Street sleeping all over the house, three and four in a bed.

Feeling a bit like a traitor and preening in my knowledge of a wider world, a witness to mysteries unknown to the other Jewish kids, I luxuriated in descriptions of what I had seen and been told of the Italian festivities. Given warm welcome in Italian houses mainly because my mother was available at all hours for emergency help and advice, my closest friends were Italian. I liked the shouting and laughter, the plants in backyards, the bossy, powerful grandparents, and the thrilling disrespect with which Italian mothers gave their kids wine with their lunchtime spaghetti so that they spent the afternoon school sessions sleeping, heads cushioned by arms folded on scratched wooden desks; fauns, children of Bacchus sleeping off Dionysian revels, my favorite anarchists.

Resenting my intimacy with Marias, Carlas, and Caterinas, the Ruthies, the Rosies, the Hannahs nibbled poisonously at me and my *krist* friends. They had additional ammunition in the obvious fact that our house was not kosher; my mother even gave our baby bacon, pig meat, *pheh*! How could I eat an Italian apple that lay in the icebox with pork? How could I play with dopes who thought the same baby was born year after year, maybe for as much as a hundred years, and decided he was God? And weren't they drunks (quoting the axiom that all Gentiles were drunkards, one of the feeble ripostes to anti-Semitism), sending their kids to school reeling, full of wine? What kind of Jew was I, anyhow? I didn't know. So I stopped displaying my ethnological enlightenments and compartmentalized my life, on one side of the street sort of Jewish, on the other, sort of Italian, yet always trying to arrange a comfortable melding: Italians were really sort of Jewish, anyhow.

Besides the holiday, the tinsel like silver rain, in the five-and-ten, and the fat Santa Claus that bent and blinked like a moron from the window of the music store on Tremont Avenue, winter meant a constant struggle over warm underwear. My tall green-eyed goddess, Miriam Silverberg, the niece of the people next door, and rich enough to wear braces on her teeth, wore high knee socks all winter and no long underwear. When I pointed this out to my mother, she countered with Miriam's age, fourteen, and my miserably few years. Also, she wasn't Miriam's mother, nor was Miriam's mine, and I had to do what the mother with whom God had afflicted me said, and no more arguments. Tomorrow morning I was to put on long underwear, down to my ankles, and long stockings, pulled all the way up, attached to metal garters that hung from a cotton vest. For years, until I was old and strong enough to refuse to go to school so grotesquely dressed, I went through a stubborn ritual: out of the house in the morning, and into the cellar behind the furnace where I pulled down my stockings to become fat sausages twisted and rolled below my knees. Up went the underwear to make even fatter sausages about my thighs. Just before I got to school and snoopy teachers, as bad as mothers, the elaborate process was reversed. School out for lunch, down the stockings and up the underwear; around the corner from the house, down the underwear and up the stockings, and so on through eight changes each school day. Four fat rolls on baby-fat legs made awkward walking but I felt splendidly fashionable as the winds and winter rains froze my knees, and triumphant. *She* thought she had won, while, really, I had, my first experience of silent battles and silent victories.

I liked her much better late winter afternoons when we went to the butcher together and she smiled her small aristocratic Warsaw smile when the butchers made their coarse jokes aimed mainly at the country *yupkes* who came in bright-eyed and smirking. The men in broad, bloody aprons looked like giants, one with the bushy eyebrows of the huge cop in Charlie Chaplin films. The store was warm with light, with the glisten of entrails, of fat, of the big shining meat grinder and big hooks hung with livers and hearts that seemed still to be quivering, like live flesh, like the big bloody hands that cut and pulled and ripped carcasses apart. The warm, fatty air was full of the butchers' ringing voices: "Come, my beauties of Israel, my Esthers, my Shebas, take what I've got—and have I got!" "You want breast? Me, too, I want breast, *tsotskele* [cutie]." While he sawed up marrow bones (a delicacy, incidentally, that belonged to our father exclusively) or ground beef that came out like red worms, one of the men would tell the story of a butcher who suspected a woman of stealing a chicken and stuffing it into her blouse. The butcher quickly reached in to encounter an innocent featherless breast, and being a witty fellow, like all butchers, asked calmly, "Already plucked?" The men roared, the women tittered.

Never quite sure of how much Yiddish we understood but suspecting it was enough for dirty jokes (the reason our parents began to tell their jokes in Polish, which we children had mostly forgotten), my mother sent me out of the store to wait in the street as the spirits grew high and salacious. I didn't mind too much, if it was snowing. The street lamps were rippled like ballerinas' skirts and it was lovely to see the snowflakes come out of the dark sky, brighten along the ripples, glow for a second or two in the full light, float down to darkness and melt, a ballet to music too delicate to hear.

Visits to the butcher shop were only pauses, periods of détente, in the

170

"you'll catch a cold" battles. One constant battle concerned itself with wearing rubbers, which still strangle, as throttled fury strangled me then. I wouldn't wear rubbers because they were ugly, a nuisance to take off and put on, and an impediment to the trials of endurance I was launched on. My father would complain that I was eating up his life by ruining my shoes, my mother would warn that I was inviting pneumonia and would have to go to the hospital where people died, but I had to try to endure the icy slush that seeped into my shoes, gathered in my stockings, and froze my feet blue and painful. As I had to climb the two-story rocks behind the hat factory (and made it a couple of times), egged on and sneered at by the practiced boys who flew ahead of me.

One solution to the rubbers controversy was to tear out of the house without them, clattering down the stairs while my mother called after me to come back, reenacting a Tobie-Fannie Herman scene. My frenzied Tobie flight and my mother's suddenly shrill Fannie-voice always return when weather and reason, fighting passionate unwillingness, force me into a shop to try on overshoes or even sleek waterproof boots. They fit. Yet they strangle, as they did in childhood, and I give them away, self-doomed to dragging ruined shoes and blue feet through icy slush for the rest of my life.

from

FAMILY

HERBERT GOLD

Life in America offered so many choices to Jewish families. Little by little, they were able to do what Jews in other parts of the world could not—become part of a vibrant, multicultural country.

Taken from Herbert Gold's novel Family, *a memoir of five generations of Russian Jews making their way from turn-of-the-century Russia to modern-day Cleveland, Ohio, this excerpt examines the unexpected changes in traditional family roles.*

Born in Cleveland, Gold is the author of more than seventeen novels and numerous stories and essays. He is a former Fulbright, Guggenheim, and Ford Foundation Fellow and has lectured at Harvard, Stanford, Cornell, and the University of California.

In the beginning was the thought, then the preparation, then the urgent anxiety and clatter; finally came the beach. A restful family Sunday meant screaming and hollering to get ready to holler and scream in the park. Sometimes my father actually started to back the Pontiac down the driveway without her while I fixed my eyes on the Indian brave hood sculpture and said, "You won't do it."

"I will, I will, I'm a Stalin when I get mad, I swear I will," he muttered. The worm of anger slithered in his cheek. He was trying to break the cycle of mother's running here and there, in and out, remembering vital items for the picnic baskets, switching off lights, testing the gas. She believed— so he told us—electricity would leak out through the sockets of electric lights. He knew her ways, Sam Gold *knew* her ways. When she went into Cleveland early one morning for a checkup and didn't come back till late at night, she disconnected the electric clock. Why should the hands have to turn uselessly all day like that, and maybe make a fire? Do burglars need the exact time while they're cleaning out the sterling silver?

What could a Stalin do with a wife who feared so much, poverty, bank closings, anti-Semites, electricity, gas, ruin, Father Coughlin, injury to her sons, malnutrition, the police, burglars, Negroes, Italians, Irish, beer-and-pork crazed neighbors, loose animals, bill collectors, the Depression, varicose veins, constipation, coffee nerves, and the empty-eyed men who sat on the Nickel Plate freight cars as the long trains rolled past our block? My father believed that maybe half that list deserved his personal attention, and none of it deserved constant shivering. He had the store to keep in mind, where he sold the freshest fruits on the west side. He had his idea to get out of fresh fruits and into property, which doesn't spoil overnight, as soon as he figured out what to buy it with. He had plans for empire. He didn't need her nightmare worries. What he really hated was to be kept waiting, the motor running, while his wife jiggled a faucet. "Frieda! Come on already!"

"Hold your horses, Sam. Did I pack the napkins? Do you want to eat without napkins?"

"We can use the towels, come on!"

"The *swimming* towels? Filthy! It's Sunday! You want to catch germs on Sunday? Hold your horses!"

"Frieda"—this was his ominous Stalin voice—"we're leaving."

"But I said just a minute hold your horses," and she disappeared for the third time, running through the rear door, the screen slamming. My father backed the Pontiac out, lumping in his rage over the boulder that protected flowers from wheels. She caught us at the street, triumphant with napkins, also an extra Jell-O mold and a bottle of Mercurochrome, and we didn't get away without her.

At first my brother and I were laughing as dad zigzagged down the driveway, but it would ruin not only the day but the week if we got further than the street. She would not have forgiven the insult. Even to straighten the car in the direction of Huntington Park would have caused her to strike back. Fortunately he stopped short and she ran fast enough.

"You wasn't going without me," she stated.

"Seems like not."

She wiped her face with a swimming towel. She was the 1936 Champion of the Fifty-Foot Indoor-Outdoor Driveway Dash. "Then let's don't talk about it."

"I get aggravated when you can't get going, you keep running around the house like a chicken. That's not talking about it."

"Since we're not talking about it, I'll only say you wouldn't want to come home to a burnt-down place—a fireman stands around checking on his papers like those Irishers down the street—you would like that?"

My brother and I immediately imagined the broken bricks, the smoking fallen roof, the neighbors hanging about in secret pleasure, and therefore shouted, "We're hungry! Ice cream! Cheeseburgers!"

"Not before lunch," Mother said. "We're almost there."

We weren't almost there. We drove through Lakewood, past the car barns, through Rocky River, out past Bay Village, along the lake road where farms replaced the suburbs of Cleveland. "I like Jacksonburgers," Sid said.

"Me too. Their secret sauce and their root beer."

But we weren't getting any. We were getting home cooking on our picnic, wholesome and thought-out family food to make a strong mind for a strong body and also it would go bad if it wasn't used right away.

The Pontiac spit gravel around the parking lot. Fishermen arrived early; so did a few show-offs in two-piece bathing outfits and their girlfriends wearing heavy lipstick and tank suits and rubber hair etched into their swimcaps. Already the sun made the cocoa butter run. There was a balletic dance of kids tiptoeing with burns and blisters across the gravel. That year the fashion was not to wear slippers or shoes, if you were young and stalwart and planning to smoke your first butt before the autumn rains; in the meantime, harden the feet by struggling against earth, prickles, gravel, whatever perils the country brought. Some couples limped and necked already—stumbling with arms choking each other and toes getting wrecked by brutal pebbles. I wasn't yet ready for such madness. A tar and ammonia smell arose from the parking lot; then, beyond, green and sand and a dizzying fish whiff of Lake Erie.

"Everybody carries!" mother said—charcoal, baskets, bags, boxes. Dad took charge of the thermos and the bottles of soda. My brother Sid wondered why we couldn't just bring a few sandwiches in a bag, maybe a few bottles of pop; so did I; we were ready to learn real American eating from the real American eaters. We knew better than to express the unthinkable to our mother. *Just a couple sandwiches? You remember when your cousin Bernie almost got the rickets?*

For us, the park was a place to swim, run around, play ball with Sid's birthday hardwood hickory bat, yell and scream. For them it was a location for an outdoor meal, air and flies and sun and all that healthy contact with nature and card-players.

For us, to meet new kids.

For them, to find a game of rummy until an appetite got worked up.

For us, jumping the rolling white waves of Lake Erie.

For them, wading, cooling off, looking at the loose dogs and people, then a not-bad lunch with fruit Jell-O for dessert.

For me, to stare at the horizon—Canada straight ahead over there, the romance of foreign places where they speak Canadian.

For them, not. To look for the card-players. Maybe to unfold the Sunday *Plain Dealer* and kill the appetite reading about Hitler.

For me, to get sore at my father for paying attention only to the game of rummy.

For him, not just to play cards. For my father to win at cards, piling up the matchsticks which would later be exchanged for cash. For my mother to unpack the lunch and warn my father not to lose, to consider everything, his family, the future, this being a dangerous and uncertain world; to remind him also to pay some attention to the kids so they don't grow up wild, gamblers. For my father to remark that he worked hard all week and now he was playing cards and he never lost. It's not gambling if you win. For my mother to point out that he played cards every morning at the farmer's market, while they were loading the truck with produce—how could he prove to her if he won or lost?—and he should do something else, this being Sunday, a holiday for the Americans, of which their children were now examples. For my father to say, "Be quiet, Frieda." For my mother to say, "I'll shut up, that's what you want to tell me, but I deserve a relax, too."

"So relax," dad said. "The boys are holding a hand for me."

For family intimacy to continue amid the biting gnats and filmy mites and heat and languages and frantic dogs and thick August humidity.

Families and clans staked out picnic areas and occasional incursive tables within other areas. Sunday peace ruled; lack of war was the tradition between nationalities at Huntington Park. Italians were making spaghetti, Jews were making salads and slicing meats, some of the Irish were making whoopee. The rich brought ice chests. Puffed checks blew on charcoal to get things started in the WPA grates. Class distinctions made little difference among fire-starters, though there were isolated instances of kerosene. For a while mother, in her black cotton bathing dress with the modest flap of skirt, came down to the beach to watch my brother and me bobbing on the whitecaps of Lake Erie. She wrinkled her nose. "What kind of smell is that? What kind of fish?"

"Inner tube," I said.

She checked invisible Canada out there. She checked the sky for cloud or storm. She had asked a lifeguard and, although he was a goy, believed him—no sharks in Lake Erie. She warned us not to drown or let a dog bite us or pick fights with strangers. "You could catch an affection," she whispered. She waded. She said, "Oooh, ooh, it's so cold, it's nice, it's warm, don't let your lips turn blue."

Her spirit took a relax in the peace of the Christian sabbath. We would keep an eye on each other, she decided, we had friends, we would take care not to walk out toward Canada where the water got deep and there might be sharks after all (how could you prove the *lack* of something? from not being bit by even one?); we had learned to swim, we used the buddy system, we were junior lifesavers. A careful review of all the facts allowed her to go back to fix lunch. Now there was a subject which deeply engaged her. We promised to come up from the beach when the noon whistle blew.

The noon whistle blew. The beach dogs yapped and yipped at the high-pitched sound; one of them extended its throat like a wolf and howled. Regretfully we left the sand spit, my brother and I. We could imagine potato salad and sliced tomatoes and tunafish, also cold pot roast with horse radish and pickles, and for once our mother seemed to have some good ideas. Swimming, jumping waves, and making contact with new close friends and their Goodyear inner tubes were a few of the basic causes of appetite. I promised a wiry Protestant to return to the beach in half an hour. Sid asked a responsible Catholic to guard the sand city they were building together and to keep the animals from running through it, especially that nervous dog over there, which was making shrill squeals and running in circles, chewed by fleas or maybe just overheated. My brother wanted to bet with me—the fruit Jell-O would be melted. "What's melt?" I asked him. "How soft is melt?"

In some ways I took after my father and mother, ever questioning. The parochial school boy, Timmy his name was, only answered questions.

Sid waved to the Catholic and he waved back. The gravity-defying dog was lurching sideways up the hill through the wild asparagus, snapping at tufts of grass and making hurt undog voices, like a person imitating a mongrel. Maybe it had reason to believe it was a person.

We climbed the slats from the beach to the picnic area above. Lake sand gave way to mixed sand and dirt into which trees and shrubs had sunk roots. It was gradual and mysterious, like how children change into people who are allowed to eat whatever they want, grass into asparagus, good nature into other. From the farms nearby, asparagus seeds had blown, and taken hold, and spiky straggles clung to the edges of the shore. These energies of the vegetable world interested my brother and me. The yipping dog interested us both as it ran in little circles, and yet moved through these circles up the slope, making wasteful progress, sending sandspins and avalanche lumps down toward the lake. It didn't seem to have enough good sense to use the slats on which barefoot kids climbed, getting slivers in their toes and soles, toughening up for the end of the summer. The dog whirled upward against gravity, emitting that odd high-pitched gargling squeal.

Our picnic table was piled with goodies. Dressings of raisins—no, sun-kissed flies—picked and chose. The air was filled with mites. My brother's baseball bat lay across the napkins. "Oh-ho, have I got something good for you," mother said, as if we didn't know. "Call your father first. He don't come when I call him."

It was my job, as the elder, to claim him away from the card-players. I didn't like this job, although he only held his grudge until something else came up. Something else always came up. But his scowl was enough to darken the sky. Interruption did not please him. When a loser, he was peeved; a winner, irked; no way for me to come out ahead in this job. I struggled to break even with my father. "Dad," I said, "time for lunch."

"Is your bathing suit wet?"

"Everyone's waiting."

"You can't eat with a wet bathing suit."

"Dad."

"They can wait five minutes. You see I'm busy don't you? I'm finishing the hand."

I hung nearby a moment. One of his friends winked at me. There would be no further communication from the author of my being, not at this moment in the perilous history of rummy. I limped on my bruised toe back to mother. "About a half hour," I said.

The dog which had yelped and followed us, spinning sideways up the slope, suddenly speeded its endeavors. It was howling and snapping at invisible enemies. It was a ginger animal with the face of an alligator—a sharp and blunt alligator's snout—soapy foam at its lipless mouth. My brother looked frightened and pulled closer to me. I pulled closer to him. Mother was thinking out loud, "Sex crimes I thought they commit in parks, that's why we pay our taxes—"

I tried to understand her.

"For the police. But this stuff besides the stuff you wouldn't even know—the dogs also bite persons when they're not even hungry—"

And someone screamed. The dog had nipped a baby on its blanket, raking the flesh and tearing off its bootie. The shriek came from a parent; the child's mouth was open; it had not yet discovered its pain. Something new was detonated in the animal by the taste of pink bootie threads, ropy droplets of blood, and now suddenly it seemed to be biting in all directions as a howling and crying arose from the flutter of Sunday newspapers, the spill of food, the splattering charcoal fires. The dog was snapping the air and what was in the air. The dog was not biting to eat. The dog was simply biting. The dog was mad.

Fur and spit hurled among the picnickers. Bottles and paper cups tumbled. Spaghetti like white worms suddenly crawled in an immense heap on the beaten ground. A loose puddle of thick tomato blood dripped from a bench. A mother screamed without words and a father screamed instructions. From far away, when I looked at my own father, I seemed to catch a puzzled glance at the commotion as he raised a winning card in his slapping slamming gesture. The dog made torture noises, barks, snarls, broadcasts from a central office of destruction. I smelled something like what my father put on his face after shaving. The mad dog was almost a familiar enemy. I wished my Catholic new friend had come up from the beach to see. The dog made abrupt squeals and darts and its eyes were red and blank.

Terror switched everything around. The faces of the kids in the park, suddenly deprived by fear of their childhood, looked like ancient agonized adults. The faces of the grown-ups, helpless with fear, deprived of their maturity, suddenly became thin and skeletal and childlike as they shouted and ran and tried to hide babies behind their bodies. In Europe, dive bombers were aloft, and Hitler came to kill. Here we were lucky, and yet even here on Sunday a mad dog was loose. I stood without moving, the moment printing itself on me, until my mother jerked me around, seizing my arm, and I stumbled; and then as I skidded alongside the path where the dog headed into me, my mother fell forward toward the animal, which seemed up close the size of a wolf, a horse, a gorilla, spewing noise and saliva and clots of mud and perhaps skin from those it had bitten—she fell on it. I could feel its panting heat like a piece of machinery near my neck.

My mother fell on the dog with the bat in her hands, and bounced away from it. As she pulled off I saw that the dog's head had been smashed, a crumple of brains leaking inside, the blood-spotted eyeball hanging by a cord, staring at me; the grinding of half a dog's head continued, a death thrash from somewhere deep in nature; and the bat came up again and again—I didn't see my mother's bat come down—the dog being broken into earth in a shape of fur and teeth and muck.

The screams continued. A haggard circle gathered about the destroyed animal, bloody meat and bones and eyeball hanging by a string of flesh into the distressed brain. The body heaved and twitched as if it still needed to bite. It steamed with some mortal internal cookery. This was also nature. A park policeman in a green twill jacket gave orders: "Stand back, stand back now. This could be dangerous."

Someone began to curse him in Italian.

"All right, you. You're in this country now. Cleveland ain't Naples—we don't use that ilk of language here. I may have to report you to the county officer."

The curses rolled on and the park policeman said, "I'm doing this Sunday crowd handling best I can without any help. Stand back. Stand back, you people."

Mother leaned slack and wet against a tree. The policeman said, "Give this Jewish lady some air, people."

The ambulances rolled and bumped across the green. The children—why was it only children?—who had been bit were strapped onto gurneys. One mother insisted on holding her child; both of them were crying.

My father said, "Frieda, that was *schoen* what you did."

"You wasn't here. You was playing cards."

"I didn't see. You handled it good."

"Mother," I said.

"Easy," she said. "When you got to live with anti-Semites, everything else is easy."

"What does that have to do with it?" I asked.

"My bat is all dirty," my brother said. "I need a new hardwood hickory."

"You'll get it," my father said. "Frieda. Frieda." I think this was the first time I saw him simply put his arms around her. "You want to go home now? Maybe we left the screen door unlocked."

"Wait a minute. No jokes. Tired."

She bent out of his grasp and reached for my shoulder, as if she needed help to lie down. But resting wasn't her business. Mother, this crazed protector, this heavy lady leaning against a tree, slid toward the ground and kneeled, holding my chin in her fingers like a flirtatious woman. She stopped running history through her mind and took my head in her hands. "If I had a girl," she said, "I suppose I wish I did, but I'm not sure she'd be pretty."

Did she want me to argue? To insist I'd be pretty if I were a girl? I wouldn't do that.

She kissed me on the lips. I had never received such a kiss, not that I could remember. "Your father got me, he don't need a girl. And I got you. And we sure had a picnic today."

She did not want me dying in her lifetime; I would have to die in my own. "Can I go say goodbye to a nice Catholic?" I asked. "He's watching our stuff. Can I tell him how I almost got bit?"

"Don't go. Stay here with me."

My father went to huddle behind a tree with his friends. They were settling up, matches for money. He returned smiling. He had won nearly forty dollars. He was sorry to miss the dog, but a man can't be everywhere at once. Fortunately he had a helper, but he was also puzzled. "She can do a thing like that, grab a kid's bat, take care of that hound when all these big strong Eyetalians was only yelling. So why can't she make a picnic without it's got sand in the potato salad?"

She held my chin and drew me closer for inspection. "No," she said. "You'll fight. I don't know if you'll win."

Again she was not answering my father, not listening to me. But she was thinking. I smelled the slaughtered beast in the air, and very soon I took to reading the newspapers to try to find out what such things mean, what my mother meant.

PART III

New Voices: Growing Up as

an American Jew

"WHERE IS IT WRITTEN?"

ADAM SCHWARTZ

Exploring the contrast between the traditional closeness of Jewish family relationships and a dysfunctional single mother and her son, Adam Schwartz ushers in the next wave of American-Jewish writing. The Jewish experience is much more diffused here than in earlier stories and plays a secondary role to the focal point of this story. Instead, this is a study of a family in modern culture—a child of divorced parents trying to find a "normal" life for himself.

    Tired of caring for his neurotic mother, Sam persuades his father to sue for custody three months before his thirteenth birthday. It turns into an ugly battle, one that Sam is not entirely comfortable with, but he was "only thirteen, and . . . didn't know that love can be as obdurate as the changes you long for."

    Adam Schwartz teaches writing at Harvard University. His work has appeared in The New Yorker, *and* Wigwag *and in the book* Writing Our Way Home: Contemporary Stories by American Jewish Writers.

Three months before my thirteenth birthday, I persuaded my father to sue my mother for custody of me. This was in late August, near the end of a two-week visit with my father. I wrote my mother a letter informing her of my decision. I told her I knew she might be disappointed, but I wasn't rejecting her; I only wanted to spend more time with my father, to know and love him as well as I knew her. I also told her not to call me. We could discuss this when I returned home, if she wanted to.

She called the second the letter came. Phyllis, my father's wife, answered the phone. "Hold on, Sandra," she said, and held the phone out to me, her palm covering the receiver. I shook my head. Phyllis gave me an exasperated look, and told my mother I was busy. She called three more times in the next hour. I knew this was going to happen, but I was not even thirteen, and I wanted to forget how well I knew my mother. Phyllis agreed to relay her messages to me: How long should she preheat the oven for my lemon-chicken recipe? Should she run hot or cold water when

183

scrubbing the sink with Comet? What should she do if the washing machine stopped in mid-cycle? I had typed out three pages of instructions before I left, but the calls kept coming right through dinner. Could she use ammonia on Formica surfaces? Should she use tap or distilled water in the iron? Finally, Phyllis exclaimed, "Jesus, Sandra, we're eating. He'll be home in two days." Then I watched her face darken and imagined the blast my mother was delivering: "Don't you tell me when I can talk to my own son. I'm his mother, and when I tell you to get him, you jump—understand?" Phyllis hung up the phone and sat back at the table, her lips drawn across her face like a thin white scar. Ten seconds later the phone rang again. My father and Phyllis looked at each other. I felt like Jonah hiding in the bowels of the ship, knowing the storm above was all his fault. No one moved. "Mommy, the phone is ringing," shouted Debbie, my little stepsister. "Maybe you should answer the phone, Sam," my father said. I stood up from the table very slowly, giving myself every chance that the phone might stop ringing before I reached it.

"What's the problem, Mom? I wrote everything down."

"You little bastard! Don't bother coming home. If I never see you again I'll die happy!"

My father wasn't enthusiastic when I asked him to sue. "Lawyers? Court? Not again." My parents divorced when I was four, and the episode still bothered him. He had wanted to work things out quietly, but my mother staged a grand opera. She asked for an exorbitant amount of alimony and minimal visitation rights for my father. She accused him of being an adulterer and a wife beater. My father was a rabbi in a small town on the New Jersey shore and brought in many members of his congregation as character witnesses. My mother had no witnesses in her behalf. She lost every point she argued for.

"But, Dad," I implored, "she's driving me *crazy!*"

He and I usually didn't have a lot to say to each other, but I expected the word *crazy* to explain everything, as if I were revealing to him that we shared the same inherited trouble, like gum disease or premature balding. I pitched my case to him, describing how she moaned during meals about her haywire menstrual cycle, how she slept on the couch every night, sometimes with a cigarette still burning in her hand.

"Do you know how dangerous that is, Dad?"

He pressed his palms up his cheeks, a gesture that always led me to imagine he was trying to stretch his beard over his eyes and forehead. I envisioned him doing the same thing the day he met my mother. When I had asked her, the year before, how they came together—a far more mysterious question to me than where I had come from—she answered, "In the shower." Both were on an archaeological dig in Israel. My father, recently ordained, was covered with soap in the primitive communal shower when my mother walked in, nineteen, naked, enthusiastic about everything. Several months later they were married, but my mother was bored by the life of a rabbi's wife. She had no interest in charity work or Sisterhood meetings. She saw an analyst five times a week and signed up for courses in Sanskrit and criminology. Once she planned a lecture at the synagogue on Gurdjieff's centers of consciousness. Three people came.

I told my father I was fed up with cooking and cleaning, washing and ironing.

"I thought you liked doing housework," he said.

"Not all the time. I want to have a normal life, Dad."

He touched his beard lightly, thoughtfully. I had found the right word.

"Sometimes her boyfriends sleep over. I see them on the sofa bed when I get up in the morning."

"All right, all right."

"Dad, I'm telling you, this is an open-and-shut case. I'm old enough to live with whoever I want. That's the law."

I knew about the law from my mother. She sued everyone. Landlords, universities, car dealers, plumbers, my father. She stayed up all night researching her cases and planning her strategies. In the morning I would see her asleep on the couch, openmouthed, beneath a blanket of ashes and law books and the sheets of legal paper on which she outlined her complex and futile arguments. Years later, after I graduated from law school and returned to New Jersey, many of the older lawyers around the courthouse told me that my mother indeed had a reputation as a compulsive but extremely knowledgeable and creative litigant. "I always thought the law was a metaphysical exercise for her," one of them said to me. " 'I can sue you: therefore I exist.' "

I also learned the art of exaggeration from my mother, the art of how to invent something when the truth is boring or makes you nervous. I had seen her on the sofa bed with a man only once. The year before, she had come into my bedroom very early one morning to tell me that Sy, her sometime boyfriend, had spent the night. "You don't mind that he's here?" she asked, sitting on the side of my bed. Her weight was comforting, as were her warm, heavy, sleepy odors. I told her I didn't mind. "I slept in the other room," she said anxiously. "But I'm going to lie down next to Sy for a couple of minutes."

"All right," I said, and went back to sleep. I knew she liked Sy. She had told me that he had always wanted a boy to raise, that he was personal friends with Joe Namath, that he had a home in Florida. He bought me books, bats, tickets to ballgames. In two years he would go to jail for fraud and income tax evasion, but that morning my mother and I both believed in him. When I went into the living room, he was asleep on his side. My mother was awake, pressed up against his back with an arm around his chest. She smiled at me, as if Sy were some wonderful secret between us, something valuable she had found.

My mother's explosion of telephone calls came on Thursday night; late Sunday afternoon I took the bus from my father's house to the Port Authority. My mother usually met me inside the terminal, but I didn't see her anywhere. I called home six times in the next hour, counting twenty-three rings on the last attempt. The next local bus across the river didn't leave for two hours. I found a bench at a far end of the terminal and, sitting with my suitcase between my knees, watched everyone going home, everyone except for the panhandlers, the proselytizers, the old men sleeping against walls, teenagers who had run away.

My mother wasn't in when I arrived home. She hadn't left a note, and by ten o'clock I still hadn't heard from her. I knew what she was doing. She was letting me know how it felt to be abandoned, to suddenly be alone. I knew she would return the next day, but still I was in tears by the time I was ready for bed. My room felt like the loneliest place in the world that night, so I pulled out the sofa bed. I had never slept in the living room before, and I couldn't orient myself, couldn't gauge the black space around me.

Gradually the darkness lightened into shadows and the shadows into a dull grayness. When I could see everything in the room clearly, I began preparing for the first day of school. I kept thinking, *Now he's brushing his teeth, now he's deciding which shirt to wear, now he's pouring milk over his cereal . . .* as if, without my mother in the house, I were inhabiting someone else's life. I was all ready by six-thirty. I lay back down on the couch and watched the clock for the next hour and forty-five minutes.

At eleven thirty, during biology, the principal's secretary came to the classroom to tell me my mother had phoned. She told me I was to go right home because of an emergency. The year before, I'd been called out of class about once a month because of an "emergency" at home. Usually my mother had fought with a patient, or a married man she was seeing had stopped answering her calls, or her father had sent her another sanctimonious letter, or some judge had treated her in a cavalier manner.

186

I declined the secretary's offer of a ride and walked home. When I let myself into the apartment, my mother was sitting at the kitchen table. She held the letter I had written to her in one hand and was burning holes in it with her cigarette. She looked like a curious child torturing a small animal.

"I thought you saw a patient now," I finally said.

She was a psychologist, but had only four regular patients. She used her bedroom as an office, though she longed to have one in town. "Someplace beautiful," she would say. "Some place where I can really be myself."

"I canceled," she said, burning a chain of holes through my name.

"Canceled! What for? That's thirty-five dollars!"

She looked at me for the first time. "Would you please explain this, Sam?"

"I explained everything in the letter."

"Everything? Really? I can think of any number of things you didn't explain. Why you're leaving me, for instance. Can you explain that? Am I really that bad of a mother?"

"I told you I wasn't rejecting you."

"Look, Sam. Let's agree on one thing. Let's agree you're not going to treat me like I'm stupid." She said this slowly and rhythmically, as if I were the stupid one.

"Mom, I just don't want to live here anymore. That's all."

"That's all?"

"I explained. I want to live with my father."

"Tell me the last time he called."

"Maybe he doesn't call because he's afraid you'll sue if he says something you don't like over the phone."

"Oh, I see. Now it's my fault. I'm to blame because your father has no interest in you."

"I didn't say that."

"Then what are you saying? That I'm a failure as a mother?"

"No, Mom. You're not a failure. All right?"

"Then why? *Why* are you doing this to me?"

"God, Mom. I don't know! I just want to lead a normal life."

"*Normal!*" she cried. "What's not normal about the way we live?"

"Everything! The cooking, the cleaning, the shouting. Everything!"

"Who shouts?"

"You do. You're shouting now."

"Of course I am. My son tells me he doesn't want to live with me anymore. Can't I shout about that? Isn't that *normal*?"

"Mom, this conversation is retarded. I'm going back to school."

187

"And who asked you to cook and clean?" she shouted after me. "Not me. You love to cook. Or is that something else to blame me for?"

"Goodbye, Mom," I said, walking out the door.

"Don't come back, you lousy child! Just see how well you get along without me!"

Before I began cooking and cleaning, my clothing always came out of the wash shrunk and discolored, sending me into fits most mornings because I was embarrassed to wear wrinkled shirts to school and my mother refused to iron them.

"You iron them," she would say. "They're your shirts."

"But I don't know how!"

"Neither do I."

"Yes, you do! You're supposed to know!"

"I am? Where is it written that I'm supposed to know? Tell me! Where?"

For supper she usually boiled pouches of frozen food, and even that gave her problems. "Oh, puke!" I'd say, pursing up my face and coughing out a mouthful of half-frozen meat loaf.

Once, on her birthday, I bought her a cookbook and pleaded with her to learn some recipes.

"Oh, honey, I can't deal with recipes."

"But why?"

"Because nothing ever turns out the way it's supposed to for me."

I began with simple dishes—baked chicken and steamed vegetables, broiled lamb chops and rice. Then I moved on to lasagna, brisket in red wine sauce, curried shrimp, veal scallops with prosciutto, Grand Marnier soufflés, and poached peaches with raspberry puree. I prepared some of my most inspired meals when my mother entertained Sy.

"I don't know how you do it," she would say, anointing herself with perfume as she watched me work in the kitchen.

"It's easy, Mom. All you have to do is read the directions."

"Directions," she replied, "bore me."

When my first day of school ended, I returned home as usual to begin dinner. Mrs. Gutman, my mother's four-thirty patient and close friend, was sitting on the couch. She was a stout Romanian woman with a collapsing beehive of rust-colored hair held vaguely together with hundreds of bobby pins. "Hello, darlink," she greeted me, her accent falling with a thud on the "darlink." I could tell by the sad cast of her eyes that she knew all about my letter.

Mrs. Gutman had been seeing my mother longer than any other patient. Three days a week for four years she had journeyed from her apartment in Staten Island to our apartment in Bergenfield, where her fifty-minute session lasted for hours. She would call at three and four in the morning when nightmares frightened her awake. The ringing phone always exploded in my ears. I sat up in bed, my heart beating violently, as if it were connected to the phone with jumper cables. I couldn't hear my mother's words very clearly, but I would lie awake for hours listening to the dim, low murmur of her voice, a sound as comforting as the patter of rain after an electrical storm.

Mrs. Gutman was the last scheduled patient of the day because her sessions went on so long. Usually I would be preparing dinner when they finished, and Mrs. Gutman would crowd into the tiny kitchen to sample and advise. Pressing her bosom against my rib cage, she stirred, tasted, lifted covers of pots and inhaled deeply. "No, darlink. You must do like dis one," she'd say, sprinkling paprika into a stew that I had delicately seasoned and simmered for hours.

"Great! Now you've ruined it," I'd say, hurling my wooden spoon into the sink.

"No, darlink, was too bland. Taste now."

"Don't call me that. I've told you my name is Sam."

"Yes, Sam, darlink."

Later, after Mrs. Gutman had left, my mother would say, "Why do you have to be so mean to her? Because she's my friend? Is that why?"

"I've told you not to analyze me. I'm not your patient."

"You can't give me credit for my successes, can you? You know how important I am to Mrs. Gutman, but you won't give me credit for it."

"Mom, she's your patient. She shouldn't be wandering into the kitchen. It's unprofessional."

"Mrs. Gutman is one of my dearest friends."

"Well, she shouldn't be. You're her therapist. You're not supposed to be her best friend, too."

"Where is it written that I can't be both? Tell me! If Mrs. Gutman values my friendship, who are you to tell me it's wrong?"

That afternoon Mrs. Gutman stayed only for her scheduled time. When my mother came into the kitchen, I was already eating my dinner, poached turbot. She joined me at the table with peanut butter on stale white bread.

"That smells delicious," she said.

"It is."

"Can I have a taste?"

"No."

"Why not?"

"I'm seeing how well I get along without you."

"Oh, really? Who paid for that?"

I pushed my plate over to her.

"Look, honey, I'm sorry I said that. The truth is that I can't get along without you, either."

"Mom, I just want a change."

"But you don't have to leave. I can change. *I'll change.* You want me to cook? I'll learn to cook. I'll be the best cook in the world. You don't want me sleeping on the couch? I won't sleep on the couch. I'll rent an office in town. How's that? You'll never have to see any of my patients again. Just tell me what you don't like."

I was staring down at the table. Without looking up, I replied, "Mom, I've decided."

She yanked me by the elbow. "You think it's that simple? Do you think some judge is just going to send you to your father because you say you want a change?"

"Do you think there are any judges who don't know about you?"

"What is that supposed to mean?"

"I mean all the lawyers you've spent the night with."

She slapped me across the face. She had never hit me before, and she began to cry, holding her hand as if she had burned it on something.

"You're just like everyone else," she cried. "You're all the same."

I had hoped my mother would just boot me out, hurling suitcases and insults at me, and when she thought to call me back, to apologize and argue some more, I would already be ensconced at my father's house, too far away to hear a thing. But after my father sued, I barely heard her voice. At dinner she would occasionally glance up from her plate to look at me oddly, as if I were a stranger she had just found sitting at her table. If I attempted conversation, she'd either ignore me or say, "Ask your father." I felt sure her silence was purely strategic; I was certain that if I told her I was changing my mind, tears would well in her eyes, all would be forgiven, and she'd vow to change. Some nights, though, after I was in bed and she called up Mrs. Gutman, her voice sounded extremely faint, more so than usual. I kept changing the position of my head on the pillow, but I couldn't tune her in, and after a time she faded out like a voice on the radio during a long drive in the middle of the night.

*   *   *

At the end of September, my mother and I visited her father in Florida. He was a dentist, and we saw him twice a year to have our teeth fixed and to be reminded of things we were not supposed to do. I was not supposed to eat sweets because my teeth were low in calcium; my mother was not supposed to "use" cigarettes in public or tell anyone she was divorced. For some reason, he thought it was less embarrassing to introduce her as a widow.

"Your grandfather doesn't know about our problems," she said to me on the plane, "and I don't plan on telling him."

We always went to Florida at the wrong time—either in May or late September, when the air in New Jersey was most delicious, when the perspiration on your face was cooling as a breeze. Usually, we stayed only for two or three days, sunning by the pool of his condominium or accompanying him on the golf course for his daily 6:00 A.M. game. Neither my mother nor I played, but he was adamant that we come along, as if she and I might get into trouble if we were left alone. By the thirteenth hole she was desperate for a cigarette. She'd quickly light one up as my grandfather was bent over the ball. He'd catch a scent of it and stop his stroke. "Sandra, how many times have I asked you to refrain from doing that in public? Now, put it out." Once the cigarette was lit, she became calmer, drawing deeper into herself with each drag. "Sandra!" She let a long, elegant ash drop to the green.

"Sorry, Daddy," she'd say in a bored voice, as she grasped my shoulder for support and twisted the cigarette against the bottom of her shoe.

On this visit we went straight from the airport to the office. My mother's gums had ached for weeks, but she didn't have the money to see a local dentist. My grandfather ushered her into the chair and instructed her to remove her lipstick. She pressed her lips against a tissue, leaving a red O-shaped print, and then gave it to my grandfather as though she were handing over her mouth. "Sandra," he said over the hum of the drill, "have you heard from the Yoskowitzes' son?" Both his thumbs were in her mouth and she moved her head from side to side. I sat in the dental assistant's chair, where I had a direct view of the bloody saliva swirling underneath my mother's tongue. "No? Maybe he'll call when you get back. I gave your number to Jack and Ruth to give to him. He lives in Jersey City and sells hospital equipment. They showed me a copy of his tax returns, so I know for certain that he earned $81,000 last year. He thinks you're a widow, so don't say anything to disappoint him. Understand?" Her eyes widened with hurt. I wanted to do something. Unclasp the towel from around her neck, give her back her mouth, and tell her, Run, I'll meet you at the airport. "Let's just hope," he continued, "he doesn't mind that your teeth are so stained with nicotine."

She raised her hand for him to stop. "Daddy, I really don't want to hear this today. My life has been a real shit-hole lately, and I just don't want to hear this." She never glanced at me.

My grandfather held the drill in the air and looked up, like someone about to begin conducting an orchestra. "Some days," he sighed, "I'm almost relieved that Rose is gone." I watched my mother's eyes brimming with tears. When my grandfather noticed, he reached for a needle and asked if she needed more Novocain.

A month before the hearing, and two weeks before my bar mitzvah, I went to see a court-appointed psychologist. Florence Fein's office, in a red Victorian house, was a large room crowded with old furniture, Oriental rugs, stained glass, and antique lamps. She served me a cup of tea and then asked me what I would like to talk about. I told her I couldn't think of anything.

"Why do you think you're here?" she asked.

"Because I have an appointment."

"Perhaps you can tell me why you don't want to be here."

"Because there's nothing wrong with me."

"You don't have to have something wrong with you to come to a psychologist, Sam. Most people come here just to figure things out."

"But I don't have anything to figure out. I know I want to live with my father."

"No one is keeping you here. You're free to leave."

"Then you'll tell the judge I have to stay with my mother."

"Sam, I'm not here to penalize you for saying the wrong thing. If you really don't want to be here, I'll just write in my report that I couldn't draw any conclusions."

I was uncomfortable with Florence Fein because I knew I could never say a bad word about my mother to a stranger. For a second I wondered if my mother had anticipated this; maybe she hadn't booted me out because she knew I'd turn silent and recalcitrant with psychologists and judges.

"If I go right now, is my mother still going to have to pay for the time?"

"Why do you ask?"

"I feel bad about her spending money for nothing."

"Do you always feel bad about your mother's actions?"

"Sometimes."

"Do you think that would change if you lived with your father?"

"I don't know. . . . Don't you think people can change?"

"Of course. I wouldn't be in this business if I didn't think so." I believed her when she said this, as if change were a reliable commodity. I knew the word didn't hold the same meaning for my mother. When I thought of her pleading "I can change, I'll change!" the words sounded like *"I'm in pain, I'm in pain!"*

"Sam, you probably know that your parents' divorce was very bitter."

"So?"

"Do you think your father has put any subtle pressure on you to come live with him?"

"Did my mother say that?"

"Not at all. As a matter of fact, she argued that your father wasn't all that interested in having you live with him and that you might be deeply hurt once that became a reality for you."

"What else did she say?"

"She said she's failed at everything she's ever tried, and she doesn't want to fail as a parent."

We looked at each other for a long two or three seconds; and in that moment I felt the whole weight of my mother's life, as if Florence Fein had placed in my cup a teaspoonful of matter from a black hole weighing millions and millions of tons.

The day before my bar mitzvah, my mother informed me that she was planning on showing up. I acted surprised, but deep down I had expected it.

"You're not religious," I argued.

She was driving me to the Port Authority.

"You know this isn't a question of religion. You just don't want me to come. Admit it."

"But you're always saying that my father's friends are against you. You'll have to face all of them if you come."

"And so why should they be at my son's bar mitzvah and not me?"

"Mom, that's not a reason to go."

"Oh, and are your reasons any better? You just want all your father's friends to think you're more your father's son. You want them to think, My, hasn't he turned out so nice and polite despite his mother."

"I told you not to analyze me! I'm not your goddamned patient!"

We entered the Lincoln Tunnel, and I was truly afraid that she might stop the car in the middle of it and order me out. We hadn't talked that way in months. But she didn't say anything until we pulled up to the bus terminal. "Talk to your father that way sometime," she said, "and see how long he lets you live with him."

That evening Phyllis fixed a traditional Sabbath meal. My father invited six couples from his congregation to join us. My mother had warned me about all of them at one time or another. They were too interested and too familiar with me, as if I were a disfigured child and they were pretending not to notice. Before we had finished the soup and melon, they asked me which subject I liked the most in school (social studies), whether I was a Yankee or a Met fan (neither—the Dodgers), whether I, too, planned on becoming a rabbi (no, a gourmet chef). Everyone gave me a pained smile. I was thinking of the last elaborate meal I'd prepared for my mother and Sy, and how I loved standing in the kitchen with her, minutes before he came to the door. My mother and the pots rattled with expectancy: would this be the man to stay with her, to adjust our haphazard course? The kitchen smelled rich with promise, as if the scent of her perfume and the odors of my cooking held the power to transform our lives, to transport us from our crowded, chaotic apartment into a large house, where we all had our own rooms, where my mother would be calm, secure, loved.

After we returned from services that evening, I told my father and Phyllis that my mother would probably show up the next morning. They looked at each other.

"Oh, Sam," my father sighed. "Couldn't you have done something?"

"No, Dad. She wants to come."

"Doesn't she know how uncomfortable this is going to be?" Phyllis said.

"Mommy, who's coming?" Debbie asked.

"Nobody, dear. Nobody."

I didn't say anything, and I went to bed feeling just like everyone else.

The next morning, I stepped up to the Torah and saw my mother sitting in a row of empty seats. She waved at me like someone in a lifeboat attempting to flag a distant ship. Everyone's eyes moved from her to me. I brought my tallis to my lips and began chanting in a language I didn't understand. From behind me, the sun beamed through a stained-glass mural. The light washed over me and the colors skated back and forth across the parchment, echoing the manic movements of my heart.

After the service, she rushed over to the receiving line and reclaimed me with a long, long embrace. She had not held or kissed me in months. Several people waiting to greet me formed an uncomfortable semicircle around us. She tightened her hold, as if I were a charm to ward off bad spirits. People began to file away. Soon we were standing alone, like two strangers who had wandered into the wrong celebration. Then Phyllis came over to tell me that the photographer was set up for a family portrait. My mother squeezed my elbow.

"You stay right here, Sam."

"We'll only be five minutes," Phyllis said impatiently. "Come, Sam."

She reached for me and my mother slapped her hand away. Phyllis looked at her hand as if she had never seen it before.

"I'm his family," my mother said. "If the photographer wants a portrait, he can come over here."

"Crazy woman," Phyllis murmured, and turned away. My mother caught her on the side of the head with her purse. Phyllis whirled around, crying "Oh! Oh!" more in disbelief than in pain. My mother lunged at her. Both women grabbed at each other's hair and face. They teetered back and forth in their high heels. I could hear nylons whispering against nylons. My father rushed over, his hand raised and his black robes billowing. I ran out.

I kept running until I reached the beach, breathless. Each gulp of the November air stung my lungs. I wrapped my tallis around my neck and walked rapidly through the sand. Then I heard my mother shout my name. I turned around. She was perhaps a hundred yards behind me, her shoes in her hands. She crossed them above her head, signaling me to stop. I walked down to the shoreline.

I recalled how she and I used to come to this same beach on winter afternoons when my parents were still married. She hated the summer crowds, but liked the remoteness of the beach in winter. Once we came with a helium balloon she had bought me at a nearby amusement park. At the shoreline she had bent down beside me and we placed our fingertips all over its shiny red surface. "We're sending a message," she said, "to your Nana Rose." I let go of the balloon, and we watched it sail up into the brilliant blue air and disappear over the ocean. She explained that when the balloon reached heaven Nana Rose would recognize our fingerprints. Perhaps I looked at her quizzically, because she then said, "Trust me, sweetie. We're already on the moon."

I watched the waves explode and dash toward me, watched the froth top my shoes, and at almost the same moment felt my socks turn to ice.

"Sam, dear, why are you standing in the water?"

She was about five feet behind me. I didn't answer or turn around.

"Honey, you'll ruin your shoes."

"Good."

"You'll catch pneumonia."

"Good."

"Won't you at least step out of the water?"

"No."

"No?"

"Maybe I want to go for a swim."

I really didn't want to swim. I just wanted to lie down in the surf and close my eyes and drift, like a toy boat or a bottle, to the other side of the ocean, washing up on the shore of a new country.

"Darling, it's too cold to swim. Wait until June. Then you can go in the water."

"Don't talk to me like that!"

"Like what, sweetie?"

"Like I'm crazy. Like I'm about to jump out a window. You're the one who's crazy, not me."

"Oh, Sam, don't criticize. Not now. Not after what I've been through. Don't be like everyone else." I turned around, ready to shout, "Why can't you be like everyone else!" Then I saw how bad she looked. One eye was half closed and her nostrils were rimmed with blood. Angry red welts laced her windpipe. She dropped to her knees and began crying noiselessly into the sand.

I was only thirteen that day, but I knew my mother would never change. She would never have a beautiful office like Florence Fein's. She would never have more than three or four patients, people like Mrs. Gutman, who were as chaotic and pained as she was. I knew she would always feel like a stranger on the planet.

Two weeks later a judge sent me to live with my father. The fight with Phyllis, and the depositions provided by nearly everyone in my father's congregation, weighed heavily against my mother. I was sullen with the judge, though he was gentle with me. Perhaps I could have said something kind about my mother, but I was only thirteen, and I didn't know that love can be as obdurate as the changes you long for. Perhaps I could have told him that after I turned around and saw her bruised face, I lifted my mother to her feet. I pressed my tallis against her bloody nose. Then I rolled it up into a tight little ball, and we trekked back up the beach together.

"THE LEGACY OF RAIZEL KAIDISH"

from

STRANGE ATTRACTORS

REBECCA GOLDSTEIN

"To the older generation, it seems, Jewishness was so much more of a barrier," Rebecca Goldstein said in an interview. "It was something they had to break through. . . . I come from an Orthodox family. I am not quite sure how I Jewishly identify myself now, but I still have ties with Orthodoxy through my family. But I am not concerned with my Jewishness. I take it for granted."

"The Legacy of Raizel Kaidish" is about Rose, a girl whose identity is defined by a fourteen-year-old heroine of Buchenwald who unsuccessfully tried to save the life of her friend. Rose's mother, also an inmate at Buchenwald, remembers how courageous Raizel Kaidish was, and never wants her daughter, Raizel's legacy, to forget that. Unlike Goldstein herself, Rose is incapable of taking her Jewishness for granted, and in fact must break through much the same barrier as the older generations of Jewish immigrants.

Rebecca Goldstein is the author of a collection of short fiction, Strange Attractors, *and three novels:* The Mind-Body Problem, The Late-Summer Passion of a Woman of Mind, *and* The Dark Sister. *She lives with her husband and children in New Jersey.*

In 1945 the following incident took place in the death camp of Buchenwald.

There were two young Jewish girls, each the last survivor of her family, and they had become very devoted to one another during the few months of their imprisonment. One morning one of them woke up too weak to work. Her name was put on the death list. The other, Raizel Kaidish, argued with her friend that she, Raizel, should go instead. She would tell the Germans there had been a mistake, and when they saw how strong and fit for work she was, it would be all right. Someone informed on the girls and they were both gassed. The informer was rewarded with Raizel's kitchen job.

I'm named after Raizel Kaidish. My mother knew her from the camp. It's noteworthy that, though the war took all her family from her, my mother chose to name her first child, her only child, after an outsider—the heroine of block eight, Buchenwald.

My mother's moral framework was formed in Buchenwald. Forged in the fires, it was strong and inflexible. One of her central concerns was that I should come to know, without myself suffering, all that she had learned there.

My moral education began at an early age. It consisted at first of tales from the camp.

People in my real life were nice or mean, usually a little of both. But in the tales there were only saints and sinners, heroes and villains. I remember questioning my mother about this, and her answer to me:

"When times are normal, then normal people are a little nice and a little mean together. But when there are hard times, when there's not enough to eat or drink, when there's war, then you don't find a little nice and a little mean mixed together. You find only greatness. Very great badness and very great goodness."

The people in my life didn't seem so real to me as the people in the tales. When I closed my eyes I couldn't picture the faces of my friends or family. All that I could make out of my father was a vaguely sad face around the glinting rimless glasses. Even my mother's features wouldn't come into focus, only the outline of her: tall and always erect, in the gray or dark-blue suit and the white blouse, her light-brown hair in a low bun at the nape of her neck.

But my images of the camp were vivid and detailed. The pink rosebuds on my wallpaper weren't so real to me as the grayness of the barracks, the brown of the mud. It seemed to me that I knew the feel through decaying shoes of the sharp stones in the main square, the sight, twice daily, of the terrifying roll call.

It seemed I, too, had quickly glanced up at the open sky, and wondered that others outside saw the same sky.

My father, like my mother a doctor, didn't approve of the tales:

"She's too young. You'll give her nightmares, traumas. A child this age shouldn't know."

"A child this age. You know you would never consider her old enough to know."

"And why should she know? Can't we forget already? Can't we live like others?"

"Would you really want it, Saul, to live like the others? To join the mass of sleepwalkers, with the glazed eyes and the smug smiles? Is that why we lived when all those others didn't? Is that what we want for Rose?''

And at this point I can hear my father's sigh, the deep drawn-out sigh so characteristic of him, which had always seemed to me, when I was young, to hold the slight tremor of a sob. My father's sadness was something I felt I could almost reach out and touch, like my mother's goodness.

The arguments between my parents continued throughout my childhood. And my father, so gentle, was a man who hated to fight. In the quiet of the night, awake in my bed, I would catch the cadences of their voices, my father's sad and low, so that I missed much of what he said, my mother's burning with the pure flame of her certainty.

And the lessons continued, the simple stark tales of cruelty and sacrifice, cowardice and courage, which always came back to the story of my name-sake. My mother would tell me that she had honored both Raizel and me in choosing my name. She sometimes called me Raizel, or even Raizela, in rare moments of tenderness, stroking back my hair.

When I reached fourteen, my mother, deeming me to have arrived at long last at the age of reason (and also, perhaps not coincidentally, at the age at which Raizel had lost her life), began to instruct me in the moral theory she had worked out in Buchenwald.

The theory is elaborate and detailed, reminiscent of the German my parents spoke to one another: complications nesting within complications. The brief account I give here is necessarily inadequate, and perhaps not intrinsically interesting. But I feel that the picture of my mother is incomplete without a description of her moral outlook.

My mother believed that the ethical view is the impersonal view. One is morally obliged to look at a situation without regard for one's own identity in it, and to act in the way dictated by this impersonal view; to act in the way one believes will minimize the sum of suffering.

My mother's emphasis was always on minimizing pain and suffering, never maximizing happiness or well-being. She explained this to me once, when, much older, I asked her:

''I know what is evil. To know suffering is to know evil. None of the attempts to identify the good have this same certainty.''

So far there's nothing, except for its pessimistic cast, to distinguish my mother's view from the great bulk of utilitarian theories. The special twist comes in the foundations she claimed, and it's a twist that mirrors her personality: her uncompromising rationality.

Ethics, she believed, is nothing ''separate''; it's a branch of logic. The moral obligation is nothing over and above the obligation to be logically consistent, and virtue reduces to rationality.

Why is this so? Because, she explained, to deny the obligation of acting on the impersonal viewpoint, one would have to maintain that one's self has some special metaphysical significance, that it makes a difference that one is who one is. And how can this consistently be maintained once one has recognized the existence of other selves, each of whom is who he is? Only the solipsist can consistently be unethical.

To use one of my mother's favorite analogies: the person who acts only in his own interest is like a person who says there is always something special about his own location, because he can always say, "I'm *here*," whereas everyone else is merely *there*.

Once one has granted that there are other subjects of experience, other selves who suffer, then one can maintain that one's own pain matters—and who would deny *that*?—only if one grants that the pain of everyone else matters in exactly the same way.

Raizel Kaidish's behavior was therefore, by my mother's accounting, paradigmatically ethical. Viewing the situation impersonally, this fourteen-year-old had seen that the stronger child would have a better, although slim, chance to survive. She acted on this view, undeterred by the fact that it was she who was the stronger, she who was unnecessarily risking her life.

In fact, I have no doubt at all that my mother's ethical view was the straightforward consequence of taking Raizel Kaidish as her paradigm, and not the other way round. The heroic action of that child was the real foundation of her theory—which, like my name, honored the girl's memory.

After the liberation my mother returned to Berlin to continue her formal training in medicine. She also began her lifelong study of philosophy. She was curious to see who among the philosophically great had shared her discovery.

She considered Kant to be the most worthwhile ethicist. Socrates she loved for his devotion to the ethical questions, for his conviction that nothing ought to concern us more than the questions of how to live our lives. Hanging over my bed, the only piece of embroidery I've ever known her to do, was the Socratic quotation: "The unexamined life is not worth living."

But for the most part my mother found the great philosophers of the past a supreme disappointment. The truth, so simple, had eluded them, because they had assumed the separateness of the ethical realm. Some had grasped pieces of it, but few had seen the seamless whole.

It was contemporary philosophers, however, particularly the positivists and their "fellow travelers," who aroused her genuine wrath.

For here were theorists who dismissed the possibility of all ethical theory, who denied the very subject matter of the field. Instead of conducting inquiries into the nature of our moral obligations, they offered analyses of the grammar of ethical propositions.

She would look up from some contemporary philosophical book or journal, her eyes blazing their blue fury:

"Positivists." The intonation she gave the word was similar to that she gave "Nazi." "They don't see, because their eyes aren't turned outward but inward, into the tabulae rasae of their own minds. To forsake the important questions for this dribble! To spend your life examining endless quibbles!"

And I? How did I feel about my intensive moral upbringing?

The object of so much attention, of all the pedagogical theorizing, the fights in the night: I felt ignored, unloved, of no significance.

And, especially as I grew older, I felt angry: an unvoiced and unacknowledged outrage.

It wasn't just a matter of the rigidity of my upbringing, the lack of laughter in a home where one could reach out and touch one's father's sadness and mother's goodness.

It wasn't just the fact that I was always made to feel so different from my friends, so that I often, though always with an overwhelming sense of guilt, fantasized myself in another family, with parents who were frivolously pursuing happiness, and didn't have numbers burned into their arms.

It was something else, more elusive and more potent, that infuriated me.

Of course, there's nothing unusual in a daughter's resentment of a mother. My friends, from early adolescence onward, were always enraged with one or the other of their parents. But theirs was the pure clean indignation unashamed of itself.

Hadn't she suffered enough? Shouldn't I try to do everything to make it up to her? By hating her, I joined the ranks of her enemies. I allied myself with the murderers.

And so the resentment was folded back on itself, again and again, always thickening, always darkening.

I never spoke it, not even to myself. Its acknowledgment came only years later, after my mother had died, during the years I spent deliberating over whether to have a child of my own. The mental delivery of that decision was so much more agonizing than the physical birth.

In debating the reasons for having a child, I asked myself whether any reasons could ever be right, whether one was ever justified in bringing a person into being for some reason of one's own? But if not for one's own reason, then for whose? It seemed a moral inconsistency woven into the very fabric of human existence.

The solution really only came to me after I was a mother: It's possible— it's right—for the reasons one had for creating a child to recede into insignificance when faced with the fact of that child's existence. Whatever considerations went into the decision to have a child lose themselves in the knowledge of the child itself.

In my view, this is the essence of good parenting, and once I finally knew this I knew at last what I had felt all along to be wrong about my mother and myself. I had known what no child should ever know: that my mother had had me for some definite reason, and that she would always see me in terms of this reason. I sensed this in my mother, and I hated her for it.

I said that my anger never showed itself. Actually there was a brief rebellion, whose form was so typical of my family's peculiarity that now, years later, even I can see its comic aspect and smile.

My first semester of college, while my friends developed their own conventional modes of rebellion, I worked out mine. I became a positivist. I took Introduction to Philosophy with a self-intoxicated young professor, a new Ph.D. from Harvard, and, although this wouldn't be his own description, a neopositivist.

He told us during the first lecture that he was going to show us, over the course of the semester, why we were lucky, insofar as we were philosophy students, to have been born now; that it was now possible to see that previous generations had devoted themselves to pseudo-questions concerning the nature of Reality, Truth, and the Good; and that such questions were expressions of logical confusion. These fine big words don't name anything, and thus there is nothing there whose nature is to be explored.

I sat there, drinking in his words, thinking: "This is it. This is why I came to college."

All through that term, Monday, Wednesday, and Friday, from ten to eleven, while others dozed and doodled, I listened in a state of delirium, following the arguments with a concentration I've never attained since. My mind bubbled over with the excitement of this illicit doctrine, this forbidden philosophy.

And the most forbidden, and therefore enticing, view offered in the course was that devoted to ethics, or, rather, to the dismissal of ethics.

202

I memorized whole passages out of my favorite book, A. J. Ayer's *Language, Truth, and Logic*:

> We can now see why it is impossible to find a criterion for determining the validity of ethical judgements. It is not because they have an "absolute" validity which is mysteriously independent of ordinary sense-experience, but because they have no objective validity whatsoever. If a sentence makes no statement at all, there is obviously no sense in asking whether what it says is true or false. And we have seen that sentences which simply express moral judgements do not say anything. They are pure expressions of feeling and as such do not come under the category of truth and falsehood.

I was inexpressibly moved by the sparse beauty of the arguments. How had I never seen it before, never seen that my mother's supposedly impermeable theory was nothing but an insubstantial confection fabricated of pseudo-statements?

My preparations for final exams were trivial compared with my cramming for the visit home during intersession. I arrived back about eleven at night, too late for philosophical debate. But my mind was so teeming with my professor's methods of query that when my mother wished me "good night" I almost challenged her: "What do you mean by that? What do you mean by *good*?"

The next evening, after my mother and father arrived home from the hospital, we all sat in the living room, while Bertha, our housekeeper, finished dinner. I was waiting for the right moment for launching my attack, poised to pounce on any comment that was mildly speculative.

But my mother, with her practiced perversity, was being very concrete that night. She asked me about the food at school, about my roommate, even told a funny story about her own roommate, in Berlin, before the war. Then, finally:

"You were always so brief on the phone when I asked you about your classes. Tell me more about them. You seemed to have enjoyed them very much."

"They were wonderful. Especially philosophy. I'm going to major in it."

"Really? And are you thinking of this as a profession?"

"Absolutely. It's it. There's nothing else I'll even consider."

"Well, that's interesting. Very interesting."

"That's *all:* interesting? Are you pleased, horrified, what?"

"At the moment maybe a little baffled. To tell you the truth, I've always thought it a rather funny kind of profession. Every person should of course

203

think about the big questions, but it seems an odd way to earn one's living.''

"But what about teaching, Marta?" my father, the eternal peacemaker, asked. "Don't you think it's important to have people teaching philosophy?"

"Well, yes, that's true. Yet I suspect that most of them don't think of themselves primarily as teachers, but as thinkers, professional thinkers, however peculiar that sounds. Well, we can ask Rose here. What do you fancy yourself, a teacher or a philosopher?"

"A philosopher, of course. The need for professional training in philosophy is no different than anywhere else, no different than in medicine. People think they can just jump in and start philosophizing and that they'll make sense. They rarely do. It takes technical training. Years and years of it."

"Oh? I disagree very much, as you know, with this emphasis on technical training. Instead of humanizing the mathematical sciences, they try to mathematize the humanities. Translating into a lot of fancy symbols doesn't show the truth of what you're saying."

"But it does often show its meaninglessness."

I brought out this positivist buzzword with all the provocative emphasis I could muster.

"Do you think so?" responded my mother, not even lifting an eyebrow. "Yes, I can see how that might often be true."

Impossible woman! What was wrong with her? Her kindling point was usually so frighteningly low, but tonight she wouldn't burn. She wouldn't even flicker.

The explanation, of course, would have been obvious to anyone not occupying my vantage point. She was, quite simply, very happy to see me.

I had no more patience for her unwonted tolerance. I abandoned my hopes for a smooth transition.

"Mom, there's a question about ethics that's been bothering me."

There. I had opened the door. Now I had to walk through.

"Yes? Tell me. Perhaps I can be of some help."

"You've always said that the moral obligation is nothing but the obligation to be logically consistent. But why do we have to be logically consistent?"

My mother smiled.

"I must say, you surprise me. Such an antirationalist question. And after a whole semester of college! The answer is, of course, that the truth is important. And logical inconsistencies can't be true. If you ask me, as I can see you're about to, why the truth is important, I can't give you a noncircular answer. Anything I say is going to presuppose the importance of truth, as all rational discourse presupposes it. And this impossibility of a noncircular answer is itself the answer.''

"I don't understand a word you're saying!'' I exploded. "The Truth! The holy Truth! What's the Truth? Where's the Truth? Let me see you point to it! What can it possibly mean to say, 'The Truth is important'? What cognitive content can it possibly have? It's nonsense! Emotive non-sense! And the same with all the other so-called truths of your so-called theory! You claim to be so rational, so superior and so rational! But you're only emoting—eternally emoting—and I'm sick to death of it!''

My speech was not delivered in that calm voice of detached reason I had so obsessively rehearsed. Instead it tore out of me with a force that frightened me, sweeping me along.

The effect was immediate. My mother's face had the capacity for in-stantaneous transformation I've observed in my own young daughter. In fact, I often find myself wondering whether this is a trait characteristic of early childhood, or whether it's something my daughter has inherited from her grandmother, along with her name.

My mother had never raised her voice to me, and she didn't raise it now. As always, her eyes did all the screaming.

"Positivist!''

Her intonation wasn't the usual one. There was anger, but it was softened by sadness.

"After all that I have taught you, you lose everything in one semester of college? Do you have so little substance that at your first exposure to the jargon of these antithinkers you disintegrate?''

I had no answer for my mother. The brilliant arguments spilling over in my mind only the night before were all vanished. My head was so hollow it felt as if it were floating away from the rest of me. The deadening fog, of shame and guilt, was settling back over everything.

Dimly, I saw my father sitting there, staring out at us over the wall of his sadness. My mother's voice cut through the haze.

"You disappoint me. You disappoint us all. You aren't worthy to be named after Raizel Kaidish.''

Soon after my wedding, when my mother was fifty-six, she learned that she had ovarian cancer and didn't have more than six months to live.

She reacted to the news of her impending death as if she had been preparing for it her whole life. She looked at it with her customary objec-tivity: Yes, she was relatively young, and there were still many things that she would have liked to experience, particularly being a grandmother. But that she, a Jew from Berlin, had been given these past thirty years was a fact to which the proper response was gratitude, not a greedy demand for yet more years.

She never complained. Her grief seemed entirely focused on the anguish her terrible illness was causing my father and me.

She died as I had always known her to live: with superhuman discipline, courage, and rationality.

A week before she died, she told me that it had been she who had informed on Raizel Kaidish. She asked my forgiveness.

"THE LOST WORLD"

from

A MODEL WORLD AND OTHER STORIES

MICHAEL CHABON

Taken from Michael Chabon's first collection of stories, "The Lost World" is about sixteen-year-old Nathan Shapiro adjusting to life. His parents are divorced—his father has a new wife and they are expecting a baby; his mother has just been remarried to a man who is an "acquired taste." Nathan is looking for something to rely on, something he can count on, and is surprised to find it in a girl he hardly knows.

In an interview with the Baltimore Jewish Times, *Michael Chabon said, "I definitely consider myself an American writer. To some extent, I suppose, I'm a Jewish writer. I'm Jewish and some of my characters are Jewish. But I'm not sure what role Judaism has in my work." Like other Jewish writers of his generation, the presence of the Jewish experience in Michael Chabon's writing is secondary to the exploration of modern-day family relationships.*

Michael Chabon was born in Washington, D.C., and raised in Columbia, Maryland. He is the author of one collection of short stories, A Model World and Other Stories, *and two novels:* The Mysteries of Pittsburgh *and* The Wonder Boys.

One summer night not long after he turned sixteen, Nathan Shapiro drank four tall cans of Old English 800 and very soon found himself sitting in the front seat of a huge, banana-colored Ford LTD, with his friends Buster, Felix, and Tiger Montaine. They had swallowed the malt liquor while bathing in Buster French's hot tub (the Frenches were from Los Angeles) and, as a result, were driving around boiled, steaming drunk, and in various stages of undress. Buster and Felix E. still had on their scant Speedo bathing suits, Tiger Montaine wore only a black mesh tank top and one sanitary sock, and Nathan, through some combination of glee and desperation, was naked from head to toe.

Two weeks before this, his mother, in a modest and homemade little ceremony, had married a man named Ed, a kindly, balding geologist from Idaho whom she had been dating for six months. And then just this evening, an hour before Nathan went over to Buster French's house, Dr. Shapiro had telephoned jubilantly from Boston to announce the first pregnancy of his wife, Anne. Ricky, Nathan's brother, had been living in Boston for a year now, and he went on and on over the phone about the little bubble of life that had blossomed in the vial of Anne's home pregnancy test, which Ricky had taken to his room and placed between his soccer trophy and a photograph of his mother and father and Nathan standing in the wind at Nag's Head.

All of these developments, though he did his best to welcome them, had left Nathan somewhat more than normally confused. He liked his new stepfather, who had been to Antarctica and Peru and Novaya Zemlya and returned with all sorts of hair-raising tales and queer stones; in his own way he was genuinely as excited as Ricky by the prospect of a new baby; and he was old enough to regard these changes as the inevitable outward expansion, as of an empire or a galaxy, of what once had been his family. He was happy for his parents in their new lives, the way he had always been happy for them, all along, as step by step they had dismantled their marriage; and so he was looking for a reason, an excuse to feel so unmoored, at once so angry and nostalgic; and alcohol seemed to be doing the job. He had no idea of where he and his friends were going, and it was not until they had been lurching aimlessly along the empty, fragrant streets of Huxley for what seemed like hours that he understood that they were headed—as Buster French put it—to the crib of Chaya Feldman.

Buster, driving Mrs. French's car, made this declaration just as the drink, the deep velour seats, and the sweet smell of lawns flowing in through the open windows had begun to lull Nathan to sleep, and at the mention of Chaya's name Nathan sat bolt upright. Buster then called Chaya a "skeezer," which meant, as far as Nathan had been able to determine, that she was certain to permit them—all four of them—those dark liberties of which he was still very much ignorant, a notion which filled him only with wonder, and with solicitude for Chaya, whom he had known since he was six years old. She was a quiet girl, with a serious brown face and tangled hair, and her parents dressed her like a doll. He remembered her as someone who was always coming upon orphaned puppies and sparrow chicks with broken wings, in meadows and along roads where anyone else would have found nothing at all, and then trying imperfectly and with an eyedropper full of milk or sugar water to nurse them back to health. Her chief social art—until recently, at least—had been that, upon request, she could draw you an extremely realistic picture of an eyeball, with a sparkle on the iris, and fathomless pupils, and the finest tracery of veins.

They had never really been friends, but from time to time Nathan still thought about one distant afternoon when he and Chaya had somehow ended up playing together, in the fields behind the Huxley Interfaith Plexus. In the tall grass and the weeds they had played a game of Chaya's own invention, called Planet of the Birds. Nathan had been an intergalactic castaway trying to survive in a windy, grassy world, and Chaya's hair had tossed like a crest of feathers as she sang to him in a variety of cries. Chaya even claimed that when she grew up she was going to write a book set on this imaginary planet, whose name, she said, was Jadis; in the dust she scratched a map of its oceans and aeries. As with all of those blissful Sunday afternoons he had ever passed with some child with whom he never played again—every childhood has a dozen or so—his memory of this vanished afternoon was luminous and clear. In the three years since his liberation from Hebrew school he had seen Chaya twice, from a distance, coming out of a movie with her parents and her sister, Mara. Now Nathan was suddenly afraid for her, and he was afraid, for the first time ever, of the raucous bodies of his friends.

"Hey, Buster," said Felix E. Scott, leaning forward so that for an instant his thigh lay smooth and cool against Nathan's, "what you going to do to Chaya Feldman?"

"Don't tell me you don't already know, Felix E.," said Buster, heaving the LTD into a small cul-de-sac which Nathan recognized, from some long-ago car pool, as Chaya's street.

"Cut the engine," suggested Tiger Montaine, who excelled in stealthy behavior. He ran his battered little Fiat on siphoned gasoline, filched cigarettes from the supermarket, and had for several months, with Nathan's shocked connivance, been replacing Mrs. Shapiro's codeine pills with extra-strength Tylenol, one at a time. "Don't be waking up that mean Israelite daddy." Chaya's father, Moshe, an oncologist, had been born and raised in Israel, and was, in fact, the most humorless and stern of the one hundred and five fathers Nathan had known in his life. He had a dense black beard and crazy eyebrows, and it was widely half-believed that he kept an Uzi submachine gun, from his days in the army of Israel, hidden under his bed.

Buster turned off the ignition and the car began to glide silently toward Chaya's house. The sudden calm cast a pall over the party and no one spoke; perhaps they were only being careful. Nathan pictured Chaya, asleep, her legs tangled under a light summer blanket; a skeezer! Then, because the ignition had been cut, the steering wheel locked, automatically, and before Buster could do anything they had hopped up over the curb, and came to a stop halfway across somebody's front lawn.

"We're there," said Buster, and everyone laughed. "Now who's going to go knocking on that skeezer's window?"

"I'll go," said Nathan. "I know her."

All of the other boys turned to regard him. Although Nathan felt fairly confident that his friends held him in a certain esteem—his naked presence among them was testimony to that—he had never distinguished himself for his daring, and in fact generally had to be persuaded even to perform minor feats such as dancing with Twanda Woods, or wearing his sneakers without any laces, an affectation which drove his mother out of her mind. And all of the boys knew, for Nathan had been unable, despite himself, to conceal it, that he had never made love to a girl. Emboldened by the malt liquor, he reached out and pushed Felix E. and Tiger in their faces, so that they fell backward into each other.

"I went to Hebrew school with her," he explained.

Perhaps it was only their shock at this uncharacteristic display of fearlessness, but as Nathan stepped out of the car, he noticed a strange look in the eyes of his friends. It was a kind of blank, blinking puzzlement, as though the game had gone awry. Nathan wondered if the whole thing was a lie, if Chaya was not a skeezer at all, and the boys were all of them virgins, and none of them knew what fate awaited him as he began to make his way, naked, barefoot as a child, across the soft grass. He glanced toward the car, toward the three shadowy heads now drawn together in what looked like anxious parley, and almost turned back.

The next moment, however, he felt an entirely new kind of drunkenness; the air was warm against his skin, his lips, his forearms, and—incredibly—moonlight fell upon his penis. He wished that it were a mile to Chaya's house, and not a few short steps, so that he might walk this way a little longer, like a fairy on a moonlit heath. Just this summer—just this month—his body had begun to grow lean, and he strode across the grass with the jangling gait of a young man, delighting in the purpose of his legs. He came to the Feldmans' driveway and zigzagged quickly around to the left side of the house, where he was confronted with a gated, wooden fence. He stopped and contemplated the latticed gate. His breath came quickly now and there was sweat in his eyebrows; a drop spattered against his cheek. Just when he felt the water on his face he saw, through the spaces in the lattice, that a swimming pool, long and unusually narrow, lay beyond. It was not a pool for a pleasure swim; it was a lap pool, no wider than a pair of racing freestylers. Nathan remembered hearing that Dr. Feldman required himself and his family to swim a mile every day.

Pretending for the moment that he was tricksy Tiger Montaine, Nathan held his breath, eased up the steel latch, and slowly let open the gate, without a sound. He walked to the railroad ties that formed the near end of the lap pool and curled his toes over their edge. Thus perched he stood a moment, looking at the reflected moon on the black water and trying to force the tumult in his stomach to abate. He was so nervous that he forgot why he was nervous, and simply hovered at the edge of Chaya's swimming pool, shaking. What was he doing here? Where were his clothes?

He crouched and then slipped, like a deer fleeing a forest fire, into the cool water. He swam across the pool with a light and leisurely stroke. The exercise of his arms and heart in the cold water cleared his thoughts, and left him with a pleasant chlorine sting in his eyes, and when he arrived at the far side of the lap pool, he felt a greater trust in himself and in the general benevolence of a Tuesday night in July. He pulled himself from the pool and tiptoed around to the back of the Feldmans' house. There were some bedsheets, striped pillowcases, and a pair of bath towels hanging from a revolving clothesline in the backyard, and he considered taking a towel and tying it around his waist. But he felt, obscurely, that there was some advantage in his nakedness, an almost magical advantage that Tiger Montaine, for example, would never have surrendered, and he went over to the windows of the daylight basement in which Chaya had always had her room and stood a moment, with his hands on his wet hips, looking into the dark windows, preparing to wake her. The pool water streamed down his chest to his thighs, raising goosebumps along his legs and arms as Nathan drummed lightly on the glass, attempting a sort of suave seductive rhythm that came out, inexorably, as shave-and-a-hair-cut, two-bits.

A light snapped on inside. Someone sat up in the bed—in Chaya's bed—and this someone did not appear to be Chaya. She was too tall, and her hair was fuller and darker, and through the armhole of her sheer short nightgown he saw the startling contour of a woman's heavy breast. He turned and began to hightail it out of the backyard, but the door opened almost immediately, and he turned sheepishly back.

"Is, uh, Chaya here?" he said, in a tone which he hoped would make him sound too stupid to be doing something illicit.

"Nathan? Nathan Shapiro?"

"Chaya?"

"What are you doing here? Where are your clothes?"

The light spilling out around her reduced her to a silhouette and he could not tell if she looked angry or merely puzzled. Her voice was a cracked whisper and sounded rather plaintive in the dark, as though she were also afraid of getting into some kind of trouble.

"I swam in your pool," Nathan offered, uncertain if this would explain everything adequately.

"Well, you'd better get out of here. My dad is sleeping and he hasn't been well."

"Okay," said Nathan. "Good-bye. You got so big, Chaya." He was staring.

"Puberty," she said. "Ever hear of it?" She stepped back into the light of her room and smiled a sort of frowny smile she had always had, and then Nathan felt that he recognized her.

"Chaya, I feel so weird," he said. At the sight of her familiar, serious face he was all at once on the verge of tears.

"Well. Okay, come inside. You have to be quiet."

"Okay."

Nathan followed Chaya into her room, which had the drop ceiling and damp-carpet odor of a basement. On one paneled wall there was a print of *The Starry Night* and an El Al poster with a picture of the Old City of Jerusalem; on the other wall was a painting that Chaya herself must have made, a picture of a palm tree full of bright parrots under a double sun, and Nathan remembered the day he had spent on the Planet Jadis. Beside the painting was an old mounted deer's head, with a split ear, wearing sunglasses and a purple beret. On the table beside her bed was a squat jug lamp with a green shade, a package of Kool cigarettes, and a book by Erica Jong that Nathan had twice been admonished against reading by his grandfather. The circle of light from the lamp seemed to fall almost entirely on the bed, and Nathan averted his eyes, so intimate was the sight of the exposed white sheets and the deep declivity in the pillow. The imprint of her sleeping head, the whole idea of Chaya asleep, struck him as terribly poignant, and he could not look. He heard the creak of the bedsprings and the rustle of sheets as she climbed back into bed.

"I mean you're not ugly, or anything, Nathan," said Chaya, "but put something on, okay?"

"I'm naked!" said Nathan. He looked down at himself, and knew that he was naked. And he saw, as through Chaya's eyes, that in assuming some of its manly proportions and features, his penis had also begun to take on a concomitant forlorn and humorous aspect, sort of like the Jeep in Popeye cartoons; and he made an apron of his hands and forearms. This did nothing to conceal, however, the whiteness of his thighs, or the soft, sad divot of hair around his left—but not yet his right—nipple.

"There's a towel on the chair."

"I'd better go," said Nathan. He turned and began to walk out the door, attempting now to cover his probably ridiculous-looking rear end.

"It's okay, go ahead, put it on, Nathan," said Chaya.

"They brought me," he said, turning again and crab-walking over to the chair beside Chaya's desk. "The guys. Tiger and Buster and Felix E." Hurriedly he wrapped the towel around his waist and tucked in one end, in the fashion that his grandmother had always referred to, for some reason, as Turkish. It was a scratchy white towel that had been stolen, to judge from the illegible Hebrew lettering that was woven like a pattern into one side, from some hotel in Israel. The lopsided situation of his chest hair remained a keen embarrassment, and the towel was so skimpy that the knot at his hip just barely held.

"Are they out there?"

"Yeah. They sent me in. They said—"

"Your hair is all wet." She folded her hands over her stomach, on the pleat of the bedclothes, and stared at him. She seemed all in all only mildly surprised to see Nathan, as though he were visiting her in a dream. Her face had grown wider, her cheekbones more pronounced, since the last time he had seen her, and with her tawny skin and her thick eyebrows and that big, wild hair Nathan thought she looked beautiful and a little scary. He sat down and hugged himself. His teeth were chattering.

"Okay, now I better go." He stood up again.

"Wait," said Chaya. She patted the sheets and indicated that he sit beside her. He came to sit gingerly at her feet, keeping hold with one hand of the tenuous Turkish knot.

"Nathan Shapiro," she said, shaking her head.

"Chaya Feldman."

"Mrs. Falutnick's class."

"Kvit chewink your gum in fronta da /-/adio," said Nathan, repeating a favorite inscrutable admonishment of Mrs. Falutnick's in an accent he had not mimicked for six or seven years. Chaya laughed, but Nathan only snorted once through his nose. It had been so long since the days of Mrs. Falutnick's class! He saw himself sitting in a flecked plastic chair at the back of the droning classroom in the Huxley Interfaith Plexus, defacing with moustaches and monkey's fur the grave photographs of Emma Lazarus and Abraham Cahan in his copy of *Adventures in American Jewry*, furtively folding all ten inches of a stick of grape Big Buddy into his mouth when Mrs. Falutnick turned her enormous back on the class, and at this he was unaccountably saddened, and he sighed, startling Chaya out of her dream.

"I heard your parents got a divorce," she said. She looked down, and her long hair splashed her folded hands.

"Yeah," said Nathan, hugging himself again. The shiver that this word produced in him never lasted more than a second or two.

"Why did they?"

"I don't know," Nathan said.

"You don't?"

He thought about it for a few seconds, then shook his head. "I mean they told me, but I forget what they said."

"It's complicated," Chaya offered, helpfully. "People change."

"I think that was part of it," Nathan said, but he didn't believe that there was really any explanation at all.

"Does your dad still live around here?"

"He moved to Boston."

"That's cool," said Chaya. She lifted the curtain of hair from her face and smiled another crooked smile. "I wish my dad would move to Boston."

Nathan said automatically, "No, you don't." He had hitherto managed to forget about the fearsome doctor and he glanced over his shoulder. In the far corner of the room he noticed three large plastic suitcases and a guitar case, neatly lined up as for an imminent departure.

"Where are you going?" he said, gesturing toward the luggage.

"Jerusalem," said Chaya. "Tomorrow. Today, I guess. Later this morning."

"With your family? Or all alone?"

"All alone."

"Are you ever coming back?"

"Of course I am, you," she said. "My father thinks I've gotten—he just wants me to learn to be an Israeli."

"Oh," said Nathan. He was not certain what this entailed, but he suddenly pictured Chaya operating a crane on the bristling lip of a giant construction site in the desert, lowering a turbine generator or a sheaf of I-beams down into the void, the dust of the Negev blowing around her like a long scarf.

"Did they tell you I put out?" said Chaya. "Those guys?"

"Kind of," said Nathan, taken aback, before it occurred to him that this was admitting he had come here for sex, when in fact he had come—why had he come? "It was more like a dare, I guess," he said. "They sort of more or less dared me to come."

"None of them's ever sat on my bed the way you are," said Chaya.

Nathan wondered for a moment exactly what she meant by this, and then, in the next moment, leaned toward her and kissed her lips. This was done only on an off chance and he did not expect that she would take such forceful hold of his body. Startled, without a clue of what he ought to do next, he put one hand on the nape of her neck, the other at the small of her back, and then he lay very still in her arms. He could feel the bones of her hips pressing against him, like a pair of fists, and his lips and somehow his breathing became entangled in her hair. The laundered smell of her bedclothes was overpowering and sweet.

"Are you a virgin, Nathan?" she said, her mouth very close to his.

He considered his reply much longer than he needed to, trying to phrase it as ambiguously as he could. "In a manner of speaking," he said at last, blushing in self-congratulation at the urbanity of this reply.

Her grip upon him relaxed, and she drew back slowly and then fell back against her pillow, looking calm again. He had the feeling that she had been hoping for some reply totally other than the one he had given. Then Chaya sighed, in a bored, theatrical way that to Nathan's ears sounded very grown up, and he was afraid, at last, that she really might have become a skeezer, that it really was possible to lose track of someone so completely that they turned into someone else without your knowing about it.

"Can you still draw eyeballs?" he said.

"Eyeballs?" she said, her face blank. "Sure, I can."

"Chaya! Mara!" called Dr. Feldman from somewhere in the house. His voice resounded like an axe-blow. "That's enough!"

They both started, and stared a moment at one another as children or as lovers caught.

"Can I tell you something, Nathan?" she said. "When I get to Israel I'm *not* coming back."

"You have to come back," he said, taking her hand.

"Chaya!" thundered Dr. Feldman from very far away. "Go to sleep."

"I'll write you," said Chaya. "Give me your address."

"Sixty-four twenty-three Les Adieux Circle. Is he going to come down here?"

"No," she said. "He thinks you're my little sister. I'll never remember that address. Let me write it down."

"Oh, that's all right," said Nathan, getting up. "You don't need to write me a letter."

"No, wait. Hold on."

She climbed out of bed again, grinning, and went to a blue wooden desk, under the stairs that led up to the first floor of the house. Nathan watched the play of her nightgown across her little behind as she bent over to open a drawer, and then scrabbled around in it, looking for a pen. She found a sheet of pink stationery and began to scratch across it with a Smurf pencil.

"Chaya, I'd better go," said Nathan. He headed for the door.

"Wait!" said Chaya. She was writing furiously now, in a pointed, ribbony script almost like cursive Hebrew, and he waited, one hand on the knob, for her to finish, and hoped that Dr. Feldman would not call out again. When she put down her pen she took a red, white, and blue airmail envelope from another drawer, folded the slip of pink paper in half, slid it into the envelope, and ran her tongue along the flap. Then she bent over the desk again and, brushing her hair from the face of the envelope, wrote out what Nathan knew even from a distance to be his name and address.

"There, I wrote you a letter from Jerusalem," she said, turning toward him. "Don't read it until tomorrow."

"Okay," said Nathan. "Good-bye." He hugged her awkwardly, afraid that he might get an erection, and then eased open the basement door. "Have fun in Jerusalem."

"But I'm already there," she said, continuing in this teasing and mysterious vein. She put a hand on each of his shoulders and kissed him on the cheek. Nathan took the letter from her, a little uncertainly. Probably it was just a bunch of scribble, or an apology for not wanting to have sex with him.

"I know what you're doing!" said Dr. Feldman, with that weird Yisraeli accent of his, and Nathan went out naked into the night. He was not quite so drunk anymore, and this time the trip around the house, past the swimming pool, did not seem especially fine or ominous. The dog next door to the Feldmans' caught wind of Nathan and began to rail at him, and he ran the rest of the way, all the while trying to determine if Dr. Feldman and his Uzi were in pursuit. As he was running across the Feldmans' yard and into the neighbors', the white towel finally slipped from his waist and fell away, nearly tripping him; he left it to Chaya to explain how it got there, and went naked the rest of the way.

He came around to his side of the car and hesitated with a hand on the door. They were asleep, all three of them, Felix E. and Tiger slumped in opposite corners of the backseat, Buster stretched out across the front seat of the car. The radio played very softly and threw green light across Buster's thighs. They were snoring with the lustiness of children, and Nathan felt a surge of pity for them and wished that they might just keep on sleeping. When he got into the car, he knew, his friends would want to know what, or rather how much, Chaya had given him; and when he showed them the letter, they would want to read what she had written. He was afraid that its contents might somehow embarrass him, and now he looked for somewhere to conceal it.

At first he considered retrieving the discarded towel, but he was afraid to go back, and anyway, if he wrapped the letter in the towel it would make a pretty suspicious bundle. Then he looked around at the lawn on which they were parked, to see if it held any place in which he could hide the letter, but there was only the silver expanse of lawn, an entire neighborhood of grass and flat moonlight. Under the front windows of the neighbors' house stood one small row of bushes, and he tried poking the envelope deep into this, but you could see it from a mile away, reflecting the light of the moon like a shard of mirror glass, and he retrieved it and looked around again.

Just when he was about to give up and try to hide the letter somewhere in the Frenches' car itself, under a mat, or even in the glove compartment, he spotted a bird feeder, about twenty feet away, hanging from the low branch of a young maple tree. It was shaped like a small transparent house, with a peaked plastic roof and glass walls, about half-filled with birdseed. Nathan unhooked it from its wire and turned it over, his hands shaking with fear and with the aptness of his plan. He pulled off the plastic base of the bird feeder and laid the letter within, burying it amid the smooth and rattling seeds. When he returned the little house to its hook, the letter was nearly invisible, and he trotted back, with a certain air of coolness, to the big yellow LTD.

His friends clambered upright when Nathan climbed back into the car; they were sober and embarrassed, and slapped Nathan constantly on the side of his head. They demanded to know what had happened to Nathan in Chaya's room, and as they drove slowly home he made up a story, filled with sophisticated orgasms, and accurate anatomical impressions, and some bits of sexual dialog in half-remembered Hebrew. The other boys seemed on the whole to believe him, although they were surprised, and blamed malt liquor and hormonal agitation, when halfway through the tale Nathan suddenly burst into tears—then stopped, and resumed his lying account.

The next night Nathan sneaked out of the house after his mother and Ed had gone to sleep. He rode half an hour on his bicycle, through the darkness, to retrieve the letter from Jerusalem. There was no moon, and black shapes seemed to dart and loom across his path. He pulled up in front of the Feldmans' house and contemplated it for a moment, straddling the hard bar of his bike. There was no sign of the towel he had dropped. He hated it that Chaya was not there in her house anymore, that she could so quickly be gone. He had a great curiosity to read what she had written him, but when he crept across to open up the little bird feeder, past the two long scars in the lawn from the wheels of the LTD, he found there was nothing inside it anymore but birdseed. The hairs on the back of his neck stood on end, and he whirled, half expecting to see Chaya, with the letter in her hand, laughing at him from behind the curtain in the low side window of her bedroom. He looked around on the grass, in the row of low shrubs, in the branches of the maple, but the letter was nowhere to be found, and after a few more minutes of baffled searching he got back on his bicycle and pedaled home. As he lay in bed that night he tried to imagine what she might have set down in her letter, what professions of love, what unhappiness, what nonsense, what shame, what news of the planet of her childhood. Then he fell asleep.

One Saturday a few weeks afterward, Nathan and his stepfather were in the kitchen, trying to work their way out of an incipient argument about whether or not tuna salad ought to be made with chopped gherkins, the way Ed's grandmother had always made it. The dispute was merely the latest and perhaps the most trivial in what was becoming a disheartening routine for Nathan and Ed, and this particular volley of intransigent politeness had just begun to make Nathan's stomach hurt—without inclining him to capitulate—when Mrs. Shapiro-Knipper entered the kitchen, carrying the Saturday mail.

"Two things," she said, handing Nathan two envelopes, one of them tricolor and heartstopping.

"I'm going to put pickles," said Ed. "You'll see. It's an acquired taste."

This time, though everything Ed liked to eat, from raw oysters to pizza with pineapple and ham, seemed to be an acquired taste, Nathan let it pass. He rose from the kitchen table and carried the two letters out into the hallway and down to his bedroom. The second, in a plain business envelope, was evidently from his father, who had never before sent a letter to Nathan, and Nathan sat on his bed for a long time without opening them, just thinking about mailmen, and sealed envelopes, and the mysteries of the post.

He supposed that the neighbor had found Chaya's letter hidden in the bird feeder before Nathan could retrieve it, and had finally gotten around to affixing a stamp to it and sending it along. Since, in the past weeks, Nathan had decided that he was in love with Chaya, and had been busy erecting all the necessary buttresses and towers and fluttering pennants in his imagination, the surprise arrival of her letter, which he had presumed lost, was a delicious addition to the structure, and he delayed as long as he could stand before finally tearing open the envelope.

Dear Nathan,
   Sometimes it is very hot here. I have a thousand boyfriends.
It is scary if a gun goes off in the night.
   You made me laugh a lot of times in class I remember.
   "Take it easy."

Love,
Chaya

He was sharply disappointed. He hated the fact that he had made her laugh, for one; and it angered him, unreasonably, he knew, that all of the other things—and there were so few of them—she had written were hypothetical, as insubstantial as her Planet of the Birds, or as his parents' marriage, or as the baby that was growing in his stepmother's belly. He stuffed the bogus letter back into the envelope and tore it to pieces.

He was still feeling bad when at last he brought himself to open the letter from his father. It was a brief, barely legible note, on a sheet of legal paper. After some facetious chitchat about the Red Sox and Ricky's karate lessons, Nathan's father had written, "Your mother tells me that you have made some new friends and she is a little worried because you're going around with your shoes untied. Tie your shoelaces. Don't be angry with us, Nate. I know that everything seems different now but you have to get used to it. I will always love you as much as I will love any new Shapiros that come along."

"Nathan?" his mother called to him through the door of his room. "Come on and eat."

"I hate it with gherkins," said Nathan, but his heart had gone out of the argument, and he stood up to join his mother and Ed for lunch. Hastily he dried his eyes, and scrambled to gather up the letter from his father and the scraps of Chaya's letter that were scattered across his bed. It was as he laid them carefully in the Roi-Tan cigar box in which he kept his most important papers that he noticed the strange and beautiful postage stamp in the torn corner of the airmail envelope, and the postmark, printed in an alien script.

Permissions